I'll Fly Away

The true story of how one American mother found herself
trapped in Beirut with her two daughters,
rejected by her husband's family
because she refuses to convert to Islam.
Forced to live under Sharia law, where she and her daughters are
not much more than possessions, she realizes that
she will never deny her faith and makes plans to escape.

Kelly Nielson

෯ঞ

This book is dedicated to my daughters: Layla and Nadine.

I hope that you will never forget this story, which is your story.

I pray that you will never take for granted the freedoms that were gained for you, but live your lives with grateful hearts and choose to walk in God's light and embrace His wonderful plans for your lives.

May you walk in truth, my daughters, and always seek His face.

And last but not least, remember that one of the most important decisions that you will ever make is deciding whom you will marry.

May your future husbands know God, love God and love you with all their hearts.

May they be men of honor, compassion and respect and may you find the true joy in marriage that God always intended since the beginning of creation.

෯ঞ

Some of the proceeds of this book will be donated to the Call of Love Ministries, which was founded in America in 2001 by Mike and Samya Johnson. The ministry focuses on delivering God's message of hope and truth to Muslims and aids the persecuted Christians in Muslim countries.

∞ ∞

"Do not be yoked together with unbelievers.
For what do righteousness and wickedness have in common?
Or what fellowship can light have with darkness? What harmony is there
between Christ and Belial (devil)? Or what does a believer have in common
with an unbeliever? What agreement is there between the temple of God
and idols? For we are the temple of the living God."
(2Corinthians 6:14-16)

∞ ∞

CONTENTS

Part X: AN OPEN DOOR

Part XI: TAKING FLIGHT

Author's Note

This is a true story. Some names and identifying details have been changed to protect the privacy of certain individuals. I have reconstructed dialogue from memory, which means that it may not be word for word, but the essence of what was said is accurate.

This story almost didn't make it to print. It has been denied and rejected so many times by agents and publishers that I have lost count. The reasons given were many - that everyone is tired of hearing how an American woman escaped her Muslim husband (been there done that) - that my story is unbelievable because it couldn't have been that bad in Beirut, Lebanon as I described it. Surely I had other options because as an American citizen I have certain inherent rights. These are the same people who don't understand that under Sharia law there is no separation of church and state, and because I was married to a Muslim I was subject to this law the minute we entered Lebanon, and any former rights I had were gone. For many agents, my story was too heavy, too religious, too politically incorrect, and too intolerant. Suggestions were given to lighten it up so it would read more like a romance novel.

I would like to warn the reader that this is not a romance novel, nor a politically correct story devoid of any religious convictions, or even a quick read during your vacation weekend. It is simply my story, with all the good, the bad, and the ugly. I also want the reader to know that I harbor no unforgiveness or resentment in my heart toward my ex-husband or his family in any way shape or form. I have forgiven completely, but forgiving someone does not mean that you are admitting that what he or she did to you was right, nor does it mean that you have to be in a relationship with him or her. It simply frees you from harboring bitterness in your heart that only hurts you.

I also harbor no ill will or resentment toward those who follow the Islamic faith. I do not have to agree with their beliefs, nor do they with mine, but I do have the right to discuss our differences and explain why I choose to be a Christian and not a Muslim.

I have no agenda with this book, save one, for people to be inspired to search for the truth. Theology is the study of the nature of God and religious belief and I believe that we all practice it everyday regardless if we call ourselves an atheist, an agnostic, a Muslim, or a Christian to name a few. Each of these requires a belief system that ranges from the belief that there is no God and what we do doesn't matter anyway because we are just a random accident, to the belief that we are created by a loving Father who invites us to be part of His family.

What a person believes directly influences how he or she lives their life. How different will a person act and behave when he believes that he is not a random accident but a precious child created by a loving God who knit us together in our mother's womb? How differently will you pray when you believe you are God's child rather than His servant? How will you treat your daughters and wife if you believe that women are inherently inferior to men, compared to those who believe that both men and women are created in the image of God and deserve to be treated with the same dignity and respect?

This story was very difficult to write, but it is my hope that you, the reader, will understand my journey, and that it helps you on your own personal journey through this gift called life.

Prologue

"I picked three lemons in life, Kelly," my grandmother would begin, leaning over so she could look me directly in my eyes, holding up three fingers with her right hand. "Don't do what I did," she would admonish me. Every time we went to visit her, she made sure she told me the story of The Three Lemons. I could recite the story verbatim but always acted as if I had never heard it before, respectfully giving her my utmost attention as she began down memory lane. Her lemons were the three men she had chosen in life, each one worse than the previous, and I knew the stories well.

My grandmother was born during the Roaring Twenties, in a city that was one of the largest and most notorious copper mining towns in the American West, Butte, Montana. Copper was in great demand at the time because of the need for copper wires in the development of electricity, and during World War I where it was used in every single rifle bullet. Butte was named the "Richest Hill on Earth" and my grandmother grew up during its heydays, the only daughter of a very successful interior designer, in a beautiful home where her mother kept her dressed in silks and satins. Her life changed forever, however, when both of her parents suddenly died of pneumonia, leaving her an orphan in her early twenties. Her sheltered upbringing left her unprepared for this tragedy.

Alone in the world, she was thrown into the harsh realities of living in a rough town where hundreds of saloons and an infamous red light district serenaded hard working miners, tempting them to trade their hard earned money for transitory pleasures. After World War I, and the onslaught of The Great Depression, people were desperate, and a young, inexperienced woman naïve to the ways of the world was easy prey. A charming Irish man named John serenaded her, asking for her hand in marriage. My grandmother hastily agreed for she was in love for the first time in her life. Soon after they were married, he borrowed money and opened a bar of his own which at first brought them hope for a new life, but he eventually ran it into the ground

Penniless now with three children and a wife to provide for, he went to work as a miner for the Anaconda Copper Mining Company, trading clean air and sunshine for the suffocating darkness of the pit. It didn't take long for him to drown his sorrows in alcohol, frequenting the bars after work with his dusty coworkers, squandering his family's sustenance on drink. Paydays, my grandmother would wait for him to come home, so she could shop for groceries, but all too often, he would stagger in late at night, drunk, and pick violent fights with her while the children ran upstairs to hide. When my mother was 3 years old, he abandoned them and left without a word. My mother didn't see him again until she was 15 years old at his funeral. He had died from cirrhosis of the liver. At his funeral, my mother's older sister asked her why she wasn't crying and she remembered looking at the stranger in the casket responding, "I never knew him."

My grandmother was alone in the world again but now with three little children to take care of. Hard times followed. That Christmas, desperate, she sold her wedding ring to provide Christmas presents for her children – underwear and socks - the necessities that others took for granted. Boots were a luxury even in the cold Montana winters where snowdrifts piled high. Her children wore plastic bread bags over their shoes, held with rubber bands so the cardboard that covered the holes in the bottom wouldn't deteriorate in the deep snow.

A widow with three children would seem a burden to most men, but my grandmother was still a beautiful woman, and it didn't take long until another suitor pursued her. Lemon Number Two was a tall, chiseled German named Shockey who worked in the mines like her late husband and he pursued her passionately.

"He was the most handsome man," she would say looking off into the distance as if remembering his face. "But, he was also the cruelest," she would add, a flicker of anger in her eyes. They had met at a dancehall. My grandmother loved to dance - it made her forget her troubles - and not only was she a good dancer; she had the most beautiful legs. She always wore dresses and heels, even when doing housework. It didn't take long until she was mesmerized by his devilish good looks and they were married.

The day my grandmother introduced him to her children, my mother knew he wasn't going to be a nice stepfather. She remembers her little brother John smiling at him, playfully grabbing his hat when all at once this stranger yanked her brother's arm and spanked him hard, while her mother just stood by and watched.

My grandmother gave birth to another little girl in that marriage, and although her second husband was a good provider, the violence he meted out made her first husband look like an angel. She wanted to leave him but he threatened to kill her if she tried, so she prayed. She prayed that he would lose interest in her and leave her for another woman, and soon, her prayers were answered, just as she had asked.

She never did talk about "Lemon Number Three" and when I asked my mother about it, she changed the subject. He must have been the worst to be unspeakable, or maybe there was more shame involved than the others. I will never know.

All I do know is that when my grandmother was younger she believed the best about people. She was open to life and open to love but she unknowingly placed her heart in the hands of men who didn't honor or cherish her. It was hard to see her as she neared the end of her life. Although she kept her hair dyed the same chestnut brown and cut in the same curly bob she had in her twenties, her big, bright blue eyes were softened now with sadness, and her beautiful legs were grossly swollen, lined with twisting, purplish veins. Life had made her afraid and she more or less became a recluse, living alone and trusting only one friend, her son John. She clung to him until the day she died.

Once a year, we would visit Grandma in her little apartment in Silver Bow Homes, the same place where she raised her family. A candy dish of pink mints was put out for our visit and she would offer us a "poor man's dessert" – white bread slathered in butter with sugar sprinkled on top. Then she would look at me and begin with her stories. It was always directed at me – my little brother escaped the lessons running to the backyard to play. I was her first granddaughter and maybe when she looked at me she saw herself. I certainly had inherited her thick, wavy hair and big, blue eyes, but I was also timid and soft-spoken, accommodating to everyone around me, and painfully shy.

I wasn't assertive, bold, or confident like my street-smart mother who had to fight for everything as a poor child growing up in Butte. Looking out for number one was not a choice for her – it was survival and my mother had taken great pains to isolate me from the harshness of her childhood, controlling every detail of my life and providing everything for her children that she had lacked in hers but I had lost something of myself in this exchange and I think my grandmother saw that.

At the time, her stories seemed a million years away, and I wish I could say I learned from them and never made the same mistakes she did, but I didn't. I couldn't see how they applied to me at the time, nor did I know that more history is repeated in families, not because of genetics, but because we recycle our pain, our past, right into the next generation. My mother didn't escape this and neither did I.

I shared the same simple dream my grandmother had - to simply love and be loved in return, and like her, set out on my quest ill-equipped and unprepared. However, unlike her, my first lemon almost completely annihilated me.

Part I Courtship

EXODUS

For one brief moment, I forgot that we were squeezed into these cramped cubbyholes called seats. Apprehensively, I gripped the bony armrests and stared intently at the overhead screen displaying our flight's progress. I followed the little white plane with my eyes, with an uneasy feeling in the pit of my stomach as I watched it leave Maine, the last northeastern tip of America. Like a ride on a rollercoaster, I swayed against it, as if I could steer it away from the ocean in front of it, but it kept moving forward, following the trajectory of the red line in front of it.

My face must have betrayed my feelings, because my eight-year-old daughter, Layla, reached over and grasped my trembling hand in her small, but firm one. I forced back the threatening overflow and looked into her trusting eyes. They reminded me of soft doe eyes, large and innocent, now searching my face for answers.

"Are we finally going to be happy there Mommy?" she asked.

I swallowed hard, searching for an answer to alleviate her fears, and forced a smile, "Yes, we will, my love. Baba is going to open up his very own pharmacy so we can finally settle down ...and you will be going to an excellent school – and you will have so many cousins to

1

play with!" I responded as enthusiastically as I could muster for her sake.

Layla laughed, showing a big, toothy smile. "I love you, Mommy," she said nestling her head into my chest, her long auburn curls falling over her face.

As she put her headphones back on to resume her movie I once again pulled the navy blue blanket over my three-year-old daughter, Nadine, and tucked it under her little chin. She was sleeping with her head on my lap, her legs and arms stretched every which way. Her sun-kissed light brown hair that I had carefully braided this morning was now all undone, wildly shooting out from her small almond-shaped face. Under her closed eyelids, her eyes were moving furiously in unison with her dreams. Every so often, she would murmur in protest to some unknown shadow she was fighting and kick off her blanket in anger.

I glanced over at my husband two seats away. He was fast asleep; his head tilted back, arms folded over his chest. His face was flushed from the nightcap of three travel-size bottles of liquor, and he was snoring loudly. His profile resembled Michelangelo's David, with his strong chin, full lips and large Roman nose. But then the forehead sloped back, as though the sculptor ran out of marble, and slanted into his fast-receding hairline. Wavy black hair sprinkled with gray was cropped close to his head. His flawless olive skin didn't betray his forty years or his daily habit of smoking. I felt irritated at how peacefully he slept and how oblivious he was to my inner turmoil. To him it was just another move, move number fifteen to be exact. Fifteen moves in fourteen years of marriage. This time was different, however. This time we were moving to his homeland, Beirut, Lebanon.

As the flight attendants dimmed the lights, the tension in my face returned. My pretense of calmness wasn't needed in the dark and the anxiety that had been gnawing at me for months resurfaced. *"How had it come to this?"* I pondered yet once again. *"What am I doing on a plane with my daughters headed for Beirut?"*

INTRODUCTION

College was our introduction. After attending a lifetime of private Catholic schools, I decided to transfer to a public university. The door to my small world was opened the minute I stepped into my dorm room at Idaho State University. Here I met people from all kinds of backgrounds, races, religions and countries and it fascinated me. It was as if a whole new world was introduced to me. And, I met a guy who rocked my world.

The yearly International Festival in the spring of 1986 was one of my first introductions to a world beyond my hometown. This campus festival was a celebration of the foreign students who attended ISU; it was a chance for them to proudly display their native dress, music and food. My good friend, Mareta, invited me. She was from American Samoa, a small island in the South Pacific, and she was excited to share her culture with me.

She had spent all afternoon helping set up for the Festival at the school gym and wanted me to meet her that night at the entrance door. I almost didn't recognize her when I first saw her. She was transformed into an island beauty. Her bronzed skin was glowing against the deep purple sarong she was wrapped in, her long black hair swung around her tiny waist.

"I am so happy you could come!" Mareta gushed, embracing me in a big hug when she saw me. "This is so exciting!"

"Wow, you look beautiful!" I smiled, always warmed by my friend's enthusiastic affection. No one had ever made me feel so important and genuinely liked as this little foreign friend from some far away island. It struck me as strange, how two people from opposite ends of the world could become so close.

My eyes widened as I fixated on the stage behind Mareta, where a student from Tonga, dressed in nothing but a loincloth, was twirling fiery batons to the loud beating of drums. Students brushed past me, in bright colorful costumes speaking their native tongue. I suddenly felt

3

out of place in my 501 blue jeans and oversized gray sweatshirt. Strange, unfamiliar aromas of curry, cumin and saffron invaded my nostrils as Mareta grabbed my hand and led me to some long tables arrayed with exotic dishes. I followed closely behind her, clutching a paper plate to my chest.

"Mareta!" a deep heavily accented voice suddenly boomed out. "How are you my friend?"

I looked up across the food-laden table and saw a pair of dark seductive eyes staring at me. I felt naked under his stare, the way he was looking at me so intensely. I averted my eyes to my roommate.

"Abraham!" Mareta squealed. "How are you?" She noticed his eyes were focused on me and introduced me immediately, "This is my roommate, Kelly!"

"A pleasure to meet you," he said, reaching out his large hands, clasping my small right hand in both of his.

"Nice to meet you," I replied uncomfortably, trying to take my hand back from his while he held on. Mareta interrupted and began conversing with him. While they were talking, my eyes took him in. He was tall, at least 6'2", broad-shouldered, and his light creamy olive complexion was offset by thick, wavy black hair. I could see every perfect white tooth in his smile. His looks screamed Italian with his large Romanesque nose and full pink lips.

"Would you like to try some of my baklava?" he asked in a thick French accent, pointing to a tray of diamond cut pastries. "It has pistachios and rose water and it is delicious!"

"Oooooh, how beautiful!" Mareta blushed. "It looks wonderful!"

He placed a piece of baklava on each of our plates and poured some thick clear syrup on top.

"Thank you," I replied, my eyes staring curiously at the pastry, now extremely confused about the ethnicity of this French-speaking Italian, with a Jewish name, serving a Greek pastry.

"I hope you enjoy it," he smiled, his eyes lingering on me.

Mareta and I sat down to enjoy our food as we watched the rest of the dances on stage. Every so often I would glance over at him only to see him staring intently back at me. After the last dance, a Basque folk dance, we rose to leave. As we passed by him, I avoided his gaze and grabbed Mareta's hand, firmly pulling her with me, walking quickly towards the exit door.

I'll Fly Away

"Goodbye Abraham!" Mareta called out, looking over her shoulder as I whisked her into the brisk night air.

*****

Weeks passed and I hadn't even given him another thought until one afternoon, when Mareta bounced into our dorm room while I was lying on my bed, vacillating between daydreaming and studying.

"Kelly! Do you remember my friend Abraham whom you met at the festival?" she asked, plopping herself right next to me, her face only inches from mine. Personal space was a lost concept on Mareta, as was hiding her emotions.

"You mean that guy who served us baklava?" I answered calmly, trying to appear nonchalant, as I put my book down.

"Yes! Yes – that's the one!" she clapped her hands together. "Well, guess what he said?" she asked, and then answered her own question. "He said you have the most beautiful blue eyes in the world!" she swooned, leaning in even closer, right into my lap, her big brown round eyes staring wide-eyed into mine.

"Well, that was … nice," I answered hesitantly, pulling away as I tried to make some space between us, thankful that my roommate always smelled like fresh, clean soap.

"I knew he liked you!" Mareta said, bobbing her head up and down. "I know these things! So, he wanted our dorm room phone number and I gave it to him!" she blurted out, as she inched closer to me, her eyes anticipating my reaction.

I watched Mareta scan my face for the response she was looking for, but I couldn't give it to her. I hugged my knees against my chest, my back up against the wall, looking even smaller now and feeling afraid. I was flattered, but scared. He was too intense, too loud, too foreign, and too good-looking. I didn't know what to tell her.

"Well, okay. That's good," I responded politely, avoiding Mareta's gaze. I tried to show some enthusiasm for my friend's sake and smiled.

Mareta saw right through it. "I don't understand you," Mareta said softly, placing her hand on my arm, "What are you afraid of?"

"Nothing. I'm not afraid of anything," I responded, pulling away.

"You are so funny… " Mareta hesitated. "You don't even know do you?"

"Know what?" I asked, now concerned that something was really wrong.

"How beautiful you are," she answered, looking down at her hands.

"What are you talking about?" I looked up, completely surprised.

"Oh, just every time we go anywhere together," she began, smiling at me. "I will be walking with you and all these guys' heads turn to look at you. They aren't looking at me! You always walk straight ahead, oblivious to all the attention you are getting."

"What? You are making this up," I responded, scanning her face for the truth.

"Don't look at me that way!" she laughed. "My God, you are gorgeous! With your big blue eyes, blonde hair, tiny little body with curves in all the right places… and don't even get me started on your legs!"

"Now you are joking," I said without hesitating, "I am not gorgeous!" I shook my head, mentally going through a long list of things wrong with me

Mareta's face fell, her eyes now saddened, "Wow, who did this to you?" she asked. "No one ever told you that you were beautiful?"

Tears welled up in my eyes against my will as I tried to avoid her concern. I had never had a friend like this, who made me feel so good about myself. I was never that girl people called beautiful or even pretty. I used to think I was cute up until sixth grade when I had long blonde hair that fell to my waist, unblemished skin and big blue eyes, but at the beginning of 7th grade, puberty hit me with a vengeance. By the time I left junior high, my skin was an erupting volcano, and my beautiful, long blonde hair was now a short, mousy brown frizz after one disastrous haircut. Glasses were quickly traded for contacts and braces didn't help me toward the look I was going for.

My ruddy face left me open to teasing by some classmates who called me "Rudolph." It wasn't until the end of 8th grade that I discovered makeup and I embraced this miracle product that camouflaged my blemishes. My body was thin, but gangly in high school and I was so shy I rarely raised my hand in class. By the end of high school, unbeknownst to me, the ugly swan had gracefully grown into a beautiful young woman but my self-esteem had already been damaged. Even in college when I looked in the mirror, I did not see what others saw; I only saw that awkward pimply teenager. The acne was gone but the emotional scars weren't.

"Once," I replied seriously. "I had a boyfriend my senior year who said I was beautiful but I didn't believe him."

"Unbelievable," Mareta said, shaking her head. "You know when I first met you I thought you were going to be stuck-up and full of yourself but I was surprised to find you were just as beautiful on the inside – I was scared so far away from home but you helped me feel welcome and your friendship really means a lot to me."

"No, I am the lucky one," I responded as we hugged each other, breaking into peals of laughter as we tried to hold back tears.

*****

I didn't see him for another week. One afternoon I was studying in the student union building, my favorite place to study – it had just enough noise from passing students to keep me alert and I was close to an unending supply of coffee. I found a small table underneath a window near a set of stairs where I spread my books out staking my territory.

An hour into my studies, a loud voice startled me, "Kaali! How are you?"

I looked up and saw those same very dark eyes staring at me. It was Abraham, towering above me wearing a black leather jacket, and blue jeans, looking like he just stepped out of GQ.

"Good! … And you?" I answered smiling politely, wishing I hadn't chosen a table so close to the stairs.

"I am good, very good, thank you," he smiled broadly. "May I?" he motioned toward the chair opposite me.

"Sure," I answered, moving my books to make room for him.

He placed his backpack on the chair next to him and made himself comfortable.

"What are you studying?" he asked, as he grabbed an ashtray from another table.

"Finance – I mean I am studying for my Operations Productions class but my degree is Finance," I stumbled over the words.

"Oh – A smart girl! You must love numbers," he smiled knowingly.

"Yes I do," I lied. I hated Finance but I didn't feel like explaining that to a complete stranger. It was a compromise between my mother and me. She wanted me to be an Accountant; I wanted to be a Psychologist.

"So what are you studying?" I asked him, noticing he didn't pull any books from his bag. He reached into his inside left pocket, pulling out a pack of Marlboro Red cigarettes. I cringed. I hated the smell of cigarettes.

"Do you mind?" he asked lighting up one before I could even respond. "I am studying to be a pharmacist," he answered.

"Wow, that's a hard major," I applauded him and then paused. "Do you mind if I ask you something?"

"Of course not! Ask away!" he smiled, leaning forward, happy that I seemed interested in him.

"I am really confused about where you are from," I stated shyly, curious about his answer.

He smiled even bigger, "Where do you think I am from?"

"Well, honestly at first I thought you were Italian, but your accent is French…." I responded hesitantly. The way his face lit up I could tell he was pleased with my assessment.

"Well, the French accent is because I attended French Catholic boarding schools since grade school in Montpelier, France," he explained beaming. "I speak French, English and Arabic."

"You speak Arabic?" I responded now completely confused.

"Yes, I am originally from Lebanon, a country north of Palestine right on the beautiful Mediterranean Sea," he answered taking another puff, blowing smoke over his shoulder, watching my face for a reaction.

"So you are Arabic?" I asked innocently, but I saw immediately that I had offended him.

He frowned. He hated being seen as an "Arab." He saw himself as an international man and took great pride in his European dress, style and accent. He did not see himself like the other Arabs here on campus that wore scruffy beards, flip-flops and sweats in public.

"I am Lebanese. Lebanon is not an Arabic country. It is the Middle East. In fact Lebanon is called the Paris of the Middle East; everyone there speaks French as his or her second language because my country used to be a French territory. Muslims and Christians live peacefully together, side by side," he spoke emphatically. "It is a beautiful country. You can ski in the mountains and swim in the Mediterranean Sea, all in the same day."

As he continued his flowery description of his homeland, all I heard was the word Muslim and my gut wrenched. The only time I had ever heard of Muslims in my small Idaho town was during the Iran hostage crisis of 1979-1981 when 52 Americans were held hostage for 444 days.

"So are you a Muslim?" I asked as nonchalantly as I could, trying not to show my concern. "But I thought Abraham was a Jewish name?"

"It is Ibrahim, spelled with an I," he explained. "I was named after the prophet Abraham from your Bible," he answered. "I am Muslim and ...I assume you are Christian?"

"Yes, I went to Catholic schools all my life ... like you it sounds like," I answered, folding my arms over my chest. I was uncomfortable having the spotlight on me.

"Where are you from?" he asked, taking in how softly I spoke and how I avoided his eyes when answering.

"Originally from Montana; my parents moved my two brothers and me to Boise, Idaho when I was ten," I answered quickly.

"How old are your two brothers?" he asked concerned, looking over his shoulder as though they could show up at any moment.

"Corey is my youngest brother by three years – he is in college in Montana now, and Randy is two years older," I paused. "He was born severely mentally handicapped," I answered, shifting nervously in my chair. Ibrahim's eyes were too intense and the smoke curling around him reeked. I coughed.

"Oh, I am sorry," he responded with pity, crushing out his cigarette.

"Oh, you mean about Randy – no don't be," I responded strongly, defending my brother like I've done since I was old enough to understand that he was different from other people. "I mean it is sad how he was born but he gives more to me than I could ever give to him. Sometimes I feel like he took a bullet for me."

"A bullet?" Ibrahim frowned. "You mean from a gun?"

I wanted to escape this conversation. I was usually the listener, the one who asked the questions, while other people jabbered on and on about themselves. Not that I didn't love listening to others - I did. People and their stories fascinated me. But this strange foreigner sitting in front of me was different. He actually seemed to want to know more about me. His eyes were burrowing in on me now and he was waiting for an answer.

"Oh what the heck, it's like talking to a stranger at the airport – I will never see him again," I thought.

"Yes, you know, he took a bullet for me," I explained. "It's an American saying. It means that you care so much about someone that you would jump in front of a bullet headed straight for them – you know, save their life."

Ibrahim laughed, "You Americans and your funny sayings! I remember my first year in college the professor in one of my classes announced it was 'raining cats and dogs' outside and I jumped up to the window to see and the whole class started laughing at me." His face blushed with the memory, his dimples showing.

My face broke out into a grin. "I guess that would sound funny if you took it literally," I replied.

"No, but back to your brother," he said, his face now somber, puffing seriously on another cigarette.

"Well, he was born with O+ blood and my mother was O-. It's called the Rh factor, and her body produced antibodies that attacked his cells and there was no blood transfusion done or Rh-immune globin available, so it caused severe brain damage to my brother," I said looking directly into his eyes now, thinking I saw sympathy. "It's not supposed to happen to the first baby. I was the second and I know it doesn't make sense because I had O- like my mother, but I feel like he protected me somehow…" I faded off looking at my hands, surprised at myself for sharing something so private. "He's a great brother and he makes me thankful everyday for everything I have. Because of him I don't take anything for granted."

Ibrahim's eyes softened as he gazed at me. He seemed to take in my vulnerability with his gentle look. He reached out across the table and put his hand over mine.

I instinctively pulled back, not used to displays of compassion or affection towards me. I quickly collected myself and began to turn all of the attention back to him. I assumed my familiar role of listening while he talked about his family, country and travels. I learned he came from a large, well-educated family: all of his siblings had bachelors or masters degrees from the U.S. or Europe. His father was a successful entrepreneur who had done well in life. The strange tales of Lebanon's Civil War and their fight for independence fascinated me. For a small town girl who had never traveled outside of Montana or Idaho, it was like a whole new world and I had his attention - his undivided attention. Time escaped us as we talked until the sun began to cast long shadows on the table.

Suddenly, he looked at his watch and said, "I have class in ten minutes! I can't believe how late it is!"

"You're kidding!" I answered, looking out the window for the first time since he had sat down.

"Well, it has been a pleasure," he said holding my hand again like a character from an early 19th century novel.

I held his hand awkwardly and said, "Me too."

After I watched him walk away I found myself staring at an ashtray overflowing with cigarette butts.

My attention returned quickly back to my studies. It was finals week and it was time for serious cramming, endless cups of coffee, and all-nighters. Before I knew it, the last test was finished and it was time to pack up to go home for the summer. I was ready for summer to begin and Ibrahim and his stories were soon forgotten.

When I returned to school in the fall, I had a new roommate. I returned to my studies and found a full-time job at a hotel as a desk clerk. It was the ideal job, working nights and weekends and since not many people came to stay in this quiet, little town, most nights I could study at work. My life was a safe routine of school, studying and working and I liked that. I had no interest in drinking or partying not since a bad experience at Carroll College in Helena, Montana.

*****

It was my sophomore year at Carroll and I was invited to go to a concert. It was a night I never wanted to repeat:

"I am not taking no for an answer!" Michelle said. "We are here to rescue you from your boring life! I mean come on Kelly; all you do is study and work! College is about having fun!"

Michelle didn't look like a partier with her thick, black horn-rimmed glasses and straight long brown hair, but underneath that demure exterior was a raging partier.

"I can't," I sighed, pointing at my books. I have a test tomorrow and a paper on Wednesday."

"But it is the Huey Lewis and the News concert and I have tickets!" Michelle said waving the tickets in front of me. "You are coming with us!"

I finally gave in and agreed to meet her and some friends at a home she was housesitting at. When we walked into the kitchen I saw Jack Daniels shots already lined up, waiting on the counter.

"Come on Kelly, let's get this party started!" Michelle said, handing me a shot.

"Oh no, come on guys, I don't even like beer," I winced, placing it back down. My moral compass was as rigid as they came. Although most Catholics drank, alcohol was never allowed in my house growing up. I never saw my parents drink. I knew it had something to do with how both of my parents' terrible childhoods were the casualties of both their fathers' drinking. Whatever the reason, I viewed that little glass of dark amber liquid in front of me as evil.

It looked so innocent in the tiny glasses, though. "What is Jack Daniel's?" I asked Michelle.

"It's just a sweet liquor – it tastes like spicy maple syrup," she answered.

"Oh, well, I don't like maple syrup," I lied, and turned my back to it.

Michelle sighed and left to go upstairs with the other girls to get ready, realizing that just getting me to go to the concert was victory enough.

After she left I turned back around, staring at the shot glasses. I did like the taste of maple syrup and visions of hot buttery pancakes with syrup drizzled on top danced in my head.

"Well, it is so little and one won't hurt," I thought, looking around to make sure I was alone.

I picked up one glass and sipped it. It had a sweet oaky taste and felt hot running down my throat. It didn't taste like maple syrup but I liked it. It tasted much better than beer. I drank the rest all at once like I watched the girls do and waited. Nothing happened. I took another one and threw it back even faster. Nothing. In my ignorance, I thought I was supposed to feel something all at once, like an overwhelming rush. Without hesitating, I continued drinking more shots before my friend Patti saw me as she was coming down the stairs.

"Oh my God!" Patti grabbed my arm. "What are you doing? How many shots have you had?" she asked looking at five empty shot glasses in front of me, her eyes widening.

"I don't feel anything," I answered. "I think I might be resistant to alcohol."

"You are hilarious!" Patti squealed, already a little tipsy herself. "You have to give it awhile knucklehead!" and she grabbed my hand. "Come on, we have to get going. We're late already!" She pulled me behind her as we piled into the backseat of Michelle's car already crammed with the rest of the girls.

The next thing I remembered was waking up in the dorms in my bed and the ceiling was spinning. I slowly focused on a hazy figure on the bed next to me.

"Finally!" Patti said. "You're awake!"

"What happened?" I asked rubbing my eyes.

"Well, let's see… where do I begin?" she smiled. "What do you remember?"

"The last thing I remember is piling in the car to go to the concert?" I answered, more like a question, hoping that was right before I came here to sleep.

"That's the last thing you remember?" Patti asked. "You are kidding me!"

I racked my brain for more, finding nothing. "That's it," I answered, scared that I didn't remember more.

"Well, let me enlighten you as to what happened after that!" she replied. She looked at me like I had antennas sticking out of my head. "We made it to the concert and were standing in line to get in but you were having a hard time because you said you were too tired to stand, so we took turns having you lean on us. You couldn't stand up straight and you had everyone laughing until finally two policemen came over to question you." Patti looked incredulously at me. "You really don't remember any of this?"

"No! Oh my God…. cops?" I asked. "Cops? I was questioned by cops?" I sat up now holding my hands to my head, my eyes staring in disbelief.

"Yes, cops," she said, still giving me that bewildered look. "I went with you and explained to them that this was your first time drinking but they said the way you were acting it had to be more than alcohol and were convinced you had taken drugs."

I was horrified. "Drugs? They thought I took drugs?" I cried, now standing next to my bed my hands over my mouth. "Oh my God! Oh my God! My parents are going to kill me!"

13

Patti started laughing, "That's what you kept saying all night when they were questioning you!"

I looked at my friend like she was deranged. How did she find this so funny? I never got in trouble. I never drank. I never did drugs. I never did anything. How was this happening to me?

"Don't worry," she said, placing her hands on my arm, making me sit back down. "The cops finally believed me and drove us back here."

"They drove us here – in the back of a cop car?" I asked, my heart sinking, dreading her answer.

"Yes, they said to look after you so I did. You just wanted to sleep so you climbed into bed, clothes, shoes and all," Patti said. "That's it."

I suddenly felt guilty. "So you didn't get to go to the concert?" I asked, realizing what my friend had given up for me.

"No, but no big deal," Patti answered sincerely.

"I feel horrible! You missed the concert because of me!" I said, "Thank you so much for being there for me. I am so sorry!"

"Don't worry about it," Patti replied. "I wasn't too hot on seeing that concert anyway."

Just then someone knocked at my door. Patti got up to answer it.

"Phone call for Kelly," a girl announced, pointing to the phone booth in the hallway.

I looked at Patti with sheer horror on my face. "Oh no! It's my mother!" I wailed, looking at my friend for help. "The cops must have called her!"

Before she could answer, I jumped out of bed, the room still spinning, and stumbled down the hallway to the phone booth. I sat down on the bench and shut the glass doors. "Hello?" I squeaked, bracing myself for the tirade I was expecting.

"Hello honey, how are you?" my mother began too sweetly.

"She knows," I thought. *"She knows."*

I played along, "Fine... and you?"

"I just wanted to share a letter with you here that I received from your school," she answered.

"A letter?" I was puzzled. *"Mail can't travel that fast...unless they faxed it. Oh my God, here we go."*

"What does it say?" I whispered, fearing the worst.

"Well, it says here that you are on the Dean's List!" my mother responded.

I threw myself at her mercy. "Oh Mom, I am so so sorry. I didn't mean to. It was the first time in my life! It was a mistake! It will never ever happen again – I promise! I didn't know…"

"What are you talking about?" my mother interrupted me. "Being on the Dean's list is an honor. It means that my daughter is one of the best students there!"

I paused making sure I heard her right. "An honor?" I questioned. "Oh, I thought I was in trouble because, because I had been skipping a few classes!"

"Skipping classes?" she repeated. "You can't start that or you will be off the Dean's list!"

After I reassured her that I would attend all of my classes, she shared how proud she was of me. I listened quietly, amazed at this fortuitous turn of events.

When I returned to my room, still in a daze, I found Patti waiting for me.

"I am never going to take another drink as long as I live!" I announced.

I remembered that night with horror, knowing I had just escaped a major catastrophe, so from that moment on I avoided parties in college. I never wanted to tempt fate like that again.

*****

Here at ISU, I kept my routine simple: attending classes, studying and working. One night after work, I stopped by the cafeteria to grab something to eat before going home.

As I walked past a table of four, I heard a familiar voice. "Oh, there you are!"

I turned and saw Ibrahim sitting with a few friends drinking coffee.

"Great! Just great!" I thought. *"I just want to go to bed and sleep. I am so tired and I probably look like a wreck!"*

"Ibrahim," I responded, nervously. "How are you?" I patted down a stubborn flyaway hair and tried to rub away the dark raccoon smears under my eyes.

"Good," he smiled big, standing up to hug me. "But I haven't seen you all summer! I saw you this morning walking in the parking lot and I was calling out to you but you didn't hear me. I even honked my horn at you but you just kept walking straight ahead!"

"That sounds like me," I said. "I do that all that time."

"So what have you been up to?" he asked, sitting back down and motioning for me to join them.

"Oh, you know me, busy working and studying," I said, still standing, backing away from all his friends' eyes now on me.

He pulled me aside. "I just wanted to take you out to dinner tomorrow night," he whispered in my ear.

"I can't," I said. "I am working tomorrow."

"When is your next day off?" he pressed.

"Monday," I answered.

"Well, how about if I pick you up at five?" he asked hesitantly.

"Sure, that sounds good," I answered, thinking I could always cancel.

"Five it is," he said, smiling broadly, obviously pleased.

"Great," I said, forcing a smile. "See you then." I turned and walked away quickly.

"Kaali!" he called, running after me. "You forgot to give me your phone number! I don't even know which dorm you are in now!"

"Oh, of course," I said, grudgingly writing down my number on the notebook he held out for me.

"Okay, we'll see you then," he said smiling, watching me walk away.

COURTING

Ibrahim never called to give me a chance to cancel our date, so Monday night I knew he would be there, and sure enough he arrived punctually at five o'clock. He was dressed in black skinny jeans and a white crisp shirt, anchored with a slim black tie. A strong scent of cedar and sandalwood embraced me when he walked in. Suddenly I felt underdressed in my jeans, penny loafers and pink sweater.

"I thought it was just a casual dinner?" I said.

"Don't change; you look beautiful," he answered, holding out his arm for me to take. He led me to his car and opened the passenger door for me. I got in awkwardly, not used to having a date open doors for me. We pulled into an Italian restaurant and he told me to wait. I watched him jump out and run around the car to open my door.

When the waiter showed us our table, he pulled out my chair for me and I sat down in it, clumsily trying to scoot it forward as he politely tried to assist me. Ibrahim gracefully laid his white linen napkin across his lap and I imitated him feeling out of my element in this fancy restaurant.

Looking over the wine list he asked, "What kind of wine do you prefer?"

"I have no idea," I answered truthfully, "I will have whatever you are having." The only wine tasting I had ever had up to this point in my life was in communion chalices at church.

As he ordered I watched him, admiring how he talked to the waiter with a polished familiarity and charming ease. When the waiter brought out a bottle of red wine and poured a small amount into his wine glass, he expertly swirled it around in his palm, then put his nose into the glass inhaling deeply, taking a small sip, rolling the wine around his mouth, finally nodding to the waiter that it was fine.

During dinner, I took cautious sips, chasing it with water and bread. I ordered a familiar dish of spaghetti but even as I bit into the long tangled mess from my fork to my plate I looked up to see him gracefully swirling his pasta on a spoon with his fork. Feeling embarrassed, I started cutting mine with my fork, taking small bites.

The conversation turned to his childhood in France and travels throughout Europe. We discussed politics, history and current events and it fascinated me. By the time we finished dessert I didn't want to go back to the dorms.

As we drove back, he asked, "Would you like to see my place?"

"Sure, but just for a little while," I answered, hesitantly. "I have to get back – I really shouldn't have even gone out tonight – I have my first test on Friday and I really need to study."

He lived in a basement apartment by himself off of campus. It was small and old; the living room had a rickety desk with a worn out couch and a small coffee table with two ashtrays on it. He walked over to a dusty record player and pulled a record out of its colorful sleeve, putting it on the turntable. Soon Bob Marley started singing "Jammin."

"Would you like to dance?" he asked holding out his hand.

I took his hand as he pulled me in close. I found myself moving in rhythm to a calm pulsing beat, his left hand on my back, our other hands clasped together. He pulled me in closer to him as I laid my head on his chest, smelling his French perfume, getting lost in the moment with this stranger from a land I never knew existed, dancing to music I had never heard before. It was so different, yet so wonderfully alluring. After the song he offered to open a bottle of wine.

I woke out of my trance. "No, I can't. I must get back… but thank you," I answered nervously. It was softly raining outside. He instinctively grabbed his trench coat off the coatrack and covered me with it, then grabbed an umbrella. As he walked me to his car shielding me from the rain, I embraced his protection, feeling safe in this stranger's arms.

When he walked me to my door, he held my hands and said, "Thank you for a beautiful night." I looked up into his warm eyes and he bent down to kiss my lips lightly.

Later that night as I lay in my dorm bed, listening to the rain fall, I fell asleep smiling, humming to the words of that Jamaican song.

Over the next few months we were inseparable and for the first time in my life, I was in love and I basked in the warmth of this radiant new light. The whole world seemed to take on a lighter, more airy quality, raising me to a higher plane where everything took second place to this intoxicating feeling I had whenever I was with him. He had ignited a fervor in me that I never knew existed and the heat from this fire excited me, drawing me closer and closer to its hypnotic glow.

He pursued me intensely, making me feel beautiful, cherished and safe in his arms. He was four years my senior but he seemed even older and more experienced in this life, which was very attractive to me. In the isolated world of campus life, our affection for each other was not just tolerated but celebrated by friends because in this progressive, open-minded community, our differences were ignored as if our traditions, cultures and belief systems were superfluous, cast off like old clothes in the nakedness of our new love.

Here in the unreal world of campus life we were united as sojourners in the quest for what we saw as a higher purpose - those degrees that promised us self-fulfillment, a higher standard of living, the pride of accomplishment or those lucky few who simply pursued their passion and were fortunate to make a living at it. We were a tribe unto our own that welcomed everyone without discrimination, blurring the lines of principles, creeds and traditions, casting aside these encumbrances that blocked our entrance to this new way of life where we felt good, and we danced carelessly to the wild beat of acceptance, tolerance and personal liberty.

MEETING THE PARENTS

Confident in this relationship, I felt it was time for Ibrahim to meet my parents, so I called them, explaining how I had met someone pretty wonderful that I would like to bring home for Thanksgiving. I was confident that they would fall in love with him as I had. The next weekend we drove from Pocatello to Boise, and arrived at my parents' home early in the afternoon. My parents were waiting for us, eager to meet the young man that had captured their daughter's heart, but when we walked in, I saw my father's eyes widen in shock as he beheld this foreign man on his daughter's arm.

"Mom and Dad, this is Ibrahim!" I exclaimed excitedly, as Ibrahim shook both of their hands.

"Nice to meet you," my mother said politely, watching my father out of the corner of her eyes.

My father's eyebrows furrowed, as he looked Ibrahim up and down. "Let me take your things," my father said immediately, grabbing Ibrahim's suitcase. "You can stay in Corey's room. Kelly, you in the guest room," he added, making sure he separated us at least in sleeping arrangements.

When we sat down in the living room, I watched Ibrahim's eyes take in this home where I had grown up and spent most of my childhood. Crucifixes and religious pictures hung on almost every wall. The fireplace was flanked with a golden statue of the Madonna with child on one side and on the other, a large replica of the Pieta, depicting Mary grieving, holding the body of her lifeless Son. A black velvet Jesus, weeping, with a crown of thorns, hung next to an ornate shadow box housing all of the instruments of the passion that were used to torture Jesus. Ibrahim seemed comfortable with all of this as he opened the conversation by talking about his childhood in Catholic boarding schools and serving as an altar boy in weekly masses.

My father, who still had a look of astonishment on his face, asked, "But isn't Ibrahim a Muslim name?"

"Yes, it is," he answered calmly. " I was raised Muslim but I have great respect for Catholics and I have always gone to church, and, I even go with your daughter most every Sunday," he answered, smiling at me, as I nodded agreeably.

My father's eyebrows shot up again, a look of hope on his face. "So you are Catholic?" he asked.

"No, but I find the common ground between us and respect our differences," Ibrahim answered smoothly as my father tried to digest this.

"I understand that you are a priest?" Ibrahim asked my father.

"No, no, no. Not a priest," my father laughed. "I am a deacon. Big difference. I can marry, bury, baptize and preach but I can't perform mass or hear confession or confirm."

"But half the Catholic priests in Lebanon are married," Ibrahim said, looking confused.

"Well, that is because the Maronite Church allows married men to be priests but we don't," Dad explained, and added "They are, however, in full communion with Rome so we can receive communion in each other's churches."

The conversation turned from religion to politics and back again over the next few days as they tried to bridge the gap between their worlds. I sat quietly during these discussions, marveling at how well Ibrahim handled himself. In these three short days my parents noticed how inseparable we were: always holding hands, finishing each other's sentences or cuddling as we sat next to each other.

One morning, after my parents came back from daily mass, my father caught me ironing Ibrahim's shirt. He immediately became agitated, and asked me why I was doing that. I am sure he felt helpless watching his only daughter fall in love with this strange foreigner whom he obviously didn't trust. I was oblivious to their disapproval until it was time to leave. We packed our things and were standing in the kitchen getting ready to say our goodbyes, when my dad said he wanted to talk to us before we left. My mother quietly left the kitchen.

My father sat opposite us at the kitchen table, his sincere blue eyes welling up with tears as he looked directly at me and with a trembling lower lip started, "I know that you like him and he likes you," he paused pointing at Ibrahim as if he weren't there, "and the bird and the fish can fall in love, but tell me, where are they going to build their nest?"

21

I was moved by my father's emotions. The last time I had seen his lip tremble like this was when he said goodbye to me my first day of college, but I knew he had nothing to worry about; I believed Ibrahim was a wonderful person and my father would soon see that.

"Oh, Dad, it's all going to be all right," I answered, touching his hands across the table, "All we need is love, right?" I answered incredulously through my rose-colored glasses.

My father's eyes looked back at me soulfully, peering deep into my eyes, seeing that I was already too far-gone and nothing he could say would change my mind.

As we drove back to Pocatello, I wept, feeling terrible that my father was so upset by our relationship and I shared it with Ibrahim.

"Don't worry about your father," Ibrahim said, touching my knee, "He just doesn't understand us. It is a new world for him, but he will come around, you'll see."

I tried to let his words reassure me but I couldn't remove the image of my father's troubled face from my mind.

FIRST FIGHT

"My father said I have permission to marry you," Ibrahim announced rather abruptly one afternoon while we were studying at his apartment.

"What?" I asked, startled, looking up from my book. "When did you talk to your father and why, when we haven't even talked about it?"

"It's okay," he answered smiling, trying to reassure me. "In our tradition we have to get our parents' approval before we even ask the girl."

My heart surged thinking that he was talking to his parents about marrying me, but caution set in. "Don't you think it's a little soon? I mean we have only been dating a few months and I know my parents won't agree."

"That's okay," he answered. "We can get married quickly now and then do a big ceremony later for your parents."

"You mean elope?" my eyes widened. I had only heard about such wild stories of eloping whispered about my grandmother Alice, my father's mother, who against her parents' wishes, ran off and married my grandfather. "No, they would be angry and it's not the way I imagined myself getting married," I added, shaking my head.

"But don't you want to move in together this next semester – I miss you," he pleaded softly, enveloping me in his arms.

"Move in? Oh my God, my parents would kill me and never speak to me again!" I said pulling away.

"Not if we were married. Look I want to marry you. My father said yes and I want to be with you," his eyes implored me.

"So you want to run down to the courthouse and get married, just like that," I asked. "What is the rush?" I hated to be pushed or rushed into anything – especially with the most important decision of my life.

"There is no hurry," he hesitated. "Well then, we can do as you Americans do – just move in with me and we will try it at first."

"You don't understand – not all of us Americans live like you see in the movies – we all don't live together before we get married," I answered narrowing my eyes at him. "My family is very traditional and when I want to get married it will be walking down that aisle at church with my whole family present." I stood up now in front of him, explaining.

"Your parents will never agree to our marrying," he stated bluntly. "You know it and I know it." He frowned, a shadow falling across his face. "I am not good enough for their daughter."

As I looked at my new love I felt moved to sympathy for him. He was right. They would never agree to our union and I could only imagine how he felt.

"They are just close-minded and racist!" he added.

My ire was ignited. No one talked badly about my family. "My parents are not racist!" I exclaimed emphatically. "They help so many people – people from all walks of life! They visit the sick in hospitals or their homes, give so much to the poor and they are always there to help others! I have never even heard one racist word or for that matter a swear word from either one of them except the word damn! You know maybe this isn't going to work out between us!"

This was our first fight and I hated it. My family had always been there for me and the last thing I wanted was to have this friction between the people I loved the most. "I have to get out of here before I say something I will regret," I said, turning toward the door. "I am going for a drive." I left before he could object, slamming the door behind me.

I got into my little red car and started driving toward the foothills. Somehow a drive through nature always seemed to calm me down. Fall had arrived in its entire splendor - the rolling hills were on fire with warm oranges, brilliant yellows and passionate reds. Birch trees tossing their flaxen tresses; aspens trembling, their lemon yellow leaves shaking like cymbals on a tambourine; alder trees swathed in spun gold, lavishly carpeting the hillside with their soft golden leaves; sumac trees glowing like hot embers. All were proudly flaunting their exotic foliage, generously dropping leaves dipped in goldenrod, crimson and apricot. Even the plain cottonwood, with its gnarly gray trunk and dull green leaves, was now transformed: deep copper and radiant golden light adorned her limbs, now swaying to the rhythm of this autumn dance.

As I wound around the serpentine road, confetti of brightly colored leaves swirled around me. I felt the warmth of the afternoon sunshine on my face as I gripped the wheel firmly. My problems seemed a million miles away. I turned on the radio where U2 was singing, "With or Without You." I rolled down my window and turned the music up singing along with it. I drove fast but smoothly, enjoying how I handled the quick turns.

As I drove, I pondered my current situation. I had never fallen like this before. Ibrahim said he loved me and that he couldn't live without me and I felt the same way. Isn't this love? Don't you know you have met the one when you realize you can't live without them? I loved everything about him, his smile, his laugh; even his adorable accent and he cherished me, loved me and wanted to marry me. I had girlfriends who had the same boyfriend for years who lived together and they dreamed of the day their guy would even discuss marriage. But I couldn't just run away and elope – it wasn't fair to my parents. I didn't want to hurt them – I just wanted everyone to love each other and get along.

And I felt like that cottonwood tree, alive for the first time in my life and Ibrahim had been the reason. He made me feel wanted, cherished and beautiful and I loved that feeling. He found my shyness and quietness endearing, as though he could see past the walls I had so carefully placed in my world to protect myself.

"*What kind of person am I if I reject him because of the what he believes?*" I reasoned. "*Surely two intelligent, open-minded, compassionate adults can find common ground,*" I smiled as I turned my car back to town. I knew that I couldn't leave him. I loved him and he loved me – what could be simpler than that?

It was already dark when I drove back to his apartment. All of the lights were out. I walked in and heard a murmur from the bedroom. Moonlight shone through his bedroom window and I saw him curled up in bed under the covers.

"Ibrahim?" I asked, gently touching his shoulder.

"Kelly!" he said, sitting up in bed, looking relieved to see me. "I thought you left me for good."

"No, I just had to get away to think," I said. My heart ached to see him this distraught.

"Are you back?" he asked, his eyes wet with tears.

25

"Yes," I sighed. "I can't live without you," I said, smiling.

He reached out both arms to me like a child, "Promise me that you will never leave me," he pleaded.

As I entered into his embrace, I felt the wetness on his cheeks. "No, Ibrahim, I will never leave you. Never."

MUT'A

"I know how we can fix our situation," Ibrahim greeted me. I had just joined him at the school cafeteria where he was studying at one of the tables.

"What do you mean?" I asked plopping down next to him, giving him a kiss.

"We can get married," he announced.

I sighed. "You mean elope?"

"No we can perform 'mutah," he responded.

"I'm sorry," I said. "But what is mutah?"

"Mutah – it is a temporary marriage," he began. "I am allowed to marry a chaste woman who is Christian or Jewish – we call them 'people of the book' and we can do the ceremony ourselves..." he began. "No one needs to know."

"Whoa... temporary? " I asked. "Marriage is not supposed to be temporary – you are supposed to promise to be married to that person forever, richer or poorer, in sickness and in health."

"You know I want to marry you," he answered, pulling me closer. "Of course, I want to be married to you forever, but we can't wait to "be" together until then. This is kind of like a promise of my betrothal to you. I give you a dowry, we pray before God, making this promise to each other until we actually have the ceremony. This way there is no sin."

My head was spinning. "I am not following you at all. You aren't explaining this very well," I told him pulling away.

He pulled up a chair to sit directly opposite of me. "Mutah has been used for hundreds of years, especially during times of war or travel when a man was away from his country and couldn't have a marriage ceremony the proper way. It allowed him to marry a woman without sin, exchanging vows to each other. Then when they returned back to his country they could get married in front of a sheik with their families. I know how you feel about 'living in sin' and that is one of the reasons I love and respect you so much. This way we have no shame before God."

"I have already talked to my family, and to them, after this we will be considered married – husband and wife, and then the official ceremony will only be that – just a ceremony," he added.

"Okay, well, marriage to me is not just a contract but a covenant between us and God," I added slowly trying to understand this strange marriage custom. "But even in a civil ceremony, you have to have two witnesses."

I wasn't convinced and I knew that my parents, let alone the government would never recognize this 'mutah', but I could see that in his mind we would be officially married because he truly believed that. The more he talked about this over the next few weeks, I realized my mind would never believe in this temporary marriage but it wasn't my mind I was worried about; it was more carnal than that. My body yearned to be with him as husband and wife, to lie next to him naked as natural as it should be without any guilt or fear of being used and abandoned. I wanted to be his one and only, his cherished wife and abandon myself body and soul to him.

One night after a home-cooked meal of spaghetti and a glass of red wine I surprised both of us. "Okay, let's do this."

"Do what?" he asked, surprised by my demeanor.

"Let's do this mutah marriage thing," I answered, "I'm ready. But you have to promise me that we are going to get married as soon as my parents agree."

"Of course!" he said rising from his chair. "You will see. I will be the best husband ever!" and then he raced to the bedroom pulling out a piece of paper with Arabic scribbles in one hand and a necklace in the other. "Here," he said placing a heavy 22 karat gold necklace in my hand.

"What is this?" I asked, smiling. "A wedding gift?"

"Kind of," he began. "My mother sent this to me for you, for the dowry."

"Dowry?" I asked. "Really? I didn't know this was still practiced?" I stared at the thick roped necklace.

"Yes, it is," he replied and then glanced at the paper in his hands. "We also have to say a few words to each other."

"What kind of words?" I asked, frowning.

"Well, you say this," he started reading some words in Arabic I couldn't understand. "Which means 'I marry myself to you for whatever period we decide, for the agreed upon dowry, which is this,'" he said pointing to the necklace.

"For whatever period we decide?" I said shocked. "What about til death do us part?" I asked. "That's how we do marriage vows. We don't put a time limit on it just to see if it works out." I was getting upset.

"No, no, you don't understand," he tried to explain. "We can say forever. I just want to make sure I give you the dowry and do this the proper way."

"Oh, okay, well that's very thoughtful," I said smiling. "If that makes you feel better, then I don't mind."

As he spoke the Arabic words, I repeated them, feeling foolish that I didn't know what I was saying. I added my own words in English at the end, "I promise to love you forever, forsaking all others, for better or worse, richer or poorer, in sickness and in health, til death do us part."

Ibrahim said, "qabiltu!" (I accept) with enthusiasm and then we kissed. He picked me up and laid me on top of the bedcovers. To me, I now saw us as engaged, the words simply a promise of his betrothal, but the way he held me and looked at me now, I knew he saw me as his wife.

ELOPEMENT

My parents did not view this ceremony the same way I did. They soon found out that we were living together and immediately confronted me. A phone call from my mother confirmed her worst fears and soon she and my father drove down to confiscate my car. They told me I could finish my last year of college on my own since I had chosen this path. Devastated that I couldn't make them understand that we were betrothed, and feeling guilty that I had hurt them, I made a hasty decision to get married civilly, to make it official, thinking my parents would then accept us.

The day we were married there was no wedding, just a quick trip to the Justice of the Peace. The gray sky matched my mood and the wind seemed to taunt me, blowing fiercely in my face. We drove to the courthouse in silence, a heavy sense of guilt pressing down on me and I was ready to shed it. Two elderly county clerks were chosen to be our witnesses since we didn't bring any of our own, and as we exchanged our vows to each other, these women smiled kindly on us.

"You two are a beautiful couple," one said, after the quick ceremony, her face beaming and then said reassuringly, "You can tell he's a good one."

It was bittersweet, being married like this, without family or friends to share this with and it didn't feel right. There was something to be said about pronouncing your vows and love in front of everyone who mattered to you and have them share in the joy of your union. I held the little marriage license in my hand, staring at it somberly, as we drove back to the apartment and a tear splashed on it. Ibrahim noticed.

"Hey, it's okay," he said, placing his hand on my arm. "I love you."

"It feels wrong," I said. "It's not how I imagined at all."

"It's okay," he reassured me. "I promise we will get married in your church one day. It's all going to work out."

I'll Fly Away

When I called my mother with the news that we had eloped and were now officially married I couldn't have imagined that I had actually thrown fuel on the fire. She didn't believe me until she called to verify it with the county and she had a copy of our marriage license in her hands. It only made things worse. My parents were heart-broken and our relationship suffered. We talked on the phone occasionally, whenever I would call, but it was strained and the more they pulled away from me, the more I leaned on Ibrahim.

Part II The Fowler's Snare

"Keep me safe, Lord, from the hands of the wicked;
protect me from the violent, who devise ways to trip my feet.
The arrogant have hidden a snare for me;
they have spread out the cords of their nest
And have set traps for me along my path."
Psalm 140:4-5

BETRAYAL

I was only twenty-two and in this one year, I had graduated with my
bachelors degree, eloped, and moved in with my now husband.
Isolated now from family and friends, he quickly became the center of
my world. I embraced the role of homemaker, and became the
supportive wife, working two jobs while he finished his pharmacy
degree. I learned how to make his favorite dishes and kept an
immaculate house, eagerly anticipating the time he would return from
school.

One Saturday, he dropped me off at the Laundromat to do our
laundry so he could go study at the Student Union Building. A few
hours later after every item of clothing was meticulously folded and put
in the car, I thought I would surprise him with a visit before going
home. As I skipped up the stairs to find his favorite couch, I noticed a
girl sitting there, the back of her long black waist-length hair facing me.
The whole upstairs was empty, so I decided to ask her if she had seen
my husband. As I approached her, I saw my husband sitting on the
floor between her knees, his back to her, pointing to his neck where he
wanted her to kiss him. I stood utterly still as she obliged his request,
not wanting to believe what I was seeing. I couldn't move. I couldn't
breathe. I turned around and walked away, devastated. Then anger

swelled in my chest, fury building quickly. I turned back around and marched right up to them. Ibrahim quickly jumped to his feet when he saw me.

For some strange reason, I wanted to know if she was innocent in this. "Did you know he was married?" I asked her loudly, pointing at him.

She didn't respond and then I knew my answer, so I yelled even louder, "Did you know that he was married?" I pointed at her now.

She stepped right up to my face and slapped me hard on my right cheek, "Bitch!" she yelled.

I stepped back, shocked. "Why you little, you little . . . slut!" I yelled back now swinging at her.

Ibrahim jumped in pulling the two of us apart, a smile creeping up on his lips.

"Don't touch me!" I yelled, turning my entire wrath on him. "Don't you ever touch me again and don't bother following me home!" I turned and ran down the stairs running to the parking lot. He followed behind me, pleading with me to turn around.

I jumped into the car and locked the doors and began to drive away. He ran alongside, banging on the passenger side door, begging me to let him in. I glared at him through the window and finally unlocked the door to let him in. I sped home, swerving recklessly, slamming on the brakes in front of our apartment.

As I bolted out of the car, running, with hot tears stinging my cheeks, he followed me, pleading, "There is nothing going on between me and her!"

"What do you mean nothing is going on?" I turned and faced him, my small frame moving right up to his big chest, trying to push him away as he got closer. "I saw you! I saw her kissing the back of your neck as you pointed! Her legs were wrapped around your body! My God, we aren't even married a year and you are cheating on me!"

"I am not cheating," he reasoned. "She is still a virgin."

I looked at him incredulously. "What? How do you even know that? And why in the world does that matter? You are not making any sense!" I screamed.

"You are not making any sense!" he yelled back.

"I hate you. I hate you!" I said now sobbing hard, pummeling his chest with my small hands.

I felt a hard whack on the side of my head and then my legs shot out from under me as my head slapped the floor. Stunned and in a state of shock, I lay dead still, unable to move as I tried to comprehend what just happened. I felt him kneel next to me, leaning over and picking me up on his lap.

"I am so sorry," he lamented. "I didn't mean to hit you. Are you okay?"

Still confused as to what just happened I stared blankly at him, catatonic, my body frozen in shock, as he rocked me in his arms, trying to console me. I finally pulled out of my daze and quietly got up and went in the living room. I picked up the phone and called my parents.

"Mom, this is Kelly," I said numbly when she answered. "I just found out Ibrahim has been cheating on me. Please come and get me," I said, leaving out the part that he had just hit me.

"We will be right there," my mother said.

I walked in a daze to the living room and sat on the couch to wait. He tried to join me. "Don't sit next to me," I said coldly. "My parents are on their way."

"It was an accident," he started.

"No one hits me," I said quietly. "No one."

"I am an idiot!" he said, hitting himself on his temples with his fists.

"Yes, you are," I agreed. "My parents were right not to trust you."

"I don't know what I was thinking!" he said. "I was letting that girl flirt with me. She is Palestinian and always wanted to marry me and I let her get to me!"

"Whatever," I answered coldly. "Now you can marry her," I stared straight ahead.

He got on his knees kneeling in front of me, his eyes full of anguish, weeping. "I am so sorry, I never meant to hurt you! I love you and only you!"

Looking into his eyes now full of remorse, reminded me of my own heart now in pieces, lacerated from his actions. Tears spewed out against my will as my lower lip trembled, "Why? Wasn't I good enough? After all I gave up for you and did for you? Why? Is it because she's Arabic and I am not?"

"No, no no," he answered trying to hold me as I pushed him away. "I am an idiot! A real idiot! You are my beautiful wife and I don't deserve you!"

His pleas for forgiveness continued as I tried to push him away. My mother and brother were on their way but it would be four hours from Boise to Pocatello, and he used this time wisely, wearing me down with his apologies and professions of love. His tears matched my own and in a few hours we were holding each other.

"I swear that I will never even talk to another woman besides you!" he proclaimed, making bold promises. I just wanted to be held and be reassured that it wasn't me that he wasn't attracted to, not realizing it had nothing to do with me.

When my mother and brother drove up, I was sitting on the porch steps, waiting for them. After I hugged them hello, my mother quickly assessed the situation.

"You're not coming with us are you?" she asked, narrowing her eyes at me.

"Everything's okay Mom," I said, avoiding her eyes. "It's not as bad as I thought," I tried to reassure her. "I am sorry you had to drive all this way, but everything is okay." Ibrahim stayed in the house, not daring to come out while I talked to them. After they drove away, I walked back into the house and sat on the couch.

"Are they okay?" he asked sheepishly.

"Fantastic," I answered sarcastically. "Just fantastic."

"Well, I am going to bed," he said yawning. "I am exhausted."

I stayed up the rest of the night, feeling guilty that my mother and brother had driven all this way only to turn around and go back home. When the morning light shone through the windows, I walked to the bedroom and stood over my husband observing him. He was snoring loudly, sleeping like a baby; seemingly oblivious to all the pain he had caused my family and me. I felt sick to my stomach.

I grabbed a suitcase and started packing my few belongings and took out a piece of paper and wrote, "I am leaving you. Your car is at the airport." I left the note by the phone. I drove to the airport, threw his keys in the car, locked it, and went inside the airport to rent a car.

When I arrived home four hours later and walked through my parents' front door, unexpectedly, they were overjoyed. Their daughter had come home and everything was going to be okay.

CONFLICT

"Why didn't you tell me he hit you last night?" my brother Corey asked after I shared every detail of the night before over breakfast. "I would have shown him what it feels like!" he said, throwing a punch in the air angrily.

"We are so proud that you left on your own," my father interrupted. He smiled, "I think it's even better this way."

My family was happy I was back and I quickly filed for divorce. I bought a $40 divorce kit, which was sufficient since we had nothing to split up; everything I owned was in my little suitcase and I didn't want his car. I was proud of myself for leaving and I felt strong and safe here with my family, but it still hurt. I had loved him, given him all that I was and compromised many things for him and in return he had broken my heart, leaving it in pieces. I knew that leaving him was the right decision but I still ached for him lying next to me, ached for the dream that I thought was real. At first I slept a lot on the couch, wrapped up in blankets, barely eating. I was bruised, inside and out and I needed time to heal. After a few weeks, my parents encouraged me to get a job to start moving forward so I quickly made up my resume and started looking for work.

My mother gave me a lead from one of her friend's husband who was looking for a secretary. The day I interviewed it quickly became apparent to me that he wanted more than a secretary when he invited me out to lunch the next day to finish our interview. When he picked me up at my parent's house he said that after lunch he would like to take pictures of me, after he commented that he liked my hair better down. I politely declined and after he dropped me off at home, I immediately shared this with my mother who was in the kitchen making dinner.

"Mom, your friend's husband is a creep!" I told her, still shaking.

"What are you talking about?" she asked.

"He asked if he could take pictures of me some afternoon, just the two of us!" I answered, looking for a response.

"Oh, Kelly," she smiled, still busy chopping her salad, "He is not a creep. So he takes pictures? That's his hobby."

"No, he is a creep and I am not working for him," I said, trusting my own instincts.

"You are exaggerating and that is a very good job," my mother answered. "He owns that company and the pay is good."

"I don't care," I said. "I can find another job." I left the kitchen to follow up with other job opportunities. At that moment the phone rang.

My mother shot me a stern look. "He's still calling," she said, referring to Ibrahim, warning me. "Don't answer it."

I hadn't answered the phone since I had been there and had no intention of it now. "I can't believe he has the nerve to keep calling like this," my mother said.

"I have no intention of ever speaking to him again," I announced confidently. "I can't believe he had the gall to ask Dad if he could talk to me."

My mother looked carefully at me for a long time, searching my face for any cracks in my resolve. "You need to get a job," she finally said.

I applied everywhere now, for any job, and I felt confident that I was going to be okay. Yes, I had some sadness but everyday I was getting stronger and healing was right around the corner. I was twenty-three, had my bachelor's degree, no children to take care of, and had my family behind me. I was going to be okay. I had only been home a month and I knew I would eventually find a job, move out and start again.

One early afternoon after coming home from an interview, I walked into the house to be greeted by my father. His eyes were wild, his face white with fear. "What's wrong, Dad?" I asked, alarmed.

"You have to get out of here," he said grabbing both of my shoulders, pleading with me.

"What?" I asked, my heart racing. "Why? What happened? " I looked around, expecting Ibrahim to be in the next room. "Is he here?"

"No, no," he answered shaking his head, his eyes not focusing on me but wildly scanning the room for what unseen monster I couldn't tell. Then he stopped again and eyeballed me somberly warning me, "Trust me. You need to get out of here as soon as possible. It is for your own good."

A sense of dread fell on me. "Why? What happened?" I asked completely confused. "What's going on?"

I followed him to the living room where he sat on the couch looking frazzled. "Is it Mom?" I asked.

He didn't answer my question. He got up from the couch. "I have to leave," he said, heading for the garage. Before he left he looked at me again and said, "You just need to get out of this house as soon as possible. You just need to – trust me."

A sense of dread fell on my shoulders as I numbly walked to my bedroom, my ears still ringing with his words. I sat on the bed and pulled the covers around me and began to weep uncontrollably. I was left alone with a million thoughts running through my head.

"You are just the biggest disappointment to your parents. What a loser – here you are twenty-three, already getting a divorce and you can't find a job! They help you out with college and this is how you repay them? Loser! I don't blame your mom for wanting you out of here!" I thought.

I dried my tears and started cleaning the house. It was already clean but I always cleaned the house when I felt guilty and wanted my mother's approval. When we ate dinner that night, I saw the flicker of anger and disappointment in my mother's eyes and the way she talked to me as I did the dishes and cleaned up. That night they left for awhile and I sat on the couch staring out the window feeling full of despair. All of a sudden, the phone rang, startling me out of my stupor. I knew it was Ibrahim. We didn't have an answering machine and it kept ringing and ringing. I jumped off the couch ready to confront him.

"Hello?" I said boldly.

"Kelly?" Ibrahim responded. "Is that really you?" I heard the hope in his voice.

"Yes," I responded coldly. "What do you want? And why do you keep calling? I want nothing to do with you!"

"Listen.… Listen to me," he began, his voice dropping low. "I have been trying to get ahold of you forever! I called your grandpa in Montana and spoke to him. I called your Dad, and even had Mareta send you a letter."

"You talked to my grandpa?" I asked. "Why did you bother him?"

"I told him your parents won't let me talk to you!" he answered speaking quickly.

"What did he say?" I asked curiously.

"Well, he said that he heard that I hurt his granddaughter," he began. "But I told him I was sorry. It was an accident and that I still love you!"

I sat down on the fireplace, pulling the cord of the phone its full length. "You still love me?" I asked. "Didn't you get the divorce papers?"

"Yes but I don't want that. Do you?" he responded.

"Yes I want that!" I answered hotly. "After what you did to me! Of course I want that!"

"I am an idiot. I promise I never slept with that girl and I never should have touched her...." he began slowly. "But I am nothing without you! I can't live without you! I miss you more than anything! I love you Kelly, I really love you!"

Silence. A heavy weariness shrouded me as I felt an ache of love for him that I thought was dead. I buried it quickly.

"I have to get off the phone," I said sadly. "We are through – please don't call here again!"

But it was too late – he heard the softness in my voice and before we hung up he said, "Look for the mail I sent you. I hid a love letter in some of the things you left behind."

After I hung up the phone, I went to find the big manila envelope he had mailed a week prior with some papers I had forgotten to take with me. It was in my bedroom in the nightstand's drawer. I took it out and shuffled through the papers and found an unusually thick old birthday card from my parents. I looked closer and saw a two-paged letter folded up and taped inside. I unfolded the letter and began to read,

Dearest Kelly, my wife, ...

I put the letter back down, thinking I should destroy it but I was compelled to finish it. It went into detail about the anguish he felt waking up and finding me gone. How he called Mareta to help him find his car and about the letter she sent trying to get us back together. I remember reading Mareta's letter, thinking she didn't understand, and feeling betrayed that she was helping him. Then he poured out his heart telling me how we belong together and that he was so sorry for what he had done.

After I read the letter, tears streamed out involuntarily. *"Why was he making this so hard? Why can't he just be the jerk I thought he was and just forget me and move on?"* I thought angrily.

The next day I was tormented with conflicting thoughts. My emotions went from despair to elation depending on what I thought. I didn't share any of this new information with my parents. I knew I was on thin ice as it was with my mother and I didn't want her to be even angrier with me.

I continued going through the motions for the next few days trying to shove Ibrahim's words out of my mind. I went job-hunting everyday, putting my resume everywhere I could, helping at home even going to daily mass at the Catholic Church with my parents when they went. I kept the house clean and stayed out of their way falling into the familiar family routine, including the family rosary. As we chanted the 53 Hail Marys and 7 Our Fathers, I watched my parents' faces: my father mumbling his words, nodding off as my mother tenaciously recited every syllable. I loved my parents but I understood the family dynamics. My mother ruled the house, and my father followed, and although he was happy that I was home, it was obvious that I was creating tension. I didn't expect my Mom to embrace me with loving arms and words of encouragement after I returned because we had never had that kind of relationship and I felt unworthy to even be here. I knew I was an embarrassment, and the longer it took to find a job the more tension it created between my mother and me. I began to feel desperate.

A few days later when I was home alone, the phone rang again and I answered.

"I am driving to Boise to see you," Ibrahim said, answering my hello.

"No!" I said, alarmed. "What are you talking about?"

"We need to talk in person," he answered strongly. "If you don't meet me somewhere I will come to your parents' house."

'No! Don't do that!' I answered, and finally agreed to meet him that afternoon at a restaurant near the highway.

When I walked into the restaurant he was waiting for me. The shock of seeing him again after a long month of absence grabbed me. He smiled handsomely and said, "Wow! Now this is my lady! You are beautiful!"

I didn't respond and avoided his outstretched arms and sat down in the adjacent booth, trying to keep my emotions in check.

"I want to share the good news with you," he began, sitting opposite me.

"What good news?" I asked, not knowing what to expect.

"I have been accepted into medical school!" he said beaming. "Now I will be able to take care of you properly and we can soon start a family!"

I shook my head, smiling in disbelief. "You are just assuming that we are getting back together," I began. "That is an awful lot to assume."

His tone became softer as he reached out his hands across the table to hold mine. "I love you and I know you love me," he said.

Tears streamed down my face as I angrily brushed them away. I had always loved how affectionate he was with me, constantly touching and holding me. He had always filled my aching need for affection and tenderness and I wanted to believe what he said was true. More than anything, I wanted to be loved like that.

For the next two hours he talked to me, convincing me that we were meant to be together.

"I will go back to you on three conditions," I said, finally. "One that you will never cheat on me again. Two, that you will never hit me again and three, that you will buy me a real wedding ring."

He laughed, throwing his head back, showing his perfect white smile. "I promise. I promise. I promise!"

We went back to the house and I packed up my things as he helped me load them into his car. I tore a poem out of the book, *The Road Less Traveled*, and wrote on it:

Dear Mom and Dad,

I am going back to him. He loves me and promises me that he will never hurt me again. I love you both, and I am sorry for all of this.
Don't worry. Everything is going to be okay.
Love,

Kelly

As we drove back in the darkness to Pocatello, I imagined that my mother was somewhat relieved that I was not a burden to her anymore and my father could rest easy tonight, knowing I removed any conflict by simply removing myself. Ibrahim wanted me now and his pursuit for me only confirmed how much he loved me.

ADDICTIONS

Life propelled us fast-forward when we returned and I threw myself into packing for our new adventure: Ibrahim had decided he wanted to become a doctor and was accepted at a medical school in Kansas City. After we settled, in I found a night job at the IRS to help support us. One morning, he came home early from classes.

"Why are you home so early?" I asked. An uneasy feeling in the pit of my stomach started churning when I saw the anger in his face.

"That stupid professor!" he ranted. "He will not increase my grade no matter what I do! He won't pass me in that class and I am less than one point beneath a C!"

"Well, just go talk to him again," I suggested. "Maybe you can write a paper or take another test?"

"No! I already did!" he answered. "He is the most stubborn man I have ever met! That's it! I don't need him! I have a pharmacy degree that I have never used so you know what?" he asked, smiling to himself.

"What?" I asked, knowing I would not like the answer.

"I am going to get a job as a pharmacist. Forget medical school. I mean I haven't even tried working as a pharmacist yet," he answered, pacing the room.

"But you are only a month away from the first year," I reasoned.

"No! That's it!" he answered. "No one treats me like this!"

The next few days I tried to prevent him from making this decision but he was just as stubborn as the professor. So I found myself packing again – this time for Las Vegas, Nevada where they desperately needed pharmacists. I found a job working at a local bank and doctor's office. We were earning a sizeable income between the two of us but I soon found out he had another addiction besides cigarettes – gambling.

I'll Fly Away

It called to him like a siren every night after work. I was uncomfortable with him going out alone, so I joined him. His favorite was the one-dollar slots and I watched in horror as he put dollar after dollar into these machines that hardly ever returned the favor. He would throw some coins into my plastic bucket and I would try my luck but I soon realized that the odds on these machines were in the house's favor and all our hard earned money was being wasted. When I reconciled our bank statements at the end of the month, I saw hundreds of dollars withdrawn from the ATM machines placed in every casino. His habit was costing us $2,000 a month. When I questioned him about it, he would get angry, so I avoided the subject. I started cashing in the coins he would give me, and when he wasn't looking, placed the money in my purse so we could pay our bills.

Night after night, we ate out at the buffets at the casinos that rewarded his healthy gambling habit with free dinners. Afterwards, I would sit next to him, pretending to join him, but I could have been invisible. His attention was on the machine in front of him, his eyes squinting from the cigarette smoke circling around him, as his arm automatically pulled the lever again and again. He would stop only occasionally to take a free drink from the scantily clad cocktail waitresses that he barely noticed as he returned his attention back to his machine. He wasn't alone; the casinos were full of mindless zombies mesmerized by the hope of winning the next jackpot.

We lived in Las Vegas for three years and we started to grow apart. I was now going to church alone, while he worked double shifts or slept off the night before. We had been trying to get pregnant, but it was like my womb was closed off to this idea and now his gambling losses affected his mood.

One day, after I came back from the hair salon, he was waiting for me.

"Where have you been?" he asked, in an accusing tone, as he walked toward me.

"I just got my hair done, remember?" I answered timidly, backing away. "I even bought some new conditioner for my hair," I said, holding out the little paper bag in my hand for him to see.

"How much was it?" he screamed at me.

"It was $21," I answered truthfully, holding out the receipt. The only thing I ever spent on myself was a haircut and color every two months, dying my light brown hair the blonde color that he loved.

"Twenty one dollars!!" he yelled, smacking the bag out of my hand. "We don't have that kind of money!"

"I know," I answered defiantly, staring at him. "Because you throw it all away gambling."

I heard the loud smack on my ear before I felt it, but the pain soon followed. Reeling from the sheer brunt of his large hand, I clasped my left ear from the floor where I had landed, screaming, "My ear! My ear!"

The pain was searing, like a hot poker had been shoved in my ear canal, and I thought for sure it was bleeding. I couldn't hear myself, only a loud ringing as I cried out. He immediately began apologizing.

"I am so sorry!" he said. "I didn't mean to!" He tried to comfort me but I pushed him away.

"I can't hear – we need to get to a doctor now!" I cried, grabbing the phone book and shoving it in his hands.

He found an ENT doctor close by and drove me there. "Go ahead in," he said, "I will be here in the parking lot."

The doctor saw me right away and put some medication in my ear, which quickly took the pain away. He then took a tuning fork and hit it, placing it at various locations around my head to see if I could hear. He looked worried when I couldn't hear its vibrations.

"Well, your eardrum is perforated, and it is too early to tell if there is any permanent damage," he began. "Can you tell me again how this happened?"

I repeated my story. "I was playing tennis with my husband and another couple, and the ball hit me right here, right on my ear," I said as convincingly as I could.

The doctor asked his nurse to leave the room and after she closed the door he said, "Left-eared female, right-handed male...I have seen this before. Are you sure you don't want to tell me what really happened?" His compassionate eyes burrowed into mine as I held back the tears.

"That is what happened," I explained. "I am not a very good tennis player and probably wasn't paying attention."

The doctor sighed heavily and said, "Where is your husband?"

I avoided his gaze and stared at the floor and murmured, "He had to take care of something but he will be right back."

"Fine, we will leave that on your record, but if you ever want to change it, just let me know," he said seriously, obviously concerned.

After I checked out I walked outside. The harsh midday sun and enveloping heat pounded my face. Squinting, I shaded my eyes searching for Ibrahim and found him at the edge of the parking lot. He drove up quickly and I climbed in.

"What did the doctor say?" he asked.

"My eardrum is perforated," I said sadly and started to cry softly.

"You know I didn't mean to do it," he started. "Did you tell him it was an accident?"

"I told him it was a tennis accident," I said, noticing he was more concerned about his reputation. "So don't worry, you are off the hook."

"I am sorry, you know I didn't mean to," he said gently now, touching my shoulder. I jerked away from him and faced the window tuning him out with my other ear and mumbled, "Hit me once, shame on you. Hit me twice, shame on me."

That week I was seriously contemplating leaving him again. This seemed to be a pattern with him and it scared me, but the nausea I was feeling from all of this was not just repulsion for him. I was pregnant.

MARRIED IN THE CHURCH

This news overshadowed anything else in my life. I felt a mixture of happiness and fear all jumbled together. I had always wanted to be a mother and for three years we had been trying. I saw it as a miracle. This new life in my womb was another chance for us. Ibrahim was elated and called all of his family to tell them the good news. His demeanor toward me changed. Now, I was the mother of his child. He became very attentive to me and made sure I rested. He even began cooking dinners and spending more time with me. I was optimistic and saw it as a sure sign that things were going to change for us.

When I shared the news with my parents, I could taste the disappointment in my mother's voice. Ibrahim tried to "smooth the edges" as he would say, and surprised me one day with his idea.

"You know what would make your parents happy?" he asked smiling.

"What?" I answered.

"If we get married in the Catholic Church!" he said confidently, smiling expectantly at me.

"You would do that?" I answered, my face now glowing with appreciation. "Are you sure?"

"Yes! Of course I will!" he answered, scooting closer to me on the couch, touching my small baby bump. "Your parents will be happy and accept us then and I know how important that is to you."

Tears of gratitude streamed down my face. "You are the most wonderful husband in the world," I said kissing him.

We went to my church, the Guardian Angel Cathedral in downtown Las Vegas that week and met with Father White. We were seen separately and when it was my turn to talk to him he motioned for me to sit down. He was an elderly priest with a kind face; his white hair framed two sparkling blue eyes.

"So you two want to get married!" he said leaning across his desk, winking at me kindly.

"Yes, yes we do," I answered, smiling.

"Well, I just talked to your husband, and it seems he was practically raised in the Church what with all the Catholic boarding schools and all," he said.

"Yes, and he used to attend church with me often," I answered truthfully, pleased that he liked my husband.

"Well, I will have to get a special dispensation from the Bishop for this union but that shouldn't be a problem," he answered. "Since neither of you have been married before, we will only need your baptismal and confirmation certificate and your marriage certificate of course." He paused, and then said, "But before we do all of that I have a question for you, the same question I asked him."

"Okay," I answered, eager to please.

"What is the one thing that you would change about him?" he asked, now peering deep into my eyes.

"Oh, that's easy!" I answered. "That he would become Catholic!"

Father White's white eyebrows shot up. "Oh you can't ask him to do that!" he answered, surprised by my answer.

Guilt washed over me. *"But isn't that what I have been praying for all of this time?"* I thought. *"Isn't that what the Catholic Church wants me to do?"*

"Okay, that he would know Jesus as His Savior?" I asked.

Father White just shook his head. "My dear, you just can't ask that of him," he answered kindly. "Just name one characteristic you could change about him."

I hesitated, not wanting Ibrahim to be put in a bad light. "Well, I wish he would stop gambling," I murmured.

"How much does he gamble?" he asked.

"Well, more than he should," I answered hesitantly.

"Well, there is nothing wrong with a little gambling," Father White answered, smiling. After all, he was the parish priest at the church in the middle of downtown Las Vegas where parishioners often put casino chips in the offering basket. "Everything in moderation, but my concern is - are you with him when he goes?"

"Not lately," I answered, now confused. "I really don't like the conflict it causes."

"Well, you need to go with him every time he goes," he warned me. "Don't leave him alone – that is far more dangerous, okay?"

I nodded my head and agreed. "Okay, I will," I promised him.

"Great! Now I will send for this dispensation and will have the office call you when it comes in," he said standing up to shake my hand.

"Thank you father," I said humbly and left.

On the drive home Ibrahim turned to me at one point. "You know, I like him," he said.

"What did you two talk about?" I asked.

"A lot of things, you know, serving as an altar boy in France, my home country and my family," he replied and then nonchalantly added, "You do know he made me promise to raise our child Catholic in order to get married in the Church?"

My heart swelled with hope. "He did?"

"Yes but you know we both agreed to teach them both faiths and let them decide," he answered truthfully.

My heart plummeted fast. "Yes, yes we did," I answered somberly. A wave of guilt washed over me. *Surely when presented with both faiths, my child will choose the right one,* I thought.

When I conveyed the good news to my mother she seemed skeptical. "You are telling me that he agreed to get married in the church?" she asked.

"Yes! Can you believe it Mom? Isn't it wonderful!" I said, straining to hear some hint of approval in her voice.

"So is he converting to Catholicism?" she answered.

"No, no, he isn't," I answered, my enthusiasm now deflated.

"Well where are you going to find a Catholic priest to marry a Muslim and a Catholic?" she asked.

"We already have," I answered. "We are getting married at the Guardian Angel Cathedral by Father White. We received a special dispensation from the Bishop!"

A long silence answered me. "The Bishop gave you a special dispensation?" she answered dubiously, and added, "When is the wedding?"

"January 2nd, in a few months!" I answered, waiting for her to respond with some happiness.

"I will have your father call to make sure this is legitimate," is all she said.

"It is Mom, trust me – aren't you happy?" I asked. "Your daughter is getting married in the Catholic Church?"

"We'll see," she answered. "If it is legitimate."

I'll Fly Away

I clung to the hope that we would be united together in the unity of my childhood faith - that through this sacrament surely Ibrahim would convert and then everything would be okay.

WEDDING VOWS

My wedding day found me in Father White's office that seconded as a bridal room, staring at my reflection in a full-length mirror. I was six months pregnant and it showed. My oversized ivory suit with a mid-length skirt didn't hide the big baby bump underneath. This was not how I had imagined my wedding day. My mother was standing next to me, looking mortified at her very pregnant daughter who was about to walk down the aisle among friends and family.

"Oh Mom, I am so embarrassed," I said, looking to her for comfort.

"What did you expect?" she answered matter-of-factly, "You're pregnant."

I wanted to hear that I still looked beautiful, and have my mother embrace me and tell me how happy she was for me. I scanned her face waiting for any sign of approval but she stood at a distance from me, frowning.

"Well, they are about ready to seat me," she said. "Good luck." I reached out to hug her awkwardly and she left.

I sat down on a pew underneath a stain-glassed window left alone with my thoughts. I reflected that this would actually be the third time I was marrying this man. My mind went back to two summers before when I visited his family in Kuwait for the first time. Although they were Lebanese in nationality, they lived most of the year in Kuwait, visiting their home in Lebanon only in the summer. The day after we arrived, Ibrahim asked me if we could have our marriage blessed by an imam. Thinking that any blessing would be welcome, I agreed.

That day I wore the most conservative dress I brought, an army green dress that fell mid-calve. Before we left, his mother handed me one of her scarves and Ibrahim explained that I had to wear it out of

50

respect for the imam.

"Really?" I asked Ibrahim. "But I don't understand how my hair can offend anyone?"

"It's our custom. It shows him respect," he answered simply.

"I understand," I said and took the scarf. I went to the bathroom and clumsily tied it under my chin. When I looked in the mirror, I saw a peasant woman from the medieval times looking back at me. I took it off and tried again, this time putting it on loosely, letting the ends fall over my shoulders gracefully, like Audrey Hepburn. Satisfied, I left the house for the car where his parents were waiting. When my mother-in-law saw me she clicked her tongue in disapproval and started fixing my scarf pulling it tight on my head, pushing back any offending bangs and tied it firmly right under my chin. I sighed, imagining what I looked like now, but smiled politely and thanked her.

When we arrived at the imam's house, we took our shoes off, adding to the tall pile of sandals lying outside. I was immediately introduced to a short, elderly man dressed in a white prayer cap and long gray robe. He touched his heart, smiled and bowed politely as I did.

"Salam w alaykum," (Peace be with you) he said.

"W alaykum a salam,' (With you, also peace) I responded.

I already knew the rule that only members of the opposite sex could not touch, unless they were related, including handshakes. He motioned for us to sit down on a large Persian rug on the floor, and we did, in a circle, sitting on our knees. Arabic swirled around my head as the conversation began. I assumed they were talking about my dowry when Ibrahim pointed to the necklace and earrings I was wearing and his father showed 10 crisp $100 bills that he had given me. As they continued to talk I felt left out of my own wedding, like a child at the mercy of her parents who were having adult conversations regarding them, without their input or understanding.

I could tell the imam was giving a sermon when he began talking and everyone else became quiet. I respectfully gave him my attention and nodded my head up and down like his family did, pretending I understood what he was saying. Ibrahim sat next to me but didn't translate. When the imam stopped speaking, he turned toward me.

"You have to say a few words," Ibrahim said, looking at me for the first time.

I stumbled through the words in Arabic, repeating them the best I could and before I knew it, the ceremony was finished. My mother-in-law's face was beaming as she let out a loud trill with her tongue. After we got in the car, I immediately took off the scarf that made me feel more repressed than even I was used to. When we got back to their house, my mother in law asked me a question.

"What is your mother asking me?" I asked Ibrahim who was sitting next to me on the couch.

"She is asking what your new Muslim name is now," he said nonchalantly.

I felt my face turn hot. "My new what?" I asked, shocked.

Ibrahim's eyes widened, as he looked at me then his mother.

I turned to his mother and said kindly but strongly, "I am a Christian and I will never deny my Lord and Savior Jesus Christ by becoming Muslim. I would rather die. And I will never change my name. My name is Kelly. It is the name my mother gave me and it means Irish Warrior Maiden and I am very proud of it." As I spoke, my husband squirmed next to me.

His mother listened to me not understanding. Still smiling, she asked Ibrahim to translate what I had just said. When he did, my mother-in-law's eyes darkened and a shadow fell across her face. She said a few loud words in Arabic, motioning with her hands, and rose from her chair still talking angrily as she went to the kitchen.

I turned to my husband and fired questions at him. "Why would your mother ask that? Why would she think I am a Muslim now? What did the imam have me recite?"

Ibrahim rubbed his face, avoiding me. "I'm tired. I'm just going to go lie down now." He walked away from me toward the bedroom and shut the door.

As I sat alone in the living room, I marveled how another day that should be full of celebration and joy turned sour so quickly.

*****

Two years later, sitting here in this pew, this sharp division between our worlds was still painfully present. A scripture verse rang in my head:

"Anyone who acknowledges me before men, I also will acknowledge before my Father who is in heaven, but whoever denies me before men, I also will deny before my Father who is in heaven." (Matthew 10:32-34)

I'll Fly Away

"You sure didn't leave me anyway to compromise out of this," I whispered to my Lord. "By declaring that You are the Son of God and that no one can enter Heaven except by accepting the fact that You died for us to make it possible, really does create a sword, a strong division between me and my husband," I said softly. "But I love Ibrahim. I know You love him too and I know that this will all work out somehow."

I wiped my tears away and smiled as the sunlight warmed my face. I stood up and grabbed my bouquet ready to face everyone.

It was a long ceremony with a full mass where we spent most of our time kneeling. Finally it was time to exchange our vows. We held hands as Ibrahim repeated after the priest.

"I, Ibrahim, take you, Kelly, to be my bride, my wife. I promise to be true to you in good times and in bad, in sickness and in health. I will love you and honor you all the days of my life."

I repeated the same, and meant every word of it.

Part III   Hatchlings

"See, I lay in Zion a stone
that causes people to stumble
and a rock that makes them fall
and the one who believes in him will never be put to shame."
Romans 9:33

LAYLA

Layla was born late in April and she was beautiful. She had hazel
brown eyes that glimmered like a soft dewy morning on a tender green
meadow, full pink lips, auburn hair and creamy olive skin like her
father. When I held her for the first time in my arms, all of my pain and
exhaustion evaporated. I was focused on her now – her needs, her
wants and I couldn't believe how much I loved her already. It was
overwhelming to think this brand new baby, innocent and helpless, was
now placed in my care. It was humbling to think that she would look to
us to guide her, teach her, and show her who she is in this life.

Ibrahim was a very proud father. The moment I first held her,
he took Layla from my arms, holding her up and began singing a song
to her in Arabic. At one point he placed her ear close to his mouth and
whispered something to her. I cringed when I realized it was the
Adhaan, or call to prayer for Muslims:

> "*Ashhadu an la ilaha illa Allah.*"
> (I bear witness that there is no god except Allah.)

> "*Ashadu anna Muhammadan Rasool Allah.*"
> (I bear witness that Muhammad is the messenger of God.)

I'll Fly Away

"Hayya 'ala-s-Salah ."
(Hurry to the prayer.)

"Hayya 'ala-l-Falah ."
(Hurry to success.)

"And so it begins," I thought to myself, my heart clenched with angst.

My mother was a nurse so she was there at the birth and a great help for the first week home from the hospital. After my second sleepless night in a row, I turned to her and said, "Thank you Mom, for all you have done for me. I had no idea how much a mother does for their kids - I love you so much."

My mother helped me adjust to being a mother that week and taught me many invaluable things that only a mother can teach her daughter, but the day before she left, while Ibrahim was at work, she asked me to sit down and talk with her about something important.

My antennas were up, not knowing what to expect.

"Sure, Mom, What's up?" I asked.

"Well, I am sure you've noticed, like I have these past few days, that your husband is not getting up in the middle of the night to attend to Layla when she cries," she started.

"I know, but it's because I'm breastfeeding and he is tired from work," I said defensively.

"Well, he doesn't offer to change a diaper or help with anything," she retorted. "We are sleeping here on a mattress on the floor in the living room while he is in the bed like a king."

"I know, but he works hard and it's so we don't disturb him," I answered slowly, knowing inwardly that she was right.

"That's fine, but what are you going to do when I am gone?" she asked, obviously concerned. "You know maybe in his culture only the women take care of the babies, but that is not the culture you were raised in. Your father helped me with most everything with you kids."

"I'm fine," I answered. "I can do this and I am sure that he will help me more when you are gone."

My mother hesitated, then spoke, "There's something else." Her pale blue eyes became very serious. "I'm just going to say it... You need to leave him."

"What?" I asked, shocked by what she said. "Leave him? Didn't you see how he holds Layla and sings to her? He loves her, very much!" I explained.

"Things will only get worse, Kelly, believe me," she said not wavering. "How can this child grow up in a house where the father is Muslim and the mother Catholic? This poor child will be so confused – it will never work!" she said, exasperated with me.

"How can you ask me to leave a man I love and separate him from his brand new baby daughter?" I asked incredulously.

"Two cultures from two different countries is hard enough, but it might work," she said, "but you not only have two cultures, but two different races and two completely different religions!" she explained.

"So divorce is the answer?" I asked. "I cannot believe that divorce is the best thing for this child! I do not intend to have my daughter grow up without a father and especially a father that loves her!"

My mother was immovable in her stance and I broke down crying, running to my bedroom. It was a miserable day. Once again, what should have been a time of celebration was marred by these glaring differences that I kept trying to ignore. The day she left, she hugged me and whispered in my ear, "Remember what I said."

I was alone now in this apartment while Ibrahim worked long hours but I cherished every minute with my daughter. I enjoyed being a mother and what I felt for my daughter was unlike any kind of love I had ever felt for any human being. Nothing could have prepared me for this protective, primal, fierce love that I had for her. I knew that I would die for her without question and I was just as determined to unite this family.

It was one thing to be married to someone with a completely different belief system than me. As long as he respected my right to practice what I believed, then I had no problem respecting his rights also. But now there was an innocent child involved, my child as much as his, and everything was different. I ignored Father White's advice and began to pray feverishly for my husband's conversion because my daughter's future was at stake now.

I prayed the only way I knew how, the way I was brought up. I started attending daily mass with my daughter when Ibrahim was at work. Afterward, I would join other women kneeling in front of a statue of Mary and begin reciting the rosary asking for her intercession on my behalf. I had been taught that she was not only the Mother of God but also the Queen of Heaven and Mediator for all of us. I would recite the rosary saying the Hail Mary fifty three times and the Our

I'll Fly Away

Father six times begging for her intercession:

"Hail Mary, full of grace,
The Lord is with thee,
Blessed art thou among women and blessed is the fruit of thy womb.
Holy Mary, Mother of God, pray for us sinners now and at the hour of our death."

I prayed fervently, pleading with her to pray for the conversion of my husband because I knew that if anyone could make it happen, she could. I also started going to confession every week, believing that my sins would only be forgiven if I confessed them to the priest. I felt good after leaving the confessional but my failings, my sins, added up too quickly, so I became hyper vigilant about all of them because it wasn't clear to me what was a venial (lesser) sin or mortal sin (a sin that condemns one to hell). I was encouraged to confess even my venial sins because it would lessen the amount of time I would spend in Purgatory. The more vigilant I became, however, the guiltier and more condemned I felt. I knew that missing mass on Sunday was a mortal sin so I confessed all of those times in my life that I had done that.

I obtained a checklist of possible mortal sins and confessed every thought, action or word that could threaten losing my chance to go to Heaven. The list was long- it included not fasting for one hour before receiving communion, receiving communion in a state of mortal sin, which I found out was worse than a mortal sin. It was sacrilege. All this time I thought I was a pretty good person but when I delved into this faith I realized how corrupt I truly was. And when I read that withholding confessing a sin was also a mortal sin I began covering all bases by ending with, "And for all of my other sins that I failed, or forgot to mention," just to cover all bases. All of this was my fault. I had sinned by marrying an unbeliever and now it was up to me to fix this. I did as I had been taught as a child in school and began offering up my pain for my husband's salvation.

My role models as a young girl were St. Philomena, St. Bernadette and St. Rose to name a few. I remembered opening up the big colorful Book of Saints in second grade when I had to choose a patron Saint for first communion. St. Agnes was burned at the stake and then beheaded for her belief and St. Philomena was subjected to scourging, drowning, being shot at with arrows and finally decapitated. I was horrified by all these stories so I purposely chose St. Bernadette because she didn't suffer any bodily afflictions in anyway and her body was supposed to still be incorrupt to this day.

But now I revisited these saints and began to embrace the sorrow that they suffered, especially St. Rose. She was the first saint to be canonized from the new Americas and she pursued self-affliction with a passion. She slept on a bed strewn with rocks and broken glass and used a log for a pillow; deprived herself of sleep to the point of exhaustion. She tried to mar her natural beauty by cutting all of her hair off and rubbing pepper into her face. She even wore a crown of thorns that she hid from others.

Although I didn't go to these extremes, I believed that through my suffering I could atone for the sins of others. My job was to suffer so sinners can be converted and the souls in purgatory released. I believed that through my works and Mary's intercession, I could help bring about the change I wanted in my husband. It was a very heavy burden.

RELIGIOUS DEBATES

One answer to prayer came a few months after Layla was born. We were finally leaving Las Vegas.

"I am going to go back to medical school," Ibrahim announced to me one day. "I know that I can be a doctor. That is my dream and I want to pursue it."

I readily agreed and he was soon accepted back into the same medical school in Kansas City. I was happy to leave this city that stole all of my husband's free time. Hope was renewed again as I packed our belongings with optimism in my heart.

We were like any other young couple in medical school, sacrificing the present for the future, but it worked. Life took second place to the pursuit of his medical degree and when he was home, he was busy studying late into the night. My day revolved around Layla and I soon made friends with other wives in the same situation as me.

One Sunday, as usual, I got Layla ready to go to church with me. I dressed her in a pink romper, arranging her curly auburn ringlets around her sweet face. She was two and adorable.

"Say bye bye to Baba," I told Layla as she ran to give him a kiss. Ibrahim was sitting on the couch in his blue scrubs, a pile of books surrounding him.

"She is not going with you," he suddenly said, still holding her.

Startled, I turned to look at him as he picked her up and headed for the kitchen.

"What? Why? What are you saying?" I stuttered. His demeanor frightened me.

"She is not going with you anymore to church," he said.

"But why?" I answered timidly. "I thought we agreed to teach her both faiths and let her decide when she is older?" His mother had just stayed with us flying all the way from Kuwait, and I wondered if she had anything to do with this.

"No, she will be confused," he answered. "It is about time I started teaching her how to pray. My mother brought her a prayer rug and it is my responsibility to teach her." He picked up Layla and took her to the kitchen, sitting her on the counter, handing her a cookie. He stood next to her, arms crossed.

"Fine," I choked out the word, "But why can't I take her to church?"

"Because I don't want you to," he answered glaring at me, his voice raising a few decibels, warning me not to go any further.

My face fell. I knew that tone. I knew what it could lead to and I didn't want my baby to be in the middle of that. I hugged her goodbye and walked out the door alone, and drove to church crying uncontrollably. I was hoping that this was a one-time incident, that maybe he was just in a bad mood and he would retract his stance, but he didn't.

This compelled me to begin studying his religion. I needed to understand what he was planning on teaching my daughter. I delved in, reading everything I possible could on his faith.

Soon I began what became the first of many discussions about our different faiths. It began one evening after Layla went to bed.

"Do you mind if I ask you a few questions about Islam?" I began respectfully.

"Of course," Ibrahim answered, smiling. He had noticed that I was reading his books and seemed pleased that I was exploring.

"So, who do you believe Jesus is?" I asked point blank.

"Isa (Jesus) is the son of Mary, a holy prophet of Allah, and Messenger of God who was given the Injil (gospel) from God as confirmation to the Torah," he answered.

"So you believe this Injil (gospel) was an actual book given to Jesus by God?" I asked.

"Yes, yes exactly!" he answered, pleased that I understood.

"Okay, well, that's what I don't understand. Christians have never said that the gospel was a book just handed to Jesus and the bible doesn't say this either. The gospel is just the first four books in the New Testament describing Jesus' life and teachings by eye witnesses." I answered gently.

"Oh, your bible is corrupt," he smiled knowingly and added, "but we do believe that Jesus ascended into Heaven."

"Corrupt?" I answered. "Even your Q'uran says that the Bible is a true revelation of God and demands faith in it and that no one can change the Word of God," I answered. [1]

"No, the Quran is talking about the original bible, not the one you have," he said somewhat patronizingly, as he tried to help me.

"But don't you remember the recent discovery of the Dead Sea Scrolls? Remember when every news station on TV was making a big deal about how these ancient manuscripts of the Old Testament were now going to prove what you just said – that the bible we have today is corrupt?" I said excitedly. "These manuscripts predate the authentic Hebrew text of the Old Testament by about one thousand years."[2]

"The Dead Sea Scrolls?" he asked with a puzzled look on his face.

"Yes, remember in 1947 an Arab shepherd accidentally discovered these scrolls in a cave not far from Qumran, Israel?"

Ibrahim's face look startled. "No, I didn't know about these."

I was excited. "Well after careful years of study, it was finally concluded that the Dead Sea Scrolls confirm that our Old Testament has been accurately preserved. The scrolls were found to be almost identical with the authentic Hebrew text," I explained.[3]

"Okay, so the Old Testament is pretty accurate, let's assume," he began dubiously. "But the New Testament is not."

"Why do you say that?" I asked

"Because of some of the things it says," he answered with assurance.

"You mean about Jesus?" I offered.

"Yes," he said. "You know the claims about being the Son of God, his dying and being resurrected – that is simply not true."

"Well, do you know that the Old Testament prophecies predicted the coming of Jesus, the Messiah and confirm those things that you say are incorrect?" I asked quietly, holding my breath.

"What do you mean?" he asked with a puzzled look on his face.

"There are over 100 prophecies in the Old Testament that are fulfilled in the New Testament about Jesus," I answered confidently.[4]

"Such as?" he answered, skeptically.

I quickly fired back, not stopping to take a breath, "That He would be born in Bethlehem by a virgin from the line of Abraham, that there would be a massacre of children at His birthplace, that He would be falsely accused and crucified with criminals, that His bones wouldn't be broken, that He is our sacrifice for our sins and that He would be resurrected from the dead, ascend into Heaven and is now seated at the right hand of God to name a few!"

"Where does it say in the Old Testament that Isa would die for our sins?" he asked, honing in on the one glaring edict of my faith that caused the sword between us.

I opened my bible and read Isaiah 53:5-12:

"But he was pierced for our transgressions, he was crushed for our iniquities;the punishment that brought us peace was on him, and by his wounds we are healed.

We all, like sheep, have gone astray, each of us has turned to our own way;and the Lord has laid on him the iniquity of us all.

He was oppressed and afflicted, yet he did not open his mouth;he was led like a lamb to the slaughter, and as a sheep before its shearers is silent, so he did not open his mouth.

By oppression and judgment he was taken away. Yet who of his generation protested? For he was cut off from the land of the living; for the transgression of my people he was punished.

He was assigned a grave with the wicked, and with the rich in his death,though he had done no violence, nor was any deceit in his mouth.

Yet it was the Lord's will to crush him and cause him to suffer, and though the Lord makes[c] his life an offering for sin,he will see his offspring and prolong his days, and the will of the Lord will prosper in his hand.

After he has suffered, he will see the light of life[d] and be satisfied[e];by his knowledge[f] my righteous servant will justify many, and he will bear their iniquities.

Therefore I will give him a portion among the great,[g] and he will divide the spoils with the strong,[h]because he poured out his life unto death, and was numbered with the transgressors.For he bore the sin of many, and made intercession for the transgressors."

Silence was Ibrahim's response. Then he asked, "All of that is from the Old Testament?"

"Yes," I answered "and what about Isaiah 9:6?" I flipped to the scripture and read:

"For to us a child is born, to us a son is given, and the government will be on his shoulders. And he will be called Wonderful Counselor, Mighty God, Everlasting Father, Prince of Peace." (Isaiah 9:6)

"All of this was prophesied several hundred years before Christ," I added, when he didn't respond.

Ibrahim pursed his lips and rubbed his face and said, "But you Christians believe in three gods! God, Jesus & Mary! We believe in one God, Allah!"

His answer gave me pause, seeing his only version of Christianity was Catholicism and how easily he could have been led to believe we worshipped Mary, kneeling before her staute, and praying to her. "No, we believe in One God, the Father, the Son and the Holy Spirit," I corrected him.

"How can one be three?" he asked, smiling.

"The same way a man can be a father, a son and a husband." I answered. "But we believe in one God in three separate persons."

"Aha!" he said pointing at my bible. "But where is that in your bible?"

"Matthew 28:19 where Jesus commanded us to "go and baptize in the name of the Father, and of the Son, and the Holy Spirit," I answered.

"So you believe God died on the cross?" he asked, now getting agitated. "How can God die?"

"Jesus the Son of God died," I answered. "But what do you mean by died? To die does not mean He no longer existed. Physical death is when the soul-spirit separates from the physical body. Death is the start of a new eternal life and death has no victory over Him. He conquered death."

Ibrahim seemed startled by my words. "Look, we believe Jesus, blessings be upon him, was a good prophet, a good man but He was not the Son of God," he said gently.

"Ok, well, can you tell me anywhere in the Quran or Bible where it says Jesus sinned or that He was guilty in anyway?" I asked.

"I told you, He was a good man," he answered.

"But the bible teaches that no one is righteous but Jesus," I replied. "Even in the Old Testament it says,

'For we do not have a high priest who is unable to empathize with our weaknesses, but we have one who has been tempted in every way, just as we are – yet he did not sin.'" (Hebrews 4:15)

I continued. "Even in your Quran and Hadiths, it says that Jesus was without sin."

"Where does it say this?"

I was ready. "It says that when the angel Gabriel appeared to Mary he said, 'I am only the messenger of your Lord, to announce to you a faultless son.' (Surat Maryam, 19:19, The Noble Quran) "The Hadith also says that Jesus was sinless. Your prophet Mohammed also believed that Jesus was sinless. It is recorded in Sahih Muslim (Vol 4, pg 1261): 'Abu Huraira reported Allah's Messenger (saw) as saying: The Satan touches every son of Ibrahim on the day when his mother gives birth to him with the exception of Mary and her son.'"

"Okay, so Jesus is sinless. So what?" Ibrahim answered. "That doesn't make Him the Son of God."

"But I don't understand," I answered. "Muslims call Jesus a good prophet, even the Messiah, but they reject all of his teachings. Jesus said He is the way, the truth, and the life and that no one can come to the Father but by him. (John 14:6) He even said He had the authority to forgive sins. (Luke 7:48-49) and what about John 11:25 when Jesus said,

'I am the resurrection and the life. He who believes in me will live, even though he dies; and whoever lives and believes in me will never die...'"

"I just think that the Allah you worship is not the same God as I worship," I continued. "Because in my bible it says that whoever denies that Jesus is the Christ is an anti-Christ; no one who denies the Son has the Father," (1John 2:23) I continued. "Think about it. What other prophet in any other religion claimed to be the Son of God, predicted his death and resurrection, had eyewitness to all of this including healing the lame, giving sight to the blind, even raising the dead? Mohammed never did."

I had gone too far. In my zeal to show my husband the truth, I had made the terrible mistake of comparing Jesus to his prophet.

"God does not have a son! I am not listening to this anymore!" he said, his eyebrows now furrowed in anger.

After I heard the front door slam, I realized that Jesus was still the stumbling block that separated us and always would be.

ISLAMIC SUNDAY SCHOOL

Two years of medical school went by quickly. We moved to Garden City, Michigan to finish his core clerkship in Family Medicine. We were only fifteen minutes from Dearborn, which boasts the highest concentration of Lebanese Americans in the United States.

Dearborn was like being in its own separate country and Ibrahim loved this little Lebanon where everyone spoke Arabic and most women wore veils. Muslim mosques abounded and Ibrahim soon joined one and began praying faithfully. We became immersed in the American Arab Muslim community. We shopped at the Dearborn groceries stores and butchers, buying only halal meat (the only meat that Muslims are allowed to eat according to Islamic law) and spices, oils, olives, sweets, etc. found only in the Middle East.

We would visit the famous bakeries and restaurants where baskets of hot puffy pita bread, freshly baked in a traditional brick oven accompanied every order. Chicken and lamb shawarmah (kebobs) were my favorite, along with tabboueleh (parsley salad) and hummus. Manaaeesh was Layla's favorite – mini pizzas garnished with cheese, za'atar(thyme), kashk (dried yogurt) or minced meat and onions. The sweets were unusual and unlike anything I had ever tried before: Knafeh; cheese baked in butter, between two sesame buns and doused with rosewater syrup; layali luban: cold semolina pudding with caramel syrup and pistachio nut topping; awamat: crispy small round shaped donuts soaked in syrup; and all different kinds of baklava stuffed with walnuts, almonds, pistachios. We would wash all of this down with laban, sour milk that was similar to buttermilk.

I loved this part of his culture – the delicious food and generous hospitality of his distant relatives who always made us feel welcome in their home. The conversations would mostly be in Arabic though, and I wanted desperately to understand what everyone was saying around me. I found conversational Arabic being offered at one of the community colleges and approached my husband about taking classes one night a week for two hours. He agreed, but insisted on driving me.

After a few classes, I was starting to understand more of his conversations and even began reading some of the signs written in Arabic in downtown Dearborn.

"Look! That sign reads Yas-mine….Meh…muz, Yasmine Mehmuz, Jasmine's Bakery!" I said, pointing to a sign above our favorite bakery, reading it from right to left as I had been taught. I was excited that this language was coming easily to me and now I would eventually converse with his family.

Ibrahim didn't seem to share my enthusiasm though. "Uh-huh, yeah… that's good," he answered frowning.

The next week when it was time to drive me to my Arabic class he resisted. "I can't do this anymore," he complained.

"Can't do what anymore?" I asked confused.

"Drive you to your class," he answered, pointing to a pile of books on his desk. "I have so much to study tonight."

"Well, that's just fine then," I answered lightly. "I can drive myself, you know. I mean I have been driving since I was fourteen years old," I teased. "Where are the car keys?"

"No, I mean I can't study and take care of Layla," he clarified.

"What do you mean?" I answered, now questioning his motives. "Layla is an angel. She's four year's old. Just put on one of her favorite movies and she'll be fine," I said, finding the car keys and turning toward the door adding, "It's only for two hours."

"I will drive you," he said suddenly, putting on his shoes. He took the keys from my hand and told Layla to join us. When we drove up to the school, he got out of the car and walked me to my classroom carrying Layla. He stood by my desk, staking his territory with his stance, as though he was telling everyone there that I belonged to him. It was very uncomfortable.

The next week he refused to drive me. "This is taking three hours out of my night to take you!" he yelled.

"Don't drive me then!" I answered, matching his pitch. "I don't want you to drive me! I am perfectly capable of driving myself!"

I ignored him and opened the front door to leave.

"You are so selfish!" he bellowed. "You don't understand how much I need to study!" He slammed the door shut and pointed at Layla. "How can I study and take care of her?"

I looked at Layla's little face; her big hazel-brown eyes were now round with fear looking first at me and then at her Baba, not understanding what was going on. I did, though. I knew that tone in his voice, that purple vein that now throbbed noticeably on his neck, the glaring hatred in his eyes – it all threatened to escalate into something more violent and I didn't want her to be in the middle of that.

I calmly walked away from the door and put the car keys back on the counter. "It's okay," I said evenly, avoiding his glare. "You know, you are right. I don't need to go and your studies are much more important." I walked over to Layla and picked her up. "I can learn this language on my own somehow."

Ibrahim's eyes softened somewhat. "Exactly!" he said. "You can get a book – this way it doesn't interfere with my studies."

"How about I read some books to you?" I asked Layla, ignoring him. "We still have those new ones from the library?" As I took Layla with me into the bedroom, I stifled the anger building inside me.

I went to bed early that night and when he joined me I pretended I was asleep, but he sensed that I wasn't.

"You know, I forgot to tell you, I am enrolling Layla in Islamic Sunday School at the mosque," he said.

I didn't answer and pretended I didn't hear him. I shut his words out of my heart and refused to acknowledge them. It was too much to bear for one day.

*****

"But I want Mama!" Layla screamed running after me. It was her first day of Islamic Sunday School at the mosque.

"Now Layla, you need to stay here and listen," Ibrahim admonished her. "We will be back when you are finished."

"Nooooo!!!" Layla screamed. "Don't leave me Mama!" she begged me, running toward me, latching onto my legs.

The teacher, a young woman wearing a long gray dress and scarf, offered a solution. "You know, it's okay if she stays," she said pointing at me. Ibrahim nodded and thanked her.

"Look, Layla," she said holding her hand and motioning for me to sit on a bench outside the classroom. "Look! See? Your Mama will be sitting right here the whole time while you are in class. You can see her through the window. She will not leave? Okay?" she smiled.

"I won't leave honey," I confirmed, trying to smile for my daughter's sake.

"Okay," she agreed and went to take a seat where she could see me, not taking her eyes off of me.

"I will be back in three hours," Ibrahim said to me and added, "You should fix your scarf."

I nodded numbly and tied the green scarf his mother had given me a little tighter.

As I watched, I had no idea what she was teaching but I heard the children repeat "Allahu akbar!" (God is great!), "Inshallah!" (God willing) and soon "Ya ibe a shoom alek!" (Shame on you), directed at some of the more rowdier boys in the classroom.

It was time for prayer and Layla had no idea what to do. The teacher led the girls into the bathroom where they performed the necessary ablutions (ceremonial act of washing) before prayer; another man took the boys in the men's restroom to instruct them. They washed their hands, arms, legs, head and mouth several times with water. Before we entered the main area to pray, Layla's teacher handed me an instructional pamphlet with pictures demonstrating how to pray and the words to recite next to them. "You can go with her and teach her," she said leading us down the corridor before I could protest.

After we took off our shoes I walked into a large round room with dark green carpeting, red and gold borders separating individual "prayer mats" all facing Mecca, Saudi Arabia, the holiest sight for Muslims. I went to the back of the room, holding Layla's little hand. Two women were praying a couple of rows in front of me, one, an elderly woman wearing a dark black robe and scarf and a young woman of about twenty years completely covered with a pink scarf wrapped tightly around her face. Both were completely covered except for their hands and face.

Layla was only four, not yet at the age when girls are supposed to wear a scarf, so she had a bright pink, sheer scarf loosely wrapped around her head. It was part of an Esmeralda costume I had bought her at the Disney store. She sat on her knees next to me patiently waiting for me to teach her.

"What am I doing?" I thought, my mind racing. *"How in the world did I end up here in an Islamic mosque trying to teach my daughter how to pray to Allah?*

I'll Fly Away

I watched the other women nod, bow, and prostrate, chanting the same words over and over. Muslims are supposed to pray five times a day and these women were praying their afternoon salat (prayer). The elderly woman pulled out a beautiful ivory misbaha, (Muslim prayer beads). I watched as she ran her hands over each of the thirty three ivory beads, rubbing them as she stopped to chant, "Subhanallah!" (Glory to be to Allah) at each bead and then start over again to chant, "Elhamdilallah!" (Praise be to Allah) another thirty three times ending the last round with "Allahuakbar!" (Allah is the greatest) As I watched her mouth move, repeating the same words repetitively, moving over the beads, it reminded me of how I bowed down in front of the statue of Mary and repeated my own repetitive prayers over my rosary.

"Who is this Allah that she is worshipping?" I thought. *"Is it just another name for God like Ibrahim told me? But how can it be the same God when they don't believe in the Son of God or the Holy Spirit?"*

Layla was pulling on my sleeve, "Are you gonna teach me how to pray Mama?" she asked innocently.

The older woman furrowed her eyebrows at Layla telling her to hush. "Okay," I whispered. "Just do and say what I do," I told her.

We started standing side by side and I substituted the word "Allah" for the English word "God."

I followed the illustrations and got down on my knees, placing my head and hands on the floor in front of me.

"God is the greatest!" I began

"God is the Greatest!" Layla repeated, enthusiastically.

Then I stood up and said, "In the name of God, the most kind and the most - ouch! Merciful." I tripped on the edge of my skirt. I lurched forward and caught myself with my hands. The elderly woman looked back at me, shaking her head, clicking her tongue at me. I smiled back sheepishly and continued while Layla did a handstand giggling at me.

Sitting on my knees, I read over the next few verses and frowned. I was supposed to say, "He does not produce a child, and He was not born of anyone. There is no one equal to Him." But I took the liberty to change the words.

"For God so loved the world that he gave His only begotten Son, so that everyone who believes in Him will not perish but have eternal life," I whispered.

Layla repeated this rather loudly with enthusiasm and the

younger of the two women turned around cocking her head at us, with a puzzled look on her face. I didn't want to push my luck so I bobbed my head a few more times and quickly hightailed it out of there, Layla in tow. As we rushed into the corridor I ran straight into Ibrahim's chest. He had been standing there observing us from a distance. My eyes were round as saucers, waiting for his reaction.

"That was wonderful!" he said beaming. "See Layla, that is how you pray!" and he lifted her in his arms as we headed out the door. I immediately took off the scarf, enjoying the cool breeze blowing through my hair as I followed quickly behind him.

RAFAEL

I was pregnant again, fourteen weeks along and I was tired that
afternoon. I put Layla down for her afternoon nap and stretched out
on the couch to relax, but before I could rest, Ibrahim stormed
through the door. He was not in a good mood. When he saw me lying
on the couch with my feet up he became even angrier.

"You haven't even started dinner?" he yelled at me.

"It's only 3:00," I answered meekly, rising from the couch into
a sitting position. I had the lamb already thawed out and wasn't
planning on preparing it until 4 since he usually didn't get home until 6.
"I didn't know you were coming home early," I added.

He went into the kitchen, pulling out pots and pans and started
banging them around on the stove. "I guess I have to do everything
around here!" he yelled louder.

I got up and walked to the kitchen, opened up the refrigerator
and pulled out the lettuce and vegetables to make a salad while he put
the meat in the pan and started chopping onions. "I always have dinner
ready," I said meekly. "I was just taking a breather for a minute – I
don't know why I am so tired…"

"Tired!" he screamed. "I'm tired! Tired of working and having
no sleep!" He pointed to my stomach. "And now you are pregnant
again! Just what I need - another one to take care of!"

He continued to rant and rave and yanked open all the drawers
slamming them shut looking for something. "Where did you put the
garlic press!" he yelled. As I searched in the drawers he screamed, "You
can't do anything right!" He started to swear at me in Arabic as I
handed him the press. I stood there staring at him for the longest time,
his back to me, listening to the onslaught of terrible words, cursing me,
and for the first time a hatred for him rose in me. I was holding a large
wooden salad spoon in my hands and I flung it at the back of his head.

Immediately he swung around, the momentum of his whole
body behind him, as he flung me against the entrance wall, six feet

away. My body slammed into the wall and then slid down on top of our shoes by the door. It happened so fast I collapsed into shock and then looked up to see him coming after me. I ran for our bedroom and locked the door behind me.

He banged on it. "Let me in!"

He started working on the bedroom door with a hanger and then I heard Layla's voice. She had woken from her nap and wanted me.

"Kelly, Layla needs you!" he yelled through the closed door.

I waited a few minutes and opened the bedroom door to let Layla in and pretended like I was just tired and needed to rest. Satisfied, Layla left to watch a video while Ibrahim continued to cook.

I went to our bathroom and just sat on the floor, shaking from crying. I felt the urge to use the restroom and when I looked down in the toilet and saw blood I began to wail, "Oh my God – no!"

Ibrahim was knocking on the bathroom door. "I need you to finish the salad. I'm sorry but I didn't mean to – this one is your fault – you threw the spoon!" he said.

"Well, you will be happy to know that I am losing the baby," I said spitting out the words at him.

"What?" he asked through the door.

"I am bleeding. The toilet is full of blood!" I answered.

"Let me see," he said.

"No! Just stay away from me!" I yelled through sobs. "Don't touch me – just go away!"

He left quietly and went back to the kitchen while I stared at the blood trickling down my leg.

I put a pad on and slipped into bed thinking that if I lay really still the bleeding would stop. Ibrahim came in carrying one of his medical books and opened it and began to read, "Miscarriages this far into pregnancy are very common. They happen within the first thirteen weeks of pregnancy."

I looked at him incredulously. "So you think that throwing me into the wall had nothing to do with this?" I asked bravely, my lower lip trembling. "Are you kidding me?"

He had never admitted guilt before and wasn't about to start now. "This is very common. It happens all the time but you just need to rest right now. It doesn't mean you are miscarrying because you see a little bit of blood," he continued.

But I knew as only a mother can, my baby was dying within me.

The next morning the sheets were covered in blood. Shocked, Ibrahim drove me to the emergency room to a downtown Detroit hospital with Layla. The waiting room was full and we passed through a metal detector before we were even registered. Finally I was admitted and called back. A nurse put me on a gurney and wheeled me down the hallway and placed me against a wall, explaining that all the rooms were full. Ibrahim stood there uncomfortably next to me and then took Layla back to the waiting room. As I lay there bleeding for over an hour, watching hospital staff walking past me, I felt forgotten and completely alone.

Finally, a doctor confirmed what I knew – I was miscarrying the baby and there was nothing he could do. Since it was within the timeframe of normal miscarriages, no questions were asked and I didn't offer any answers. I was sent home and for the next month I bled and mourned the loss of this child. Although I never laid eyes on this child, I longed for him. I named him Rafael which means "God has healed" hoping God would heal this agony in my heart.

The loss of this child left me extremely depressed and I didn't realize at the time that depression is anger turned inward. I was angry – angry with him but mostly angry with myself for getting into this situation in the first place.

"*This is my punishment,*" I thought often. "*I am reaping what I sowed. I made my bed and now I must lie in it. This is what I get for being unevenly yoked and marrying someone outside of my faith.*"

As a Catholic I believed that even though I had repented of my sins and God had forgiven me, I still had to suffer temporal punishment (suffering in this lifetime). I searched for a way to alleviate this punishment for my past sins and found in my Catholic faith that I could make reparation for these sins by performing indulgences, which I found in the Handbook of Indulgences Norms & Grants. I could get a partial indulgence, which only remitted a portion of my punishment, but when I found I could get a plenary indulgence that would remove all my punishment, I pursued this passionately.[5]

TETA & JIDO

Spring in Detroit, Michigan was uneventful in this flat concrete city. The dismal gray rain only made me long for home. I sat by the living room window, daydreaming of the small western town of Boise where I had spent most of my childhood. True to its name, "City of Trees," every spring Boise would come alive with vivid greens, vibrant pinks and velvety cream blossoms on every kind of tree. Bright yellow, red & pink tulips would herald the beginning of this season and the sweet sound of songbirds promised that summer was on its way. Today there was no promise of anything in this austere city of Detroit, except potholes and angry drivers.

"Teta (Grandma) & Jido (Grandpa) are coming!" Ibrahim suddenly announced to Layla, startling me out of my somber trance.

"Yay!" Layla responded, clapping her hands together as she danced around her father. Visits from his parents always meant gifts and lots of sweets for her.

I always looked forward to seeing them because this sparse apartment where I spent most of my time alone with Layla became alive. My mother-in-law filled the house with delicious aromas as she bustled around in the kitchen, and my father-in-law engaged my husband in loud animated discussions in his big, grandiose way. I loved it because it meant Ibrahim stayed home more and Layla was the center of attention, spoiled with gifts and kisses. I had always wanted a big family, deciding early in my life that I wanted at least six children running around the house, filling my life with love and laughter.

I remembered the day I decided to have six children. The Newell family came to visit our quiet home in Boise for the first time when I was just starting adolescence. When I first met this family with six children, I remember being struck at first with their bubbly enthusiasm and warm laughter. I watched in wonder as they filled the house with their light-hearted presence and listened to their musical

74

flow of conversation where giggles erupted without warning. They spoke their minds with a polite confidence about them; it was obvious that they were secure in their love and place in their family.

I remember feeling envy for the first time in my life as I watched their father affectionately tease his daughters, hugging them, praising their accomplishments and obviously taking great delight in all of his kids. When their father turned his attention to me and asked me questions in front of everyone I became embarrassed and stumbled over my words, not used to being in the limelight. The kids affectionately befriended me and invited me into their games and I became like them for that day – their joy was contagious. When they left, the house was even lonelier than before and I quietly returned to my room, my mother to the kitchen, and my father to his books.

A big, happy, messy family full of life and noise – that's what I wanted. Ibrahim grew up in a big family- his mother gave birth to thirteen children – ten survived – eight boys and two girls. Born the third son, he was his father's favorite and he didn't hide this from his other children. I saw pictures of my husband when he was small - an adorable child with light olive complexion, big dark brown eyes and full pink lips with wavy black hair. Most of his brothers were darker in skin color with tight wiry hair but Ibrahim was the handsomest of his father's sons and his father loved to show him off in the marketplace, where people would admire him by pinching his cheeks and thanking Allah for this angel.

Jealousy ran deep among the brothers, however, and he found that while his good looks drew women to him like a magnet, he wanted something more substantial to rely on. Ibrahim still wanted his father's approval and that was the driving force behind his decision to be a doctor. He was going to be the first doctor in the family and his father was proud of his son's accomplishments and bragged about him to everyone.

As we spread a tablecloth on the floor and filled it with dishes made by his mother, I noticed the resemblance between Ibrahim and his mother. She was once the most beautiful woman in her village in southern Lebanon, and Ibrahim's father pursued her passionately. From earlier pictures I saw she was strikingly beautiful, a strong woman with long ebony hair, light skin and piercing eyes; if I didn't know better I would have thought she was Greek or Italian in the picture where she wore a peasant dress with a beautiful headdress.

But now her eyes quivered from side to side, and her body had thickened so much over the years that she moved slowly, with great effort as she walked. I followed her in the kitchen, helping her cook and taking notes on how to make these dishes my husband loved. She couldn't speak a word of English but it didn't stop us from communicating.

Ibrahim called his father Abu Ali (the father of Ali). Even though he had other sons and daughters, in his culture, a father was known as the father of the first-born son as was the mother, Amu Ali (the mother of Ali).

Abu Ali sat like a king, leaning against the couch, one knee up as we waited on him, serving him first. He was obviously pleased with me as I helped his wife and he commented, "Now this is a woman!" he told his son. He was pleased that I was an attractive match for his son and commented on my slim body and soft voice. I was raised to be a pleaser and I fit into this role effortlessly, serving others first and staying quietly in the background, happy that Ibrahim's father liked me.

My husband smiled at me as if seeing me for the first time, "Yes, yes she is," he said. "She is also pregnant with another child – this time a son I hope!" he added with enthusiasm.

"Enshallah! (God-willing) my mother-in-law said loudly. Her eyes met mine and within her dark eyes I saw hesitation, a flicker of distrust that betrayed her smile.

NADINE

"Her name will be Zaynab," my husband announced, looking down at
the small pink bundle in my arms. He seemed disappointed that he had
another daughter instead of a son but he couldn't deny how beautiful
she was. Deep brown eyes the color of maple syrup swirling with warm
honey stared back at him, intently observing him. I looked at my
beautiful daughter, admiring her long black eyelashes that delicately
framed her almond-shaped eyes. Her stubborn pink little lips protruded
out as if in protest to this name.

"No, I don't like that name," I said strongly, defending her. I
had survived three days of false alarms, being sent home each time and
just finished five hours of labor with this child, the first half without
anesthetics and I was in no mood to be crossed.

"But that is my mother's name," he said frowning.

"We will call her Nadine," I said. It was the only other
American-sounding name from the list of Arabic names besides
Jasmine and Layla that I could pronounce. In his culture the middle
name was always the father's first name and I felt that I should at least
have some say over my daughter's first name. Seeing that I wasn't
budging, he agreed.

"Nadine, my beautiful daughter," I whispered looking into her
big, captivating eyes. She was small but wiry. When I put her over my
shoulder she lifted her neck and tried to look around. "Look how
strong she is!" I marveled.

Layla held her little sister, and as I watched them I was
overcome with the joy of being a mother to two beautiful girls.

"You know her name means hope," I told Layla who was
fussing over her.

"What does my name mean?" Layla asked.

"Dark beauty," I answered. Layla smiled, showing her dimples,
obviously pleased with this.

"She is strong," Ibrahim said. "She will be soon be ready to move to Pennsylvania."

My heart fell when he reminded me of his latest decision to transfer out of the D.O. program to the M.D. clinical rotations in Harrisburg, Pennsylvania. His brothers had been riddling him lately, telling his father that a D.O. physician was not the same as an M.D. physician, and that Ibrahim was not training to become a "real doctor." In America osteopathic (DO) doctors are legally and professional equivalent to allopathic (MD) doctors, the only difference is the more holistic and preventative emphasis with Dos, but this was hard for his father who had only heard of MDs in his country to understand. Even though it meant he would have to take extra rotations, his pride took first place and I began packing.

Part IV Scattered Nest

"...A man reaps what he sows."
Galatians 6:7

LIARS

After two grueling days of driving with my colicky two-month-old baby and five-year-old daughter, we arrived in Harrisburg, Pennsylvania. I was exhausted but unpacked every box and decorated every room in the rental home we found and then flew on a plane back to Boise to visit my parents with the girls for a much needed vacation. My parents were always happy to see us on these trips and they welcomed Nadine, helping me soothe this fussy baby that never seemed to sleep.

One afternoon, after I had just successfully rocked Nadine to sleep in my room, my mother opened the door gently and whispered, "Ibrahim is on the phone."

"No rest for the weary," I said quietly, smiling.

"I need you to come back and pack again," Ibrahim said in greeting. I clutched my stomach, trying to stop my emotions from churning a new storm within me.

"What?" I answered dumbfounded. "What do you mean? I...I... just packed and unpacked everything. What happened?"

"These stupid people!" he said angrily. "They promised to accept all of my credits when I transferred but they are not giving me credit for a couple of rotations!"

79

"But, I thought we knew that?" I answered.

"I didn't think it would be more than one!" he said. "They lied to me! They promised me something and then changed it on me!"

"But you can't leave now," I begged him. "Stay with the program. It will take a little longer but it will all be worth it."

"You have no idea what you are talking about!" he yelled at me. "These rotations are ridiculous! I am running on four hours of sleep right now and I am all alone over here!"

I swallowed a big heaping of guilt. "I know," I began softly. "I am sorry to leave you, but I needed help with Nadine and I haven't seen my parents in over a year and..."

"What about me?" he interrupted. "I need you to come back right now and pack!"

His answer smacked me hard. I felt a buried anger simmer in my gut. "I was the one who packed and unpacked everything by myself," I began. "With a colicky brand new baby, and I helped drive and lift and carry and everything into the new house and unpacked everything for you, even putting the beds together for you so you wouldn't have to do anything," I answered. I felt free to speak my mind on the phone under the shelter of my parent's home, knowing he couldn't do anything to me.

Silence answered me. "I've already made my decision," he said calmly, giving me no choice. "I applied in South Bend, Indiana for some D.O. rotations and they have accepted me."

I sat on my knees on the couch, pulling myself up a little taller. "I am not flying back there to pack everything all up again and then drive with you to South Bend and unpack!" I said strongly. "This is just crazy! "

"Fine!" he yelled back. "I will hire a company to pack and move everything for me. All you have to do is just change your ticket and fly to South Bend and everything will be done!" he answered.

I paused for a long time not responding. *"Maybe I won't meet you there,"* I thought. *"Maybe I will stay right here and start over again."* I was getting tired of all of these moves. This would be move number seven for us. I yearned for stability, for a home in a community where my girls could establish roots. At this point Boise was the only place that we returned to every year that my children felt at home.

Ibrahim seemed to sense what I was entertaining and said softly, "Hey, it's going to be okay. You know, I notice that on this visit to your parents, you never call me much – is everything all right?"

"No, I mean yes, everything is all right," I answered. "I am just tired of all of this moving,"

"Don't worry," he said gently. "Everything is going to be all right. One day we will settle down and stay in one place and have our own home."

I hung onto that promise as we flew to South Bend, and walked into a strange apartment piled high with boxes.

"I couldn't afford to have them unpacked," he told me sheepishly as he caught my surprised look.

The promise of a better life and the need to create a home for my daughters were my motivation as I unpacked everything again. Layla was starting kindergarten this fall and I had to create some sense of order out of this chaos.

"Every time I come back from visiting my parents, there is always a surprise waiting for me," I mumbled to myself remembering the previous year when I had come back from Boise to our place in Michigan. I was shocked because every family photo was off the wall, even Layla's baby pictures.

When I found them tucked away in a closet and confronted Ibrahim about it, his response unsettled me. "Well, I had Kadeem over to study," he said referring to his Iranian medical student friend. "And some friends and I just didn't think it was their business to know about my family."

"What?" I asked, sniffing something suspicious. "Kadeem knows you are married."

"I know but he is a single guy and he brought some friends over to study and it is none of their business," he continued, weaving his lie.

"Were these "friends" female?" I asked, already knowing the answer.

"Yes, but they were his friends," he answered, avoiding my eyes.

I didn't believe him and my fears were only confirmed the following week when I picked up the living room phone one morning, not realizing Ibrahim was talking to Kadeem from the bedroom line.

"So do you want to?" Kadeem's sultry voice was asking my husband.

"I don't know. Are they pretty?" I heard my husband ask.

"Yes, yes, they are very pretty, and there are five to choose from," he responded.

"I don't know, let me see if I can get away," Ibrahim said.

I hung up the phone gently and sat dead still on the couch waiting for him to come out of the bedroom. He got in the shower and changed into new jeans and a freshly ironed shirt. He smelled good.

"Where are you going?" I asked as nonchalantly as I could, not taking my eyes off of him.

"I don't know," he answered, sitting on the couch to put his shoes on. "Kadeem wants to study today…"

"I heard the whole conversation!" I blurted out. I was never any good at hiding my emotions and they were spilling over now.

"What are you talking about?" he said, looking puzzled.

"You are going to meet those girls that Kadeem told you about!" I said, verging on tears.

Ibrahim remained calm and collected. He wrinkled his nose at me and said, "I don't know what you heard but I am not going with Kadeem."

"You didn't say no," I answered. "Your only concern was if they were pretty or not!"

"You are making yourself look foolish in front of your daughter," he said, motioning to Layla, who now sat next to me listening to every word. "Kadeem is a single guy – he is allowed to date."

"Well, where are you going looking so good on a Saturday afternoon?" I challenged him.

"Nowhere," he smiled at Layla, motioning for her to come sit on his lap. "I am taking my daughter downtown for some manaeesh – do you want to come with?"

I mulled over these things as I angrily unpacked our things yet again, hoping that there would be no more surprises. There was always a hint of infidelity and I would catch a whiff of it now and again in his late nights studying, strange phone calls where someone hung up when I answered, and how he never wanted us to visit him at work but nothing ever concrete materialized until here in Indiana.

ALLEGATIONS

Ibrahim walked in the front door - he was home unusually early from work again and the alarms went off in in my head. He walked past me and sat down at the kitchen table; his face was ashen white, his shoulders slumped over as he grasped his hands together, looking up at me solemnly.

"What is it?" I asked, sitting across the table facing him. "What is wrong?"

"Someone from the hospital board talked with me today," he began slowly, anguish all over his face. "They want to have a hearing with me,"

"A hearing?" I gasped. "About what?"

"About a patient's allegations," he said somberly, looking down at the table.

My heart stopped. "A woman?" I whispered, already knowing his answer.

He looked up at me startled. "Yes, but it's not what you think," he defended himself. "She is almost forty years old and nothing to look at – she is making all of this up!" His eyes pleaded with me to believe him.

I took a deep breath and pulled back in my chair, narrowing my eyes at him and whispered, "What did she say you did?"

"I don't want to talk about it because I don't understand it!" he said getting angry.

"You have to talk about it because I need to know!" I said firmly.

He looked at me again with those same sad eyes, searching for sympathy. "I don't know...She came in sick, so I began examining her. She was sitting down on the table and I began looking into her ears and checking her throat – the normal things I do for every patient. I gave her a prescription and that was it," he finished.

"Well, that's obviously not it because she is pressing charges," I

83

answered. "What did she say you did?"

"She said I was pressing up against her the whole time and touched her inappropriately," he mumbled.

"How so?" I asked.

Ibrahim stood up and shoved his chair away from the table. "She is a liar! A crazy woman! That's all I know! And now I could lose my license over this!" he exploded. "I didn't do anything wrong!"

The next few months were agonizing. I vacillated from defending him to believing my gut – I knew he did something wrong - I wasn't sure of what exactly, but it was enough for this woman to complain. At the hearing he refused to receive their offer for counseling because he thought to accept it would mean he was admitting he had a problem, so he was suspended for three days and placed on probation for the rest of his rotation. He was not allowed to see female patients. Although he was relieved that his dream of being a doctor was still intact, his reputation suffered among his fellow medical students who were fully aware of his situation.

Ibrahim couldn't wait to get away from Indiana now and after a few months I was packing again, this time for Cleveland, Ohio where he had found a coveted rotation. He was almost finished, and the dream that we had been sacrificing for was finally going to be a reality. Four years of medical school, one year of internship and two years of residency were behind us. Unbeknownst to us, however, the incident in Indiana was not.

Because these allegations were not removed from his record, he was suspended from any further rotations until the Ohio medical board reviewed his case. Eventually, we received a letter denying a medical license in the state of Ohio. The news of this dropped on our home like a bomb, shattering everything in its wake. I gingerly tiptoed around the now broken shards of our lives doing my best to attach the pieces back together. We had to move back to Nevada because he was still licensed there as a pharmacist.

Ibrahim hired a lawyer to help him remove the allegations from his records at the Indiana hospital. The litigation process slowly drudged on, taking its toll on both of us. We had moved back to Nevada in the spring of 2000. A year later we were still fighting for the removal of these allegations from his record. As hopeless as I felt I was not prepared for what he proposed.

"That's it," he said suddenly after a long phone conversation with his father one evening. "Get ready to move."

"What do you mean?" I asked hopefully. "Did you find another residency?"

"Residency?" he scoffed. "Who would give me a residency now? I sued a hospital! I am on their blacklist!" he shouted at me. "I am through with this! I will take my father up on his offer and open a pharmacy in Lebanon!"

I remained calm, ignoring his last statement. "You haven't tried to apply for a license in another state. I know there are states desperate for doctors, especially in rural areas. This isn't over yet." I told him. "You are legally a general practitioner and can work that way."

"It was not my dream to become a general practitioner, to settle like this," he answered bitterly.

"I am not going to give up hope!" I answered. "And I am not going to just pack up and go to Lebanon – that's insane!"

"Well, right now I can't deal with this," he answered, walking to the closet and grabbing his black leather jacket. "I'm going out for the night. I'll be home later," he said grabbing his cigarettes off the counter. He left, shutting the door softly behind him and slithered out into the night.

MOTHERLY INSTINCTS

Ibrahim was putting in twelve hour shifts as a pharmacist now, working from 9AM to 9PM, only to come home, eat dinner, kiss Layla and Nadine goodnight and then leave us again to try his luck at the casinos. He would stagger in around 2 or 3 AM, and fall into bed only to start it all over again the next morning.

We were back in the place I hated and the casinos called to him every night and his was the right, as he saw it, to come and go as he pleased. At first I would wait up for him and confront him when he came in but I quickly backed down when he got angry. He knew I had no power to stop him and my first priority was my daughters. They didn't need to see us fight or their mother struck. I resigned myself to tiptoeing around him and tried to create a loving environment for my girls. I took this opportunity to read Bible stories to my daughters from the same Children's bible my parents had given me and I shared my faith with them.

I couldn't seem to protect Ibrahim from himself, however, no matter how much I prayed for him and our situation. One day he came home from work early, holding his framed pharmacy license. Not a good sign. I didn't even need to ask but I did.

"Did you get fired?" I asked.

"Yes! Those sons of bitches!" he yelled, slamming his diploma on the kitchen table.

I felt myself sink into the old familiar feeling of dread. I didn't want to know why. I didn't want to face the truth. I didn't want to face what my gut had been telling me all along.

"One of those damn girls complained about me!" he said, only confirming what I felt.

"What happened?" I asked with no emotion in my voice.

"One of those Pharmacy Technicians, I don't even know her name… said I was inappropriate with her!" he said, his eyes flitting everywhere but into my own.

"What did you do?" I asked. It was as though I was talking to a stranger, with nothing invested in the outcome of his answer.

"I only touched her one time," he began. "I was rubbing some crème on the back of her neck because it was dry but I only used one finger."

"Of course," I said not believing him.

"You do believe me?" he said, now scanning my face, surprised that I showed no signs of any reaction. I nodded numbly and he was satisfied.

A sickening feeling overwhelmed me as he continued on with his story, defending himself, a familiar refrain where he was once again the poor foreigner being discriminated against. After he finished venting on me, he called his parents to complain about this terrible country.

Layla and Nadine who had come out of their bedroom at this time listened to him rant about how evil and terrible America was. Layla sat quietly next to me now, as I put my arm around her while she peered up at my face trying to determine what was going on.

"Mama, why are you crying?" she asked. "Who hurt Baba?"

"Oh, honey, Mama is just tired, so tired baby, and Baba is going to be okay," I said trying to reassure her, wiping away my tears.

As I looked into her innocent eyes the old fears now resurfaced *What if he can't clear his record and he wants to leave America? What if I can't talk him out of it?* Here in America, I had some control over the raising of my daughters, but over in his country I knew that I would lose them to his culture, his family, his belief system and I knew that their lives would be altered forever. Now more than ever, he called his family overseas and although I couldn't understand what they were saying, I could only guess that they were pressuring him to come home.

My fears were realized when after one night of a long conversation with his parents, he suddenly turned to Layla and said, "How would you like to go to Beirut with Baba and see Teta and Jido?"

"Yes Baba! Yes!" she said excitedly. "And Mama and Nadine can come too?" she asked.

Ibrahim looked over at me, meeting my gaze in a deadpan stare, and said, "No, not Mama or Nadine, just you and me."

This unexpected announcement sent shocks of terror through my body. "What?" I asked. "What do you mean – just taking Layla?" My motherly instincts screamed at me.

"It's just for two weeks," he said. "My father wants to talk to me about some things and besides, Nadine is still too young to appreciate it. Layla can play with my sister Aisha's daughters who are about the same age." He turned to Layla and said, "Aisha has two daughters, Jasmine and Farah who are waiting to play with you!"

"I will go with you," I offered immediately. "It will be a family trip."

"No, we don't have the money for all of us and Nadine needs you," he replied. "Besides, I need you here to keep in contact with our lawyer to see how things are going."

I didn't argue with him but kept quiet, keeping my thoughts to myself, and put on a mask of calm self-composure that hid the storm brewing underneath.

DUAL CITIZENSHIP

The next morning after he left for work I immediately called the U.S. Bureau of Consular Affairs and found out just how powerless I was in this relationship. A kind, female consular employee enlightened my understanding of the possible perils of having children with a spouse who held dual citizenship.

"Hello? Hi, my name is Kelly and I am just calling to clarify a few things," I began when I heard her voice. "My husband is planning a trip to his country with my daughter and I am wondering if he needs my permission to travel without me?"

"Are you divorced with sole custody?" she asked.

"No, no, we are still married... I just am a little concerned that he is taking her without me and I really don't want him to," I answered.

"Well, then just tell him you are uncomfortable," she suggested.

"No, you don't understand my husband," I replied. "That would only make matters worse and then he wouldn't trust me and then God knows what he would do."

"Does your husband have dual citizenship?" she asked.

"Yes, yes he does. He is a U.S. citizen and a Lebanese citizen," I answered.

"Oh," she responded, her voice dropping to a murmur. "That can be a problem."

"What do you mean?" I asked.

"In Lebanon, only the father can give a child citizenship. Under Lebanese law, women cannot pass on citizenship to their spouse or children.[6] So it is more than likely that he has already filed for and received Lebanese citizenship for his daughters," she explained.

"Our daughters," I corrected her. "Okay, maybe he did this without my knowledge, but how is that a problem?"

"The problem is, my dear, that the United States has no exit controls and he can have them leave the United States on a Lebanese passport. There is no requirement that foreign embassies adhere to

United States regulations regarding issuance and denial of your daughters' passports, even if you did have a court order," she said seriously.[7]

Her words struck me brutally. I was surprised I was still standing.

"Kelly?" she asked after a long pause. "Are you still there?"

I heard myself answer politely, "Yes, yes I'm here. So, there is nothing I can do to prevent him from leaving with my children?"

"The best that you can do is get a sole custody or a decree that prohibits the travel of your child without your permission or that of the court. If you can't get sole custody you may want to make certain that it prohibits your child from traveling abroad without your permission,"[8] she answered.

"But that means I would have to file for divorce and even if I did get sole custody which is unlikely - you just said that they can leave on any valid foreign passports – that the U.S. has no exit controls?" I said frantically.

She sighed and then said, "You are correct."

"Well then, what do I do?" I asked.

"Well you can ask the Lebanese embassy or consulate not to issue a passport or visa for your daughters but please keep in mind that no international law requires compliance with such requests," she explained.

"Oh my dear Lord," I whimpered.

"I am sorry. I know it looks bleak but please go to our website and links to see if any of these can help you," she said kindly.

"Thank you," I said politely, hanging up the phone.

I immediately logged onto our computer to research other alternatives but it only made me feel worse. I read terrible stories of mothers who had lost their children to their foreign husbands who fled the U.S. with their children on foreign passports never to see them again

I cringed when Ibrahim announced he had bought plane tickets for he and Layla for Lebanon with two overnight stays in Paris. I knew that he was going to discuss opening a business with his father but I was secure in the fact that he hadn't yet made up his mind since he was still waiting to see if his lawyer could clear his record. He only packed a few clothes and left everything of value, including all of his important paperwork, which reassured me. I wrote all of our phone numbers and addresses on a piece of paper and gave it to Layla telling her to keep it safe and to call me anytime.

When they reached Paris and called us from their hotel, I could breathe again after I talked to my daughter. When they flew to Lebanon I kept in contact with them everyday until they left for their flight home. The day they returned and I picked them up from the Reno Airport, I embraced Layla as though I hadn't seen her in years. This was the first time I had been separated from her and it only reinforced how easily he could have taken her overseas permanently. I knew then that I would follow my daughters to the end of the world to ensure their safety.

Layla's suitcases were filled with gifts from his family, including brochures of Catholic and International Schools that they had visited.

"Look at these beautiful schools that Baba said I can go to!" Layla exclaimed, showing me pictures of young children in plaid uniforms. "And they are Catholic, like you Mama!" she said.

I couldn't stop looking at these glossy brochures of smiling, happy children and questioned Ibrahim about it. "So you would send the girls to Catholic schools like you went to?" I asked.

"Of course, but there are many schools to choose from," he smiled. "There are also German schools and International Schools."

"Well, hopefully, everything will work out with our lawyer and we won't have to go to Beirut," I said quietly, trying to convince my husband. "I still have hope that your record will be cleared and you can work here as a doctor."

"You are a dreamer," he replied, but added, "I hope you are right."

I was careful to keep my opinions to myself now, not wanting him to have any reason to think I wasn't on his side. I watched the videos he brought back from Lebanon and agreed to get satellite so he could watch Arabic channels from home. It was clear to me that he was homesick and he talked incessantly about the pharmacy his father wanted to open for him in Beirut. I prayed even harder now, fasting and praying for a miracle. I added more saints to my repertoire of daily prayers – surely the more saints interceding in heaven, the better I thought.

9/11

September 11, 2001, Tuesday morning, I woke up and made a pot of coffee, poured myself a steaming cup, and curled up on the couch enjoying a few moments alone before the girls woke up. I flipped on the TV and to my horror saw images of the north tower of the World Trade Center on fire. The news was reporting that American Airlines Flight 11 had flown into it and that it was probably pilot error. I couldn't take my eyes off of the building now billowing with smoke but before I could register this, I watched another airplane fly into the south tower. This was no pilot error, as every American watching now knew. I jumped off the couch and ran to the bedroom where Ibrahim was sleeping off the night before.

"Wake up!" I demanded. "America is under attack! Two airplanes crashed into the two towers of the World Trade Center!"

"I am trying to sleep! Leave me alone!" he responded, pulling the covers over his head.

"But you don't understand - they think it might be a terrorist attack!" I said.

"This is my only day off this week! I need my sleep!" he replied.

"Wow!" I whispered. "I can't believe you are sleeping through this." I shut the bedroom door and went back to the TV. I turned it up so he could hear it.

He came stumbling out about a half an hour later and I made him some coffee. He sat down on the floor up against the couch, still groggy.

"Can you believe this?" I asked. "Look! Two planes were flown into the Twin Towers!" I thought maybe he didn't hear me correctly the first time.

"Uh-huh," he responded, drinking his coffee. I couldn't believe that he had no reaction to this. Our country was under attack and it didn't seem to faze him.

While he watched passively, keeping his thoughts to himself, I kept commenting out loud, conjecturing what was happening, flipping from channel to channel, trying to understand what was going on. Layla and Nadine came tumbling out into the living room and he got up to make them some breakfast like it was just another day.

"The news is now saying American Airline Flight 77 was flown into the Pentagon and that there were other planes that might have been hijacked!" I said, looking at him for some kind of reaction. He only frowned at me and continued making breakfast.

At 10:00 am, we watched as the South Tower collapsed, into a massive cloud of smoke and dust. "Oh my God!" I exclaimed.

We watched in horror as some people jumped from the other tower to their deaths. The news media showed brave men and women; first responders, firefighters, police officers and others risk their lives to help evacuate people. I couldn't believe my eyes; it was as though I was watching some end of the world movie. Thirty minutes later the North Tower collapsed. We continued to watch the events of that horrible day and like most of America began praying for those still alive and for their families.

After watching all day Ibrahim finally gave his opinion that night over dinner. "This is a Jewish conspiracy," he stated plainly. "They are behind this and now they are going to blame the Muslims as usual."

I had never realized how greatly Muslims hated the Jewish people until I married Ibrahim and studied his religion. This hatred of the Jews stemmed from their prophet who saw them as the worst enemies of Allah. He was angry that the Jews of his time rejected him and his religion so he declared war on them; beheading over 600 Jewish men and taking their women and children as slaves.[9] Their prophet saw himself as a victim of the Jews and I saw this victim mentality portrayed often in my husband's family. Ibrahim was an intelligent person but when it came to facing the truth that Muslim terrorists attacked our country, he refused to believe it.

"So you think the Jews flew those planes into the Twin Towers?" I asked incredulously.

"Of course I do!" He snapped. "I am tired of Muslims being portrayed as violent terrorists!"

"No one is being portrayed as anything; they are just reporting the facts," I replied.

"Islam is not violent, in fact Islam means peace," he said.

"No, Islam means submit or surrender," I corrected him.

"Okay, well submit to Allah then," he answered, irked that I corrected him.

"I don't know who did this, but you have to admit that these jihadist who kill others in the name of Allah are completely different than missionaries who go to foreign countries to feed, clothe and take care of the poor, spreading the message that God loves them only to be martyred," I began. "Flying a plane into a building or taking out a sword, killing unbelievers, in my humble opinion, is not the way to convert people to your faith."

"They died for their faith," Ibrahim responded.

"By killing innocent people?" I asked, not following.

"They killed themselves too!" he answered.

"Okay, well maybe they did that because they are following Mohammed?" I offered.

"Of course they are following Mohammed, but what do you mean?" he asked.

"I mean Mohammed used the sword a lot in his day," I answered. "Would you allow me to draw some contrasts between Jesus and your prophet Mohammed?" I asked.

"Of course," he replied. "Peace be upon both of them."

"So in studying Islam and Christianity I have found some very stark contrasts." I began. "Jesus never picked up the sword or ordered anyone to kill someone who didn't agree with him, in fact He got mad at Peter when he cut off a soldier's ear. Jesus picked up the soldier's ear and healed the man completely. Mohammed, on the other hand, encouraged his followers to not only kill unbelievers but he actually helped them."

"What exactly are you talking about?" Ibrahim asked.

"Well you know that Mohammed fled Mecca, running for his life with his followers and went to Medina where he sent his men out to rob caravans and killed these tradesmen for their wares."[a]

"Well Allah must have told him to do this!" Ibrahim retorted.

"Well what about Asma bint Marwan?" I asked.

"Who?" he asked furrowing his brows.

"She was a female member of the Ummayad clan who lived in Medina who ridiculed the people of Medina for following Mohammed. She dared to criticize him and because of this Mohammed asked his

---

[a] Tabari Vol 7. Pp 10-22 & LoM pp281-289

followers to murder her – and they did. A Muslim man stabbed her to death while her children slept nearby!"[b] I answered.

"She was a threat to the Prophet so she must be killed," Ibrahim answered. "Who are we to question Mohammed, peace be upon him."

"Really?" I asked. "If any prophet asked me to kill a mother just because she disagreed with me, I would not do it."

"The prophet Mohammed was a good man and we are to follow his ways," he replied. "I would kill anyone for my faith."

"But that's just it!" I replied. "I would be a martyr for my faith – that is if someone told me holding a knife to my throat and said, "Renounce your faith in Jesus Christ," "I would rather die – that's being a martyr, not killing innocent people in the name of Allah. Do you see the difference?"

"Martyrs are people who kill and die for their faith!" he answered.

"Okay, let's leave that subject alone," I sighed. "How about this – let's just compare Jesus and Mohammed in another way, okay?"

"Sure," he grumbled. "Tfaddali (after you)"

"Okay, just so you know my sources I am looking at the oldest biography of your prophet – the Sirat Rasulallah (Life of the Prophet of Allah."[c] I added.

"Where are you finding these sources?" he asked dubiously.

"Online, and in the Islamic books your brothers gave me," I answered truthfully.

"Okay, begin," he answered seriously.

"Fine. Well, let's just look at the last words of Jesus compared to Mohammed's," I began.

Jesus: "Father forgive them, for they do not know what they are doing." (Luke 23:34)

Mohammed: "May Allah curse the Jews and Christians for they built the places of worship at the graves of the prophets." (Bukhari, Vol1,

---

[b] https://en.wikipedia.org/wiki/%27Asma%27_bint_Marwan
Ibn Sa'd's "Kitab Al-Tabaqat Al-Kabir," translated by S. Moinul Haq, vol 2, pages 30-31

[c] Written by Ibn Ishaq, a devout Muslim scholar, and later revised by Ibn Hisham. It was written before any of the major works of the Hadith and is considered the most authentic biography of Muhammed. Translated by A. Guilaume into English pg 515

#427 (Mohammed said this while dying in the arms of his wife Aisha)

"So?" he shrugged. "What's your point?"

"Well I find these two so diametrically opposed," I answered.

When I received no reaction I continued, "Okay, how about the difference in the way Jesus and Mohammed treated an adulterous woman?"

"What do you mean?" he asked.

I pulled out my bible and began to read from John 8:2-11

"At dawn He (Jesus) appeared again in the temple courts, where all the people gathered around him, and he sat down to teach them. The teachers of the law and the Pharisees brought in a woman caught in adultery. They made her stand before the group and said to Jesus, "Teacher, this woman was caught in the act of adultery. In the Law Moses commanded us to stone such women. Now what do you say?" They were using this question as a trap in order to have a basis to accuse Him.

But Jesus bent down and started to write on the ground with His finger. When they kept on questioning him, he straightened up and said to them, "If any one of you is without sin, let him be the first to throw a stone at her." Again he stooped down and wrote on the ground.

At this, those who heard began to go away one at a time, the older ones first, until only Jesus was left, with the woman still standing there. Jesus straightened up and asked her, "Woman, where are they? Has no one condemned you?" "No one sir", she said. "Then neither do I condemn you," Jesus declared. "Go now and leave your life of sin."

"When Mohammed was confronted with an adulterous woman he did not have any compassion on her," I said. "This is from the Hadith of Abu Dawud #4428."

"Buraidah said: "A woman of Ghamid came to the Prophet and said: "I have committed fornication", He said: "Go back". She returned and on the next day she came to him again, and said: "Perhaps you want to send me back as you did to Maiz b. Malik. I swear by Allah, I am pregnant." He said to her: "Go back". She then returned and came to him the next day. He said to her: "Go back until you give birth to the child." She then returned. When she gave birth to the child she brought the child to him, and said: "Here it is! I have given birth to it." He said: "Go back, and suckle him until you wean him." When she had weaned him, she brought him to him with something in his hand, which he was eating. The boy was then given to a certain man of the Muslims and he (the prophet) commanded regarding her. So a pit was dug for her, and he gave orders about her and she was stoned to death. Khalid was one of those who were throwing stones at her. He threw a stone at her. When a drop of blood fell on his cheek, he abused her. The prophet said to him: "Gently, Khalid. By Him in Whose hand my soul is, she has repented to such an extent that if one who wrongfully takes an extra tax were to repent to a like extent, he would be forgiven". Then giving command regarding her, prayed over her and she was buried.""

"Don't you see – there is a marked contrast between how each man treated these poor women?" I asked.

"Who are we to question the Prophet?" Ibrahim answered.

"But Jesus treated women so different than Mohammed. Jesus healed women, taught them and let them be his disciples. He respected them and elevated them and children," I began. "Mohammed gave men the right to beat their wives if they disobeyed them. (Sura 4:34) He also took women in the spoils of war as sex slaves – they were seen as possessions not people. I know that Jesus would never do this. Allah gave your prophet slave girls as booty for him:

"Prophet, We have made lawful to you the wives whom you have granted dowries and the slave girls whom God has given you as booty;..." (Quran 33:50

"I am completely against modern slavery today, especially women used as sexual slaves and I know that Jesus would rescue these women like I would because He calls us God's sons and daughters."

"You are the daughter of God?" Ibrahim laughed.

"Yes I am!" I replied strongly. "It says so in the bible:

"I will be a Father to you, and you will be my sons and daughters, says the Lord Almighty." "(2 Corinthians 6:18)

I continued, "Jesus even taught us to pray this way,

"Our Father, who are in Heaven, hallowed be Your Name, Your kingdom come, Your will be done, on earth as it is in Heaven. Give us this day our daily bread, and forgive us our trespasses as we forgive those who trespass against us and lead us not into temptation but deliver us from evil. Amen." (Matthew 6:9-13)

"God is not our father," Ibrahim retorted. "I am Allah's slave not his child."

"Well He is my Father and I am His daughter and I know that He loves us so much that He gave his only Son, and whoever believes in Him will not perish but have eternal life," I responded confidently.

"God has no Son!" Ibrahim yelled. "Jesus was just a prophet and He did not die for me or anyone else!"

I quietly shut the books and whispered to myself, "You are wrong my dear husband, because one day every knee will bow and every tongue confess that Jesus Christ is Lord." (Philippians 2:10)

Little did I know that I had committed one of the unforgiveable sins in Islam – saying God has a son. For this to happen Mohammed believed God had to have a wife.

"They say: "God hath begotten a son": Glory be to Him. Nay, to Him belongs all that is in the heavens and on earth: everything renders worship to Him. *Surah 2.115* To Him is due the primal origin of the heavens and the earth. How can He have a son when He hath no consort?"

Surah 6.101

HONEYMOON

The aftershocks of 9/11 shook our home, unsettling the already fragile foundation that it was built on. My husband was a foreigner in a foreign land that now looked suspiciously at all Muslims. What the terrorists had done only confirmed in most American's minds that all Muslims were fighting a holy war against America. Unbelievably, there were Americans that excused this mass murder, blaming America's foreign policies as if that justified this heinous crime against innocent Americans.

Ibrahim wrestled daily with his identity now. In his youth he was a man of the world, assimilating easily into all cultures and life had been easy. But now as an American Muslim citizen, his loyalties were divided. Even at the local mosque we attended, no one dared to comment on 9/11. No one openly supported these attacks nor apologized for these 'radicals' of Islam. When I had visited different Muslim homes in different parts of America, I would often see pictures of the Ayatollah Khomeini, the Shia Iranian religious leader that overthrew the shah of Iran. He openly called America 'the great Satan' as did many other religious leaders. Ibrahim was having a hard time reconciling these two worlds now and we were caught in the middle.

He spent even longer hours at the casinos, hoping to win a lot of money, as if this would solve everything. One night he came home earlier than usual with a huge smile on his face.

Before I could say a word, he got into bed and pulled me close, "I have a surprise for you," he said smiling.

"What?" I asked, totally disarmed by his good mood.

"I am taking you on the honeymoon we never had!" he said. "I am taking you on a seven-day vacation to see Paris and Rome!"

"Did you win a vacation?" I asked dumbfounded.

"No, I saved the money and I think that after thirteen years of marriage you deserve it!" he said.

I looked at him like someone else had taken over his body,

"Are you drunk?" I asked, looking for signs.

"No, no, I just really want to take you there - you deserve it," he continued.

The next day he bought the plane tickets and arranged for my parents to watch the girls while we were gone. I couldn't be happier that my husband was doing something so wonderful for me, for us.

"Maybe people do change," I thought hopefully. "Maybe all of my prayers are being answered right now."

We began our honeymoon in Paris, France. Ibrahim became my tour guide, showing me all the places he had visited in his youth: the Eiffel Tower, Notre Dame de Paris, Tuileries Palace and the Louvre. Everywhere we went he showed off his knowledge and made sure to draw comparisons between his homeland, Lebanon and what I saw before me.

"Lebanon was a French colony at one time and that is why most Lebanese speak Arabic as well as French fluently," he told me as I watched him speak perfect French with waiters and shopkeepers.

He was the old Ibrahim, the one who had courted me in college, showering me with affection and attention. Over romantic dinners and late night conversations, I fell in love with him all over again, marveling at how quickly my love for him made me forget the past and push away my fears. But one early morning while we were standing in front of a pastry shop, I realized why we were here.

"You see all of this?" he said gesturing with an open hand to the bustling city of Paris alive with throngs of fashionably dressed people walking quickly by.

"Yes," I said smiling, looking around at Parisians drinking their Café Lattes in big bowl-like cups. The smell of fresh hot pastries enveloped me and I inhaled deeply, enjoying it.

"This is exactly like what you will see in Beirut!" he said smiling.

My face fell as I looked up at him. "What I will see in Beirut?" I repeated. "What do you mean?"

"Kelly, you know I don't intend to stay in America forever," he answered.

My fears returned softly, floating down on my shoulders, taking their former place of residence. "You never talked about living in Beirut until all of these things happened with the medical board," I said truthfully. "I thought Lebanon was still unstable. You told me it is really hard to make a living there – even most of your brothers work in different countries."

"It isn't difficult for doctors," he said, as we sat down at one of the open cafeterias.

"I can't, I won't live in Beirut," I said softly but firmly. "America is my home, it's our home."

He let out a loud snort, and chuckled, "America? My home? Are you kidding?" and added, "What has *that* country ever done for me?"

"It's not America's fault for what happened with the board," I answered gently. "We can still make a great life – you can work as a general practitioner or pharmacist and when Nadine starts kindergarten I can help by working outside the home again."

"You are such a dreamer, Kelly," he sighed, artfully inhaling his cigarettes, blowing the smoke over his shoulder. "Don't you want the best for your daughters?" he asked.

"Of course I do," I answered defensively.

"Don't you want your daughters to be children of the world – able to fit into any society? To be well-educated, able to speak three languages and work wherever they choose?" he asked me. "Lebanon is the most open country in the Middle East. Europeans travel there for vacation because of its beauty and culture."

"I don't want to take my daughters out of America, away from my family," I began.

"What about my family?" he interrupted, trying to keep his voice down. "I was sent to boarding schools at the age of twelve years old and I haven't lived near my family since then. Now my family is asking me to come home and you don't want to go?" he squinted at me taking another drag. "I have lived in your country for eighteen years now, and my parents won't be around forever."

I felt a heavy wave of guilt crash down on me as I looked down at the swirling froth in my coffee cup. I wrestled within. *"He is right,"* I thought. *"It isn't fair of me to ask him to stay in America forever."*

"But you didn't ask him to come to America," I countered with myself. *"He came on his own and the plan had always been to settle down in the U.S. and work there. I can't be responsible for the fact he was sent away at a young age because of Lebanon's Civil War. And forget all of that – what about your daughters? Do you really want them to grow up in Beirut?"*

The next few days in Paris I avoided the subject, pushing it into the furthest recesses of my mind, but the tension between us was high.

The last few days of our vacation was supposed to be a special trip just for me – a coveted trip to see Vatican City –the very holy headquarters of my Catholic faith. For some reason I didn't realize it was not a part of Italy but its own sovereign nation, an absolute monarchy with my beloved Pope John Paul II at its head, who as the Vicar of Christ, literally stood in for Jesus.

The thrill of being able to see this holy place for the first time made me forget our quarrel but Ibrahim seemed sullen and still upset that he hadn't convinced me to move to Beirut.

When we walked into St. Peter's Square, a massive plaza in front of St. Peter's Basilica, I was awestruck.

As I approached the grand entrance, I was overcome with the opulence of wealth of this beautiful building. There were too many things to look at – from the ceiling to the elaborately decorated marble floors to the walls covered with mosaics that looked like paintings. It glittered with gold like a grand palace. I had never seen anything like this before in my life.

What immediately drew my attention was a massive four-poster bronze metal canopy that towered over the high altar. It looked like it didn't belong here because it had oxidized over the years, turning the bronze black, its spiraling dark columns looked ominous. There were wooden pews in front of it and a mass was being performed. It was in Italian but I quickly found a kneeler and knelt down, following along as best I could while Ibrahim stood back and watched.

When the sacrifice of the mass had finished I walked around marveling at this church, Ibrahim beside me. There were altars everywhere and some had clear see-through coffins with the bodies of saints or popes underneath. Ibrahim shuddered when he saw me kneel in front of these dead saints asking for their intercession.

"Why are there dead bodies underneath these altars?" he asked.

"Most every altar in every Catholic church throughout the world has this," I answered proudly, happy to finally be the tour director here.

"What?" he asked. "You mean there are dead bodies under every altar?"

I laughed. "Not the whole body, silly – just body parts. We call them relics and there are three classes. The first class relic is an actual part of the body of the Saint, like their hair or bone. The second class is something owned by the Saint or an instrument of torture used against a martyr and the third class is anything that touched a first or second class relic."

"I just don't understand all these dead bodies and dead body parts everywhere," he said looking around. "It freaks me out. I mean - this is built on a graveyard inside, outside and underneath. It's like a city of the dead!"

I narrowed my eyes at him, frustrated that he couldn't see the beauty that I did. "You just don't understand how holy this site is!"

"I just don't understand why you have to sacrifice Jesus all over again and pretend to drink His blood and eat His body – it is so creepy!" he shuddered.

"It is His real body and we are drinking His real blood!" I answered angrily.

"And you think my religion is weird?" he said, looking at me with astonishment all over his face.

I turned my back to him and walked over to the altar of the Lady of the Column and knelt down and looked up at a beautiful image of a Madonna and child framed by alabaster columns. I recited an Act of Oblation to the Blessed Virgin Mary:

"My Queen! My Mother!
I give thee all myself, and, to show my devotion to thee,
I consecrate to thee my eyes, my ears, my mouth, my heart, my entire self.
Wherefore, O loving Mother, as I am thine own,
keep me, defend me, as thy property and possession.
Amen."

After I arose, I noticed Ibrahim peering at the inscriptions. "Why is she called the Lady of the Column?" he asked. "Which column?"

I was exasperated with him. "I don't know. She is called many things. Lady of the Snows, Lady of the Mountains, Queen of Heaven, Mediatrix of all graces etc..." and added, "Why does it matter?"

"Medi – what?" he asked. "Now I never heard that one in Catholic school."

"Mediatrix of All Graces," I answered. "Mediatrix- it literally means 'a woman who is a mediator.' St. Pius X said she is the 'neck' connecting the Head of the Mystical Body to us and that all power flows through the neck."[10]

"Aha! So you believe Mary is part of the Trinity," Ibrahim said.

"What?" I look askance at him. "No, she is a mediator."

"But you call her the Mother of God!" he said. "If she is the Mother than she has to be part of the Trinity."

"No!" I answered him, frustrated. "She is the mother of Jesus who was God so therefore she is the Mother of God,"

"Ah, but your logic is faulty," he smiled. "God always existed from the beginning. Did Mary?"

I hesitated. "No, of course not. She was born at a specific time and place,"

"Then how can she be the Mother of God himself?" he answered. "God has no mother – He always existed! Mary is His creation, a human like you and me!"

I looked at him like he was going to have lightning strike him here in this holy place right in front of Mary's altar but his words rung true, deep in my heart but I quickly returned to my roots, my upbringing and defended Mary's title as if I was defending a family member who had just been insulted.

"God have mercy on your soul!" I said, scanning the room desperately, searching for one of the confessional booths scattered everywhere and went into the one where English was spoken and quickly knelt down.

"Father, forgive me, for I have sinned and my last confession was over a month ago," I began, crossing myself.

"Go ahead, my daughter," a male voice spoke back with a thick Italian accent.

"I confess having doubts about my faith. I confess having feelings of anger toward my husband. I confess my past sins of not being a good Catholic and my husband's unbelief and sacrilegious behavior." I whispered. I then said an Act of Contrition.

"For your penance, go and say one Our Father, and one Hail Mary," the priest answered and then he said a prayer that absolved me from my sins.

"Amen," I replied, and left the confessional to kneel down again in the pews and recite my prayers.

Ibrahim was waiting for me to finish. "Are you ready yet?" he asked, and then seeing the hurt look on my face added, "Hey, I didn't mean anything. We have always openly discussed our religion. Let's go get something to eat. I'm hungry."

"Okay, just one more thing," I said, scanning the building. "I have to kiss St. Peter's foot!"

"Oh, okay, yeah that makes sense," he said sarcastically, walking around to help me find it.

We finally found the statue of St. Peter and I reverently kissed its right foot, now worn smooth from years of faithful Catholics doing the same. As we walked back into St. Peter's Square passing the ominous obelisk, I couldn't help wondering, *"Why didn't they just erect a big cross here in the center of Catholicism – isn't that more logical than this weird pagan pillar of Baal? What better symbol of Christianity than a cross?"*

Ibrahim seemed to read my mind and said, "Sorry, about earlier... hey, let's stop here and I will buy you a medal." We walked up to a street vendor who had a beautiful display of medals for sale. I picked out a 14-karat gold medal of the Madonna and child and added it to the chain around my neck.

"Thank you," I said smiling up at my husband, giving him a kiss.

"Don't worry about it. Let's go enjoy some great Italian food – I mean you haven't lived until you have eaten real authentic Italian pizza!" he added kissing the tips of his fingers throwing them in the air, "Delizioso!"

NO CHOICE

Any hope that had been rekindled in Europe was quickly dashed upon our return to America. Bad news came over the phone from his attorney. I listened hopefully when Ibrahim called him.

"Hi Mr. Smith, this is Ibrahim – I am just calling to check on the status of my lawsuit." Ibrahim asked. "We just got back from Europe and I wanted to touch base with you."

"Well, Ibrahim, the good news is that they offered $2,500 for any personal injury but they refuse to clear your record," Mr. Smith responded.

There was a long pause as I watched Ibrahim's face turn red. "After all this money I have thrown at you! This is the best that you can do! You son of a bitch!"

He continued to insult him in Arabic and then slammed the phone down turning his wrath on me. "I told you there is no such thing as justice in America!" he said, pointing his finger at me.

I jumped out of his way and hurried for a safe corner on the loveseat, covering myself with a blanket for protection. He towered above me ranting, swearing in English and Arabic at America, his eyes daring me to disagree with him. I stayed silent, tears streaming out of my eyes repeating the words, "I'm sorry, I'm so sorry," over and over again. I was crying, weeping profusely, because I knew now that there was no stopping him from leaving America.

It was a miserable December 2001. All sense of hope had fled and Ibrahim seemed plagued with new demons in his head. He became paranoid that no one was to be trusted – not even me. One morning while getting ready for work, he noticed a large bump on his earlobe and showed it to me.

"Look at this," he said, taking my hand and placing it on his earlobe.

"Feels like a hard lump," I said. "Maybe it's an infection?" I offered.

"No, it isn't," he said. "It's harder than that and it wasn't there last night before I went to bed."

"Well sometimes these things pop up overnight," I offered.

"It feels like a bug," he said in an accusing tone.

"A bug?" I answered. "You think it's an insect?"

"No, not that kind of bug!" He was angry. "A bug – like a listening device! Did you put a bug in my ear last night?"

I couldn't believe my ears. "You think that I put a bug in your ear last night?"

"I am asking you if you did," he said. "Because it feels perfectly round and smooth."

"Yes, Ibrahim I confess – while you were sleeping last night I surgically planted a bug in your earlobe and sewed it back up not leaving any scars!" I said sarcastically. "Are you kidding me?"

He seemed to see how absurd this was and went back to the bathroom but then came out, pointing a finger at me. "If I find out that you are on their side and planted a bug in my ear – I don't know what I'll do!"

His paranoia scared me – suddenly I was also the enemy in his eyes and I knew it wouldn't take much for him to snap and take off with our daughters. I didn't understand why he didn't trust me. I had been by his side from the beginning, supporting him by working sometimes two jobs before we had children, and even working as a nanny after the girls were born to help out. I financially sacrificed all these years, never demanding anything from him. I sincerely loved him and wanted him to succeed. I stood by him during these allegations and forgave him, choosing to move forward, but now I was seriously afraid that I would wake up one morning to find him and the girls gone. I slept very little at night and listened when he talked on the phone trying to understand what he was saying to his family.

Often I would sleep between my daughters waiting for him to come home, and as they slept I would look down at their peaceful, angelic faces, so innocent, so unaware of the dangers lurking in the shadows. I knew that to keep them safe by my side I was going to have to sacrifice yet again, but this time it would mean leaving my country, my family, and my home. I was going to have to go willingly and trust in God to take care of us because the alternative, losing my daughters never to see them again, would destroy me.

That night when I heard him opening the front door, I left the girls and crept out to meet him.

"You still up?'" he asked. I felt a twinge of pity for him now. His face was sad, dark bags under his eyes. All of this had taken a physical toll on him and he looked exhausted.

"Yes, I wanted to tell you something," I said seriously, trying to keep the tears back.

He plopped down on the couch, rubbing his face. "What is it now?" he asked. "I need my sleep."

I stood in front of him and said, "I have decided that I will go where you go, I will stay where you stay. Your people shall be my people," I quoted most of Ruth 1:16, leaving out, "and your god shall be my god."

Instead of embracing me, thanking me for this huge sacrifice that I was offering, he smiled scornfully at me and lit up a cigarette. He didn't say anything but just leaned back, putting one foot on his knee, staring at me with a look of amusement on his face. The look on his face seemed to say, "I manipulate the strings here, sweetheart, not you." We both knew I had no choice.

Tears leaking from my face, I stood my ground. "I will go on three conditions: 1) that we visit America every summer to see my family, 2) that I will attend church every Sunday in Lebanon and 3) that our daughters attend the same caliber of schools that you attended.

Ibrahim stood up now and said, "I swear to Allah that all of this will be provided and more!" with his hand over his heart.

Now I had the hard job of telling my family and friends about our departure. Ibrahim asked me not to tell our friends in Reno that we were going to Beirut because he didn't want a million questions. I felt guilty telling the new friends we had made here that we were going not to Beirut but Montpelier, France. The guilt was exponentially exacerbated when they threw me a going away party complete with a cake and a small Eiffel tower on top. But it was even harder when we shared the truth with my family.

My mother gave me advice, "Don't get pregnant again because then you will feel like you have to stay over there." My father, the ever-eternal optimist, like myself, said, "Treat it like you're a missionary, like it's a great adventure!" They hid their concern for my sake but I knew they were grieving over having their only granddaughters live overseas so far away in a dangerous country.

Ibrahim was ecstatic and prepared the girls by playing music videos from Lebanon, with beautiful young women singing against the backdrop of Lebanon, highlighting the deep cerulean blue Mediterranean Sea, brilliant white beaches, and snow-capped mountain peaks. The lively music was infectious and soon our girls were dancing along. Layla chose one of the schools from the brochures that she wanted to attend, basing her choice on the smiling faces she saw.

I began to pack. This was going to be the hardest move yet. I had no idea what awaited me on those distant shores. I could only trust that God held us in the palm of His hand, even in Beirut.

Part V Migration

"...wherever you go, I will go;
wherever you live, I will live.
Your people will be my people..."
Ruth 1:16

BEIRUT

I returned again to the guidebook for Lebanon I had brought with me on the plane. It glossed over the fifteen-year civil war that had torn apart this country, encouraging tourists to forget the violent past and look to the future where Lebanon hoped to regain their status as the Paris of the Middle East, famed for their great food and great hospitality. I clung to this fairy tale, hoping against all odds that at least some of what it said was true.

We arrived in Amsterdam's airport and walked along the brightly lit corridors admiring the chic clothing and gift shops. I felt out of place next to the attractive salesgirls who seemed captivated by my charming husband, dressed in a light gray Armani suit with a white crisp shirt. I watched him converse in French with them flashing his perfect smile. I was wearing what he picked out for me, a drab, conservative gray suit that covered everything, and I was towing along two very tired children.

After he stocked up on Cuban cigars and liquor we checked in with the Middle Eastern Airline. It was like stepping into a different world. A dreary sea of grays and blacks met my eyes. Most of the women were covered with conservative suits like mine but with scarves covering their hair. The collective mood was mournfully serious. When we walked in, all eyes were upon us. Sullen faces with critical eyes cast disapproving glances our way. Some even clicked their tongues at us, shaking their heads. Ibrahim seemed nervous here and even embarrassed by his blonde American wife.

It was a long, cramped flight. The airplanes were old and still had a smoking section, which was disregarded – people smoked in any seat they pleased. When we finally arrived in Beirut we were exhausted. I was an object of curiosity as we waited for our luggage, despite my wrinkled clothes and dark circles under my eyes. After passing through customs we walked into the waiting area of the airport where families were lined up, jostling each other while waiting for loved ones. It was a rowdy affair. Passengers were surrounded and greeted with much commotion. Bouquets of flowers were thrust upon them, amidst emotional outbursts of tears and kisses.

No such greeting awaited us though. One family member, Mohammed, his brother, stood alone waiting for us. Ibrahim clasped his brother's right hand as they kissed each other's opposite cheeks four times simultaneously saying, "il-Hamdu lillah al Salama" (Thank God for your safe arrival). Mohammed then turned to Layla and placed his hand out to her saying, "Salaam alaykum" (Peace be upon you) and she shyly responded, "wa-alaykum a salaam" (and upon you be peace). He quickly glanced at me and then lowered his eyes out of respect repeating the same, but with his right hand laid flatly over his heart, the appropriate way for a man to greet a woman not related to him by blood.

We slid into the back of his car; Layla and Nadine quickly fell asleep on our laps. I took in my surroundings. The road was dark, all streetlights were out due to an electricity outage, something I would soon experience daily. Some all-night snack bars lit up the blackness of the neighborhood by relying on private generators. The winding road soon brought us to his family's neighborhood and we drove into the driveway of his family's home – a private five-story building. Each of us carried a daughter over our shoulder and walked into the building's elevator. We got off at the fourth floor apartment where my in-laws lived.

We knocked on the oversized maple door, above which hung a large plastic blue eye, an amulet thought to provide protection from any envious visitors. I remembered that in their culture blue-eyed people were thought to carry the evil eye, another prominent reminder that I was an outsider here.

A short, chestnut-skinned woman with large excited eyes answered the door. It was Baseera, my mother-in-law's maid. She recognized my husband at once. Her mouth broke into a wide smile and in between childish giggles, welcomed him warmly. Her attention next turned to Layla. "Ah….habebti! (My love) she shrieked, pulling Layla to her chest and embracing her, smoothing her hair. After awhile I extended my hand to her and I saw her smile fade for just an instant but she quickly welcomed me, grabbing my right hand firmly pulling me down toward her, kissing my cheeks wetly four times.

At that moment, my mother-in-law walked into the foyer. "Il-Hamdu lillah al Salama!" she shouted, throwing her arms up into the air. She was a stout woman of strong build, large square shoulders accentuated by the shoulder pads in her shimmering housedress. Her reddened face was still wet from her ablution of evening prayers and it shone in the light, accentuating piercing ebony eyes that quivered from side to side. She had a perfect Roman nose perched above full lips that harbored straight ivory teeth. Her head sat squarely on a buxom body and she moved slowly, methodically, with effort.

The most supple and untiring muscle was her tongue, a phenomenon I had encountered when she would visit us in America. She could talk incessantly for hours as long as she had an audience and now this well-exercised muscle let out a litany of welcomes to all of us in a loud booming voice.

Nadine, asleep on my shoulder, woke up startled by her outburst and looked around bewildered. My husband embraced his mother warmly and kissed her slowly on each cheek four times. She looked truly happy to see him. She kissed Layla and then turned her attention to Nadine. She only spoke Arabic.

"Ah Nadine! Keefik habibti? Atini bowsi a Teta!" (How are you my love? Come and give Teta a kiss).

Nadine clung to my arms, refusing to go to her. "No! I want my mommy!" she shouted defiantly.

She finally noticed me and pulled me toward her so I could kiss her cheeks, which she did not reciprocate. We went into the kitchen where an array of food awaited us. My mother-in-law had made my husband's favorite dish – kibbe nye – raw ground lamb mixed with burghul (crushed wheat) and served cold with olive oil drizzled on top. Tabooli (parsley salad), baked kibbi, yogurt, cucumbers, olives, fresh cilantro and of course hot pita bread. I filled our plates staying clear of the raw lamb.

Abu Ali, Ibrahim's father shuffled into the kitchen wearing a soft green leisure suit that fit him rather snugly around his well-fed stomach. We all rose immediately, taking turns greeting the patriarch of his family. We sat down after he seated himself at the head of the table. Abu Ali was a large man, with a bald palate and big protruding eyes, one larger than the other due to many eye surgeries to correct retina detachments. His thick nose lurched over his neatly trimmed yet graying mustache. The back of his head was completely flat; a common sight in the Arab world, yet what stood out the most were his enormous muscular arms.

We ate mostly in silence. I found it awkward and so different than when they used to visit us in America. They seemed hesitant and careful in their language towards me. I explained it away as tiredness due to the lateness of the hour. Baseera showed us to our room where one bed welcomed the four of us. We quickly changed for bed and fell into a deep sleep.

I woke up the next morning startled out of my sleep by the call of the muezzin, the man who calls people to pray from a tall minuet from a mosque. His nasal voice boomed over the loudspeaker,

"Allah Akbar (God is the greatest)
(In Arabic) I bear witness that there is no deity except Allah
I bear witness that Mohammed is the Messenger of God
Make haste toward worship
Come to the true success
Prayer is better than sleep
Allah Akbar"

"Welcome to Beirut," I mumbled, half asleep. I got out of bed, placing my feet on the hard cold marble floor – a numbing chill grabbed my feet like I had touched ice. I turned to Ibrahim who was up now, "Can you please have them turn up the heat?" I asked shivering.

"Turn up the heat?" he repeated, rubbing his hands together. "What are you talking about? There's no central heating here."

Lebanon's whole infrastructure had been destroyed during their civil war and the power and gas lines had been totally demolished. The telephone lines had only just been reinstalled the previous year in the summer of 2000. The only buildings that had central heating and air conditioning were the finer hotels, needed to pamper the much-needed tourists. I was familiar with cold winters, but here these buildings had no fireplaces or wood stoves to keep us warm. I climbed back into bed next to the girls who were still sleeping.

"*I just need a hot bath,*" I thought. "*That will warm me up.*"

I tiptoed down the hallway and found a bathroom and turned on the bathtub faucet. Icy cold water gushed out. Five minutes later it was still cold. I returned to the bedroom and helped Layla and Nadine dress in bed. I was thankful that I had heeded my husband's advice and brought wool socks and long underwear for them.

Exhausted from our trip, we had slept through breakfast – it was already lunchtime and we were treated to a delicious feast of rice and roasted chicken topped with toasted almonds and pine nuts, and grape leaves stuffed with rice. We were starving.

Suddenly Baseera came rushing into the room holding a plunger in her hand speaking excitedly to everyone. I followed everyone out into the hallway where water was spilling out over the floor from the guest bathroom the girls had just used.

"What did you do?" Ibrahim asked me.

"I didn't do anything," I responded. "The girls just used that bathroom - that's all."

"Did they flush the toilet paper down the toilet?" he asked.

"Well, yes they did," I responded, confused.

"You can't put toilet paper in the toilet here!" he said angrily. "The plumbing system in Lebanon can't handle it. Now my father has to call a plumber and this is very expensive!"

"Well, no one told me this," I said meekly. "I am so sorry," I said to his parents who just glared at me.

"Where are we supposed to put the toilet paper we use?" I whispered to Ibrahim.

"In the wastebasket," he answered.

"The wastebasket?" I grimaced. "But that will make the bathroom smell."

"Not if you are cleaning the right way, the Islamic way," he said stiffly. He spoke down to me, as if he was trying to impress upon his parents that he was in charge of his foreign wife.

I knew what he was referring to – the Islamic way to properly clean yourself after using the toilet was to spray water from either an attached hose to the toilet or from a running bidet, using your left hand to rub yourself clean. Toilet paper, if available, was used only to dry. This tradition is the reason why it is considered unclean to eat with your left hand.

I smiled openly to him in front of his parents and whispered, "I will not use my hands. That is unclean."

"You have no choice," he answered.

My attention was now turned to my daughters as I had just noticed small red marks on their faces and arms. Alarmed I asked, "What are these?"

"Oh! Look!" Ibrahim chuckled. "Those mosquitos love their sweet blood!"

"Mosquitoes? In this cold weather?" I asked "Are you sure it's not bed bugs?"

"Bed bugs?" Ibrahim was upset. "Don't ever say this in front of my family. My mother is the most cleanest woman ever!"

I looked up at my husband and saw the anger in his face. He was waving his finger at me. His parents were watching me, frowning, not understanding but obviously aware that there was a problem already with this American wife who was unaccustomed to their ways. I never felt so alone in all my life. His family was so different to me now. In America when they would visit us they were warm and friendly, and went out of their way to communicate. As I listened to my husband admonish me, I bowed my head and apologized. This was not the welcome I had envisioned.

AMERICAN TARGETS

Our stay with his parents only lasted a few weeks because Ibrahim wanted to move into his own place. The third floor apartment had been set apart specifically for him and it was directly beneath his parents. This family building had five floors; the fifth floor belonged to the oldest brother Ali which was unoccupied since he worked with his family in another country, the fourth floor was where his parents resided in the summers, the second floor housed Mohammed and his family and the first floor was still unclaimed but currently occupied by Ibrahim's nephews who were attending college. The chauffeur and his family resided in the basement.

When we walked into our apartment I noticed that it was laid out exactly like my in-law's apartment: four bedrooms and two bathrooms, a living room area and a kitchen. It was spacious but worn. Amu Ali was our tour guide and she began in the kitchen where white linoleum with years of dirt and black grime in the cracks greeted us. Tarnished aluminum cupboards and battered countertops hung against gray concrete walls. A green fluorescent light flickered above us, and behind the kitchen we found a laundry room complete with a squatting toilet, simply a hole in the floor where putrid water lapped over the chipped white foot rests. I shivered as I saw a huge cockroach slither across the floor.

Outside the kitchen was a small balcony, adorned with only an empty clothesline frosted over with ice. In the apartments directly across from us I watched a middle-aged woman trying to secure her laundry with clothespins, wrestling with the stubborn sheets that snapped at her every time a blast from the bitter wind assailed her.

"This is where you will hang your laundry," Ibrahim said, translating for his mother. "You can not use the dryers here because the electricity isn't consistent and dryers take up too much energy anyway," he added.

"Okay," I said as enthusiastically as I could muster and smiled at my mother-in-law, trying to show her that I was up for this. "A little bleach and a lot of elbow grease and I can have this place sparkling."

Ibrahim ignored my remark and motioned for me to follow his mother to the rest of the house. The bedrooms were completely bare except one that was stuffed with old mattresses and boxes. Thankfully the other bathrooms had western style toilets, sinks and bathtubs and I was grateful.

"My parents are taking us shopping later today for a bedroom set," Ibrahim told me and I thanked his mother profusely.

All of our belongings were still on their way from America – mostly clothes, linens, books and kitchenware and the girls' bunk bed and toys. We were living out of our suitcases and still sleeping in one bed so this was welcome news. It was also a chance to leave the house and see Beirut.

That afternoon was the first time I had left the building since we had arrived. We had driven there in the middle of the night so the darkness had covered what I saw now. We drove with his parents through southern Beirut, where roads were awash with mud holes. It was a bleak picture staring back at me: narrow roads twisted and serpentine around blocks of gray concrete shops, their wares displayed for all to see. Grimy men sat in greasy mechanic shops, blackened from years of buildup of oil and dirt. Some shops were tents made of tarp and a few poles. Nothing here looked like the streets of Paris: dreary-looking apartments with frayed awnings blocked any view of the Mediterranean Sea.

My husband noticed the look on my face and said, "Don't look at this area. These people are squatters and will all be moved one day. They moved in during the civil war and built these shops without legal permits. This used to be a beautiful drive complete with well-known restaurants and hotels right on the sea but now you can't even see it."

"How long was the civil war?" I asked.

"Fifteen years," he answered. "1975 to 1990. It began with fighting between the Catholic Maronite and Muslim Palestinian forces but soon everyone was in it – Sunni, Shia, Catholics, Armenians, and Druze etc. It was just one big mess. No one wanted to live here after that – there are more Lebanese living outside of Lebanon than in Lebanon."

"I was shipped off to boarding schools in France to escape this," Ibrahim said. "It's a shame what this war did to my beautiful country."

We finally pulled up to a furniture store and picked out a simple bed and armoire for our room. His father paid for it using brand new crisp American hundred dollar bills. The salesman immediately walked over to a copier where he copied every currency and had Abu Ali sign them.

"What was that all about?" I asked my husband.

"It's to make sure it's not counterfeit. They can trace the serial numbers back to the patron if it is," he answered. "Corruption is all over the place in Lebanon."

When we arrived home, we were surprised to see Basaam, the chauffeur, waiting for us with a present for our new home. He was holding up a rusty metal cage with a lively little canary chirping loudly from it. It was one of many birds he caught and sold as a side business.

"Is this for us?" Layla asked Basaam, her face beaming.

Basaam nodded and smiled showing his few yellow teeth. He was a short man with greasy black hair and a gray mustache, his steely black eyes sunk into his tan leathered face with a cigarette dangling from his mouth. This man was more than a chauffeur to Abu Ali - he was Abu Ali's personal security guard and always wore his pistol with him for protection.

"Let's name her Tweety!" Layla announced and Nadine agreed. We brought Tweety upstairs and placed her in the living room floor. She was a wild bird, not used to captivity, and kept beating her wings against the cage, trying to get out. Her loud chirping sounded similar to basketball shoes skidding on a newly polished floor.

"Ooooh, look Mommy," Nadine said sadly. "She wants to get out and fly! Let's open the door and let her fly around!"

"No Nadine!" Ibrahim chided her. "If you let her out she will fly out the window and you will never see her again!"

We surrounded the cage watching the confused bird, frantically trying to escape. "She doesn't look very happy," Layla said sadly.

"No, this is all new to her," I said. "She isn't used to being confined like this. It isn't her natural environment. Give her time and I am sure she will get used to it." I watched her thrash herself against the bars that held her, determined to escape and I felt sorry for this confused bird.

"She doesn't like it Mommy!" Nadine blurted out, her little face pleading with me to notice the obvious. This was our first night alone as a family in our own apartment and I didn't want to start it out with tears, so I ushered the girls into the other room.

"She will be fine," I said. "Let's go look at the new bed!"

I turned to Ibrahim. "I guess the girls will be sleeping with us again until their bunk bed arrives?"

"No, my mother said we can use the bed in storage," he said.

He brought out the mattress and threw it on the floor next to our bed. It was full of holes, speckled with yellow splotches and small dark red spots.

"The girls are not sleeping on that," I said. "This one needs to be burned – I mean look- it's a nesting ground for bug beds!"

"Oooooo yuck! I am not sleeping on that!" Layla said scrunching up her face.

"There are no such thing as bed bugs Layla!" Ibrahim said loudly, ignoring me. "Your mother doesn't know what she is talking about! Teta is a very clean woman!"

"Teta is a very clean woman and she keeps an immaculate house," I said gently, ignoring his harshness. "This isn't her fault – it's just been in storage so long."

Ibrahim continued talking to Layla as if I wasn't there. "You will sleep on it right, habibte (my love)?"

Layla looked up at me, pleading with her eyes and after he left the room I said, "Don't worry honey. I will sleep on it."

That night Ibrahim went upstairs to spend time with his parents. When it was time for bed I put the girls in our bed and gingerly crept on the sullied mattress to sleep. I had covered it with two fitted sheets for protection.

Wails from Nadine stopped me. "Mommy, I want to sleep with you!"

She climbed into bed with me but only began to cry because she was scared sleeping on the floor. Finding no solution, we squeezed together in the new bed, leaving a space for Ibrahim. When he came downstairs later and saw us, he was angry and shoved me over roughly hissing, "Why isn't Layla in her bed?"

The next morning he woke up complaining that he couldn't get any sleep and insisted that Layla had to sleep on that mattress.

Layla could see the anguish this was causing me and she pulled me aside, "It's okay Mommy. I'll sleep on it. It'll be okay."

My eight-year old daughter tried to assuage his anger and protect me from his wrath as she did so often. Layla seemed to instinctively know the power she had over her father and diverted his attention away from me by gently soothing him with loving words. I had learned early in our marriage that arguing with him or defending myself only created a fiercer, meaner response from him.

"Be sweet as honey and you will see how gentle I will be and never go head to head with me because I will always win," he said often when I dared to disagree with him. But the promised reward of this gentleness never materialized. Even when I remained silent I was accused of being against him.

I wasn't about to let Layla shoulder this one though. "No, you won't." I whispered to her. "I'll put Nadine to sleep early and then I will sleep on it."

But that night the minute I left Nadine alone she cried for me. She was three, in a foreign country surrounding by strangers that didn't speak her language. She was scared and wanted me around her constantly for reassurance.

Layla came over and hugged me and said, "Mama, never mind. I can do this."

So reluctantly, I put another fitted sheet plus a blanket on top of the mattress and let her sleep on it. The next morning she had four bright red marks on one leg all lined up in a row; the trademark of bedbugs. When Ibrahim woke up we showed him the bite marks.

"Those are mosquito bites," he said condescendingly. "They sure love her blood."

"Those are not mosquito bites," I responded. "They don't even look like the other mosquito bites on her arms.

Ibrahim stood up towering above me. "You are a very stupid woman!" he said in front of my daughters. "I don't want to talk about this anymore!" He left the room and I heard the front door slam, his heavy footsteps heading up the way to his parents.

Now that his parents had done their duty and helped us move in, it was time for them to return to Kuwait. They normally spent their summers in Beirut and the rest of the year in Kuwait where most of Abu Ali's businesses were. After a long drawn out farewell from all of the family I walked upstairs with the girls, leaving Ibrahim to help his father with the suitcases. I wanted to watch his parents leave from our balcony and have the girls wave at them, so I opened the dark wooden blinds for the first time that covered the sliding glass doors and walked out onto the balcony. Layla went and grabbed her red binoculars and was peering around the neighborhood.

Suddenly my husband appeared from nowhere screaming,

"What are you doing?" he asked, ripping the binoculars from Layla's hands, roughly pushing us all inside.

"What is wrong with you?" I asked, angry that he had shoved the girls because Nadine was now crying.

Ibrahim hissed through his teeth, "Maybe you didn't notice but there is a Syrian military outpost in that building directly across the street from us and another one right there!" he said pointing to the right.

I stared back blankly, not fully comprehending what this had to do with us being on the balcony.

"The Syrian military will think we are spying on them!" he bellowed.

Layla and Nadine ran crying to the bedroom, but before I could go and console them, he grabbed my arm and said, "I do not want you on the balcony. You are an American target here, and I can't be responsible for what might happen to you. You may only raise the blinds ten inches from the floor during the day – that is it! Do you understand?"

I nodded my head somberly, still trembling from the words, "American target," then raced down the hallway to find my daughters.

That afternoon while they took a nap, I peeked out through the wooden shutters and saw the Syrian outpost across the street. They occupied a war-torn concrete building left pockmarked with small craters made from artillery fire. I noticed a lone soldier with his AK-47 guarding it. He eyeballed every car that drove by, stopping anyone that gave him suspicion. Thirty or so soldiers filed out of the building and ran in a small circle doing calisthenics to the shout of a drill sergeant.

I heard Ibrahim walking in the hallway and I quickly ran into the kitchen to make him some coffee. The rusty stove was gas but hooked up to a portable gas container. I turned it into the on position with a butter knife like Ibrahim had shown me and pulled out the rusty warming drawer, laying down to reach under the stove and lit the pilot light with my husband's cigarette lighter. I boiled the water to make instant coffee for him and we sat and talked while I began to prepare dinner.

That evening right after dinner the kitchen lights went dark and the refrigerator shuddered. I walked over to the fuse box and clicked the black knobs up and down to no avail.

"The electricity is off in this area," Ibrahim said. "It'll come back on in about four hours. Sometimes the power plants cut it off."

"How often does this happen?" I asked.

"Everyday," he answered.

"But why didn't this happen in your parents' apartment when we stayed there?" I asked.

"Because they have a generator. We have emergency lights hooked up to a battery though. We are very fortunate that my father did that for us," he said flipping on the battery light switch.

"Why don't we buy a generator?" I asked him.

"Because they're expensive! $3,000 easy," he replied.

"When you start working at your pharmacy, things will change, right?" I offered. "How is that coming?"

"We are not done with the paperwork yet," he replied.

"How much longer will that take?" I asked.

"I don't know. It could take months," he replied. "There's a lot of bureaucratic bullshit here."

"I wanted to ask you something else," I began hesitating. "I tried to call my parents this morning on our phone but I couldn't get through."

"There's no long-distance on our phone," he replied.

"What do you mean? I got through on your parents' phone," I reminded him. "Maybe I am just dialing the wrong country cod?"

"No, you are not dialing the wrong country code," he mimicked my words in a high whiny voice. "My father didn't include long-distance in our phone line."

"What?" I said, now alarmed. "How am I supposed to call my parents? I need it added!"

"Oh, you need it added?" he mocked me with a twisted grin on his face. "And how will you be paying for that? Do you know how much trouble my father had to go through just to add another phone line to this building?"

I shook my head.

"The phone company denied him because he already had three lines and they accused him of adding another line so he can "sell" it to his neighbors. This is not America. Here, not everyone can get a phone line!" He paused, pulled out a cigarette, leaned back in his chair while I waited apprehensively.

"So my father had to go down and talk to them in person," he continued, enjoying each inhale of his cigarette. "He told them not to mistake their honest paying customers for thieves who steal from them. It took a little persuasion, but they agreed to let him add another line.

He decided not to add long-distance to ours because it's too expensive and he's afraid you will call your parents everyday."

"I haven't and I won't call everyday," I said. "I've only called twice since I've been here."

"He's the one paying for all of this so we don't have a choice!" he snapped.

"How much more?" I asked.

"It will cost four hundred dollars," he replied.

"You told me that the cost of living here was extremely cheap," I began. "In fact, you told me that people who live on $500 a month live like a king here. So far, I have seen that groceries and gas are even more expensive than America. How am I supposed to call my parents? They are going to become worried if I don't contact them soon."

"Mohammed is going to hook up the computer we brought for you and bring a prepaid monthly Internet card with it. Then you can email your parents all day long for all I care," he said.

That night I went to bed with a sinking feeling in my heart. I looked over at my husband who was snoring loudly. The reality of this place was not how he had described it at all and I began to wonder how much more he was lying about.

All of a sudden, a loud boom thundered above us. I sat bolt upright in bed. Rumbles of heavy explosions were detonating in the near distance. Ibrahim woke up and walked to the bedroom window. The girls woke up screaming, groping for us in the dark.

"What is it Baba?" Layla asked, her voice reflecting the fear we all felt.

"Its just skirmishes on the border habebti (my love). Nothing to be afraid of," he reassured her.

"It sounds so close," I said, remaining calm for the girls. The next explosion rattled the windows and the girls dived under the covers.

"It's far from here," he said. "It's near the Israeli-Lebanon border. Hezbollah is probably firing on Israel."

"How far away is the border?" I asked.

"About an hour," he said. "Don't worry we are safe. We are safer here than when we were in America."

His words brought me no comfort as I prayed fervently for our protection.

A WARNING

The next morning I was awakened by a male's voice bellowing up through the floor.

"Who is that?" I asked Ibrahim who was now awake.

"It's Mohammed," he mumbled, speaking about his brother who lived directly below us.

After a good half an hour of this I asked, "What prayer is that? It doesn't even sound familiar."

"Those are extra prayers for special favors. Mohammed is *always* praying," he said, pulling a pillow over his head to drown out the noise.

The loud grating chanting blared at us in a crude monotone lacking any lilt or rhythm. I ungraciously thought that Allah was probably insulted by this petitioner who thought Him deaf.

We had our first visitors that night. Ibrahim had invited his brother Mohammed and his family up for tea and sweets after dinner. When they arrived, Mohammed's wife, Fatima, directed her four boys to kiss me and call me Halti (Aunt). The children went off to play while we sat on our rug in the living room.

Fatima was a very thin, quiet, beautiful woman. Her small pale face framed by a simple white scarf had beautiful bone structure. If I had seen her without a scarf on I would have guessed she was French. She had an intelligent face with hazel eyes clouded by a sad layer of melancholy. When she opened her mouth to speak, however, her mouth contorted and her words came out clumsily in loud bursts of expressions, a natural result of trying to be heard over her husband who had an annoying habit of talking over her.

She couldn't speak a word of English like my mother-in-law so we were at the mercy of my husband to translate.

"So, how do you find Lebanon?" she asked.

"It is a beautiful country," I edited, politely leaving out my recent discoveries.

Immediately her husband added, "But it's cold isn't it?" pointing to my two layers of sweaters and wool socks.

"My wife is always cold, always complaining – she even wears her winter coat indoors!" Mohammed laughed, pointing to Fatima's long thick coat she wore now over a thin housedress, her bare feet sticking out in rubber sandals. Fatima roller her eyes at him as he continued, "But just wait until the summer – here in Lebanon – an oven!"

Mohammed was the only son who had not gone to America to receive a college degree. He dropped out of school early and now owned his own business. He was the only son who stayed in Lebanon and he wore this fact with pride. My husband's presence threatened his unique standing in the family.

We sipped our hot tea spiced with cardamom pods and nibbled at the Lebanese shortbreads. Fatima refused any sweets and lit up a cigarette, using the tea saucer as an ashtray. She drank more tea and out-smoked my husband two cigarettes to his one.

Mohammed noticed me watching his wife and said, "You see – my wife – she is always smoking! It is a problem for me!"

Fatima just narrowed her eyes at him and inhaled deeply, exhaling a plume of smoke over her right shoulder directly at him.

"So, how do you really find Lebanon?" Mohammed asked me.

I looked at my husband. "I think it is ...fine, but last night kind of scared me," I said.

"Are you scared?" Mohammed asked me, his eyes widening, seeming to enjoy my fear.

"Yes, a little when I heard the gunfire," I answered truthfully.

His smile broadened, showing all of his tea-stained teeth. "Wait, wait...you haven't seen anything yet," he said, touching his fingertips to his thumb in his right hand, moving it slowly up and down, the Arabic gesture for "wait."

He then began a series of horror stories telling me what had happened in this city during the civil war. The Lebanese civil war lasted from 1975 to 1990. Before the war, Lebanon had a parliamentary government dominated by Maronite Christians. However, the country had a large Muslim population, which opposed the pro-western government. When the state of Israel was established, hundreds of thousands of Palestinian refugees fled to Lebanon and this changed the demographic balance in favor of the Muslim population. Fighting between Maronite and Palestinian forces began in 1975. Alliances shifted constantly and by the end of the war, nearly every party (Shite, Sunni, Druze, Maronite, Palestinian) had allied with and betrayed every other party.[11]

I heard stories about how this family building was occupied by Israelis, Syrians and Druze and how a missile landed on the roof which left a gaping hole in all the kitchens from the top on down. I learned that a family of Druze had moved into the third floor and set up residency rent-free for more than two years and refused to leave. During this war there was no civil order and laws weren't enforced, so these squatters stayed. Abu Ali had enough of asking them politely to leave and finally called on his friends to help.

"One day they came in trucks and blocked off the whole street right in front of us," Mohammed said.

"They?" I asked.

"The soldiers – Hezbollah," he answered scanning my face for a reaction. "Some of the soldiers stayed down in the courtyard with my father while others went upstairs and forced the head of the family to come downstairs in the courtyard. They made him sit down facing my father and told him, 'It is time for you to leave and thank Abu Ali for his generosity in letting you stay this long rent –free.' The man was so scared, he promised to leave the next day!"

As I listened to the rest of the story, the image of Abu Ali, my father-in-law, changed from a genial grandfather to a strong patriarch who had connections with Hezbollah, a well-known terrorist group, so much so they were called in to settle a personal matter for him.

As Mohammed continued telling me heart-wrenching stories of people being gunned down at checkpoints based solely on what religion they professed to be and how he personally had to scramble for food and water for his family, I was moved to compassion. "I can't even imagine how terrible it must have been for you," I said.

"Wait, wait... it isn't over," he said, smiling, his black eyes darkening further. "It will happen again soon. War is about to erupt here. You think it is hard now? Wait and see!"

My husband interrupted him, "What are you doing? Are you trying to scare my wife?"

Mohammed wasn't finished with his storytelling, however, and continued on with a story about another foreign woman, a German, who married a Lebanese and moved to Beirut, like me.

"She looked just like you – blonde hair, blue eyes," he pointed out. "They had two daughters just like you too. They moved here when the daughters were about nine and ten, and they lived right down here, just a few blocks from our house. Her husband opened the first grocery store in the neighborhood and they lived right above it for a few years. His business was doing great and things were going well for them, but then his wife began to complain about living in Beirut and wanted to return to Germany." Mohammed said, smiling at my husband.

"What did she complain about?" I asked.

"As her daughters became older she didn't like the way her husband wanted to raise them. She complained it was too strict, you know, she was used to the Western way of being free and doing what you want," he said grinning. "So one day, she told her husband that she and her daughters were going across town to visit someone but instead drove to the Israeli border, boarded a plane and flew back to Germany!"

"Those damn Israelis!" my husband interjected.

"Her husband followed her and flew to Germany. He found his daughters, gave them sleeping pills so he could drive them back here with no problem," Mohammed continued.

Not thinking I had heard correctly I repeated, "He drugged them?"

"Yes, and she hired some Christian mercenaries to kidnap her daughters and bring them back to Germany," he continued, his black eyes darting back and forth. "But this man went back to Germany because he is a German citizen, waited for the right moment, kidnapped his daughters again and brought them back here to live with his family!"

I felt sick to my stomach. "So is that the end of the story?" I asked, hoping her daughters were returned to her.

"No, he remarried a good Lebanese Muslim wife and now his daughters are to be married to good Muslim men here," he smiled. "And he and his new wife are now living in Germany."

Thinking I hadn't heard him correctly I asked, "You mean Lebanon?"

"No, he is a German citizen because of his ex-wife and now his new wife will have German citizenship," he said.

"But what about the girls' real mother?" I asked.

"She doesn't deserve them," he said. "She has lost all rights to be their mother!"

I was visibly upset and didn't want to react in front of my

brother-in-law. I immediately excused myself to the kitchen to make more tea. I sat down at the kitchen table and thought about this poor German woman and wondered what made her want to leave. I felt a dark heavy foreboding that unsettled me.

When I returned to the living room I found them in a heavy discussion speaking in Arabic. My husband, tired of translating for me, ignored my presence and continued talking. I caught a few words here and there but realized I needed to be fluent in this language in order to survive here, so I made a mental note to convince my husband to enroll me in Arabic classes immediately. Before they left, Mohammed helped me set up our computer and handed me a prepaid Internet card. I stored it safely away, realizing this would be my only lifeline to my parents.

Part VI Clipped Wings

"...I have been a stranger in a strange land."
Exodus 2:22

A REAL WIFE

The next morning, I woke up early and immediately tried to email my parents. I logged on, waiting for the dial up, hoping that the electricity would stay on long enough for me to write to them. At the sound of the dial tone I wrote what became the first of many emails:

Dear Mom and Dad,

I am sorry I have to email but we can't afford the long distance on our phone line. I did find an address you can mail things to. It's Ibrahim's nephew's mailbox at the American University of Beirut.

Things here are fine so far, just a little cold. We are in our own apartment and still waiting for our things to arrive. Ibrahim says, "Hi!" He is busy submitting papers everyday to open a pharmacy. It seems like a lot of red tape.

Nadine says, "I love you Grammy and Grandpa, and will you please take me to the park because Mommy won't." Actually, I have yet to see a park or playground here.

Layla sends a great big hug and many kisses. She is excited about school starting soon.

Well I better send this quickly before the power goes out.

Love you, Kelly

I turned to look at my girls. We had been cooped up in here for over a month and it was not safe to go outside. I had explained to them that I couldn't take them to any park because I couldn't drive here. We were at the mercy of others to take us anywhere. This didn't matter to Nadine who at three didn't understand and felt I was being mean to her. I felt trapped and powerless. I tried to remind myself that my daughters were better off with me being here and I was determined to live in this country and make the best of it for them. I was here now with them to protect them, because the alternative was unimaginable.

That night, Ibrahim came home in a foul mood. "I am sick and tired of people's comments when they find out I am married to an American wife!" he snapped.

"What are people saying?" I asked.

"They always pretend to feel sorry for me and tell me not to worry – that they will find me a *real* wife," he said.

"They don't even know me," I replied, frowning. "I thought I would be welcomed here, because I left my family and country behind."

"I do have good news, though" he added smiling, ignoring my comment. "We spliced the cable to the next door neighbor with his permission and we now have cable."

The girls were ecstatic to finally be able to watch TV in English. They grabbed their blankets and snuggled next to the TV. I put the portable heater next to them, thankful that they had something to entertain them.

LAYLA'S SCHOOL

It was time to enroll Layla into school. I had looked forward to this moment since arriving. We drove that morning to the school that we had chosen from the brochures she had brought home from her trip with her father. It was a few minutes from our house and as we approached the office I held Layla's hand in anticipation.

The principal of the school greeted us. He was young, tall and lanky with wavy blonde hair and green eyes. He was an obvious mixture of east and west – both German and Lebanese. As we sat down I noticed his office was completely bare, save five school manuals and some brochures, similar to the one we held, sitting on his desk.

We followed him as he took us on tour. The school was a rectangular block of classrooms with an open courtyard in the center. It was February and the cold wind buffeted our faces as we watched the students huddle together on a broken concrete playground. As we walked by them, some of the girls had pulled the sleeves of their blue sweaters over their hands and were blowing into them to keep warm.

"They are on recess," the principal said, smiling.

Nadine suddenly had the urge to use their bathroom. White, peeling wooden stalls with badly stained toilets and broken seats greeted us. There was no toilet paper, only hoses hooked up to each toilet but the water only dribbled from the clogged nozzles. I tried to flush the toilet after Nadine, but a young girl told me that they couldn't flush when the electricity was off.

When we came out, the president showed us the preschool and kindergarten indoor play area. Finally, this looked like one of the pictures in the brochure but I noticed that the teachers looked like maids from Sri Lanka and Bangladesh and they were sitting talking to each other, ignoring the children.

When our tour guide took us back to his office to discuss tuition, I felt that we weren't seeing the whole picture. I pretended

Nadine had to use the bathroom again and instead we snuck upstairs. I peeked into the classrooms that looked nothing like the brochure. The rooms were small, with dilapidated desks crammed together in unheated rooms, cracked concrete floors and grimy walls. There were no books or any hint of educational posters or supplies. It could have been a concrete storage shed.

I searched for the beautiful garden with play equipment we had seen in the brochure, but all we saw were children huddled together on concrete steps and a bent basketball hoop with a frayed net swinging forlornly in the winter breeze. I had seen enough and we went back to the office.

As soon as we left Ibrahim said, "Layla takes the entrance exam tomorrow and then she can probably start next week."

"Layla is not going to that school!" I said, emphatically.

"Mama is right Baba! It's awful!" Layla chimed in.

"But this is the school you chose," he said with a look of astonishment on his face.

"The school in the brochure and this school are not one and the same," I answered firmly.

"But this is a very good school," Ibrahim replied. "The tuition is $3,000 for one year!"

"Well, someone must be pocketing all that money because it certainly isn't going toward the school or the kids!" I said.

"Fine," Ibrahim agreed. "Let's go look at other schools."

We drove off and came to a German school and found it completely different than the last school. It was heated with carpeting and the classrooms looked similar to those in America, decorated with chalkboards and learning materials and the bathrooms were clean and modern. The curriculum was taught in German, however, which would be a definite hindrance for Layla, plus the tuition was over $5,000 a year.

"That was a clean school Mama! And it was warm!" Layla said. "Am I going to go there?" she looked up hopefully at her father.

"There are other schools to look at," he answered.

We drove by a school where children were wearing blue and green plaid uniforms, playing in pretty courtyards surrounded by neatly groomed hedges. It was a Catholic parochial school.

"What about this school?" I asked, hopefully.

"They only teach in French and Arabic here," he answered too quickly.

"Isn't that what we wanted?" I asked. "For her to speak French and Arabic?"

Ibrahim kept driving. "I want her to learn Arabic first and then French. I don't want to confuse her. "

Sensing that there was more behind his protests than what he was saying, I waited until later that evening to question him. "You don't want your daughters going to the same type of schools you went to, do you?" I asked.

"No, I don't," he answered.

"Why not?" I asked. "Your father sent you to them because of how great they are academically."

"He made a mistake," he said. "They taught us Catholicism there and I grew up not even knowing my own religion. A little sheik used to come to the boarding school to teach us once in awhile and that was all. I want my daughters to learn the Quran and Arabic."

"But that was not part of our agreement," I said.

"You are not the one to decide!" he screamed. "I am in charge over here and I have to figure out how we are going to pay for all of this anyway!"

I backed off. Ibrahim had taken over our finances when we arrived here and he kept me completely in the dark. I was worried. My fears were exacerbated that night when he asked Layla to bring him all the money she had in her little purse.

When she laid all of her rainbow of currency from Argentina, Canada, France, Kuwait, Turkey and Lebanon on the table she looked at her father and said, "I thought you gave all this to me for my collection."

"I did habebti, I did," he said. "I just want to see how much you have. Look at that! You have over 150,000 Lebanese pounds! You are a good saver! That's almost a hundred U.S. dollars!"

"Can Baba borrow this until next month?" he begged, giving her a long face.

"Sure Baba," she sighed.

"Thank you habebti. I will give you back even more!" he promised. He squeezed her cheeks and kissed her on the nose. I felt outraged that he was borrowing from our daughter's meager savings and worried about our financial situation.

"How much money do we have left in our account?" I asked him after Layla left.

"Enough," he answered, putting the money in his right pocket.

"Enough?" I answered. "Then why are you borrowing from Layla? Didn't you open a savings account with all of our money? And when are you going to add my name to the account?"

"So many questions!" he yelled. "You have no idea how things work here. I am in control here in this country and I know what I am doing!"

A shiver ran through my body. His eyes were full of contempt for me. I quickly backed down realizing I was completely dependent on him for everything.

"Don't worry," I said. "It will all work out. When you open your business this will all be behind us."

"I need a nap," he replied. "I'm going to go lay down – don't disturb me."

I sat alone in the kitchen for a long time, not able to move. I was frozen with fear. Fear that my husband was starting to hate me, to despise me. He didn't come to me for comfort anymore or even pretend to be nice to me here.

Ibrahim enrolled Layla in a school the following week. It was only a few blocks from our house. I only saw the office and kindergarten because we weren't allowed upstairs or into the other building which was locked by a gate. The office was clean and a woman in a headscarf was engaging Layla in conversation, commenting on how beautiful my daughters were. She offered us tea and made us feel very welcome.

"This is a good enough school until we can get her in a better school this fall," Ibrahim told me, holding out another promise.

AISHA

One day Ibrahim returned from his daily trips and came back with the fruits of his labors: a formal looking paper written in Arabic giving him permission to open a pharmacy.

"Congratulations!" I exclaimed.

He didn't even look at me but stared out the kitchen window.

"What's wrong?" I asked.

"I'm not sure I want to work as a pharmacist here," he said.

I couldn't believe my ears. "What do you mean? Isn't this the whole reason we came over here – so you could fulfill your dream?"

"My dream!" he retorted angrily. "What are you talking about? I had no choice. I was kicked out!"

"We can always return to America where you can work as a pharmacist or general practitioner," I said softly, hoping.

"That's exactly what you would want – isn't it?" he said staring darkly at me.

"No," I responded, frightened. "I just want you to be happy. If you stay here, you have so much medical knowledge that you can help your own people."

"My sister Aisha told me the same thing," he said quietly. "She thinks I will do well here because of my medical knowledge."

"Yes, she's right," I encouraged him. "And who knows better than her – a pharmacist herself." Aisha was his youngest sister who lived here in Beirut full time with her own thriving pharmacy.

"She was telling me that most people can't afford to go to a doctor so they go to their pharmacist who can diagnose and treat them," he replied, his countenance brightening.

I was relieved his mood had changed. I tiptoed around him, afraid to incur his wrath because I knew I was just a reminder to him of everything that went wrong in America.

"Aisha keeps inviting us over for a visit," he added. "Why don't we go tonight? Maybe she can help me."

Kelly Nielson

We drove ourselves that night, without the chauffeur. Ibrahim had obtained a Lebanese driver's license for himself and told me he was working on mine. Women were allowed to drive here, but few did because either their husbands forbade them, as was the case with Fatima and my mother-in-law, or they were too afraid to drive. Driving here was not for the faint of heart. There were no traffic lights or speed limits and traffic lanes were ignored, as was the common courtesy of taking turns at an intersection. Angry drivers incessantly honked at one another and gestured obscenities while screaming insults at each other.

When we arrived in the Shiite southern suburbs of Beirut, huge murals and long building-length posters of the Ayatollah Khomeini, Ali Khamanei, and Secretary General of Hezbollha, Sayyid Hassan Nasrallah, stared down at us with dark foreboding eyes. Banners of young men with somber faces and haunting eyes were tied onto the streetlights above us. These pictures were taken a few days before their deaths, when they made live bombs of themselves in their attack against their enemies.

Hezbollah's strongholds on this community were visible everywhere. Ibrahim proudly pointed out the hospitals, orphanages and schools for the poor, including a gas station that donated to their cause. He explained to me how the Al Shahid (Martyrs) Association, set up by Hezbollah, takes care of any martyr's family left behind. Each suicide bomber's child was given a free education at one of nine Al Mahdi schools where they are taught that their fathers are heroes and that this type of martyrdom is the ideal way to attain Paradise.

Looking up at these somber faces, I wondered if they were given all that they had been promised by their religious leaders. Were they truly given perpetual virgins as their Quran stated?

> "Reclining upon the couches lined with silk brocade…
> Wherein will be those houris (perpetual virgins),
> refraining their glances upon their husbands,
> whom no man or jinn has opened their hymens with sexual
> intercourse before.."
> (Quran 55: 54-59 Surat l-rahman -Translation by Mohsin Khan)

"I don't understand? Why are they called martyrs?" I asked.
"What?" Ibrahim responded, surprised.

136

"My understanding of the word martyr is one who dies for their faith," I explained.

"These men did die for their faith," he answered.

"They killed themselves," I continued shakily. "When I think of martyrs I think of Christianity's first martyr, Stephen, whose hands and feet were tied as he was pummeled with rocks by a mad crowd simply because of his faith or the Jewish mother Hannah and her seven sons who were killed in the second century because they refused to worship pagan gods. These people didn't kill themselves and take innocent lives with them. They were killed because of their beliefs," I tried to explain.

"These men are soldiers," he said pointing to the banners. "They are soldiers for Islam fighting against the infernal enemy!"

Without warning he slammed on the brakes, almost rear-ending the car in front of us. We were trapped in a traffic jam at a large intersection. He clenched the wheel tightly until his knuckles appeared white. It was complete gridlock. Ibrahim leaned on his horn, joining the blaring of other drivers. Angry men and women screamed at each other gesturing with their hands.

"I just know that my God would not ask us to tie a bomb to ourselves and blow other people up," I said softly to myself hoping my daughters were paying attention in the back seat.

"Well, you are not God, thank God, to understand His ways!" he remarked glaring at me.

Suddenly, a crowd of small children clamored around our car. They were in rags with dirt smeared on their faces holding out their small hands for money. My heart went out to them right away and I asked Ibrahim to open the window and give them some money.

"Don't look at them," he warned me. "They are scam artists whose parents put them up to this," he frowned and refused to look into their wanton eyes. "They are from the Palestinian refugee camps."

Their persistent pleas for "One dollar, Allah haleek (May God bless you), one dollar," tore at my insides. At that moment I wanted to save them all.

Layla and Nadine were moved to tears. "Please Baba, please give them some money!" they whined.

Finally Ibrahim shoved a Lebanese note through an open crack in his window to one little boy who grabbed it quickly. More children immediately surrounded us.

"Just great!" he said. "They noticed that you are a foreigner and now they won't stop coming!"

137

He steered around them and drove down a back alley. Finally we pulled up to an apartment building where Aisha lived. The elevator took us to the tenth floor. Her daughters Farah and Jasmine were waiting for us when it stopped and pounced on us. When Layla and Nadine saw them they were ecstatic to finally see other children their own age and welcomed their cousins' attention.

"They have been waiting all day for Layla and Nadine!" Aisha said suddenly appearing from behind her front door. "Welcome, Welcome! How are you?" She kissed us both and led us into her parlor where her maid offered us tea.

I hadn't seen Aisha in over ten years. The last time was when I visited Kuwait before I had children. She was just a young college student then and we had hit it off right away. We did each other's makeup and shared stories, giggling like teenagers. She was beautiful - the feminine version of my husband with high cheekbones, flawless skin and full lips - her deep brown eyes sparkled mischievously when she teased her older brother about how jealous he was of our time together. She was strong and independent and had convinced her father to give her permission to pursue a pharmacy degree. Numerous young men sought after her because she was the perfect combination of beauty and brains but she turned many away without a second thought. She finally chose her husband and settled down with him here in Beirut, opening a pharmacy of her own. And now she had four children.

The Aisha who stood before me now was only a shadow of the vibrant young woman I knew. Her face seemed longer, paler, with deep hollows, and a haunting sadness permeated her eyes that now had dark circles underneath where laugh lines used to be. Her mouth was pinched into a forced smile as she conversed and I noticed how the bones on her wrists protruded when she poured us tea.

She sat next to Ibrahim and nudged him, teasing him like old times. "So how have you been, habebti (my love)?" she asked me. She and her older sister Salam were the only ones to call me by that term of endearment.

"Fine," I responded, avoiding her eyes as I looked at my husband. "A little lonely but just fine."

"And how about you?" I returned.

"Il-Hamdu lillah," (Thank God, I am fine) she replied looking upward.

"So, now you are happily married with four beautiful children and your own pharmacy!" I exclaimed. "Congratulations! It must be a wonderful feeling. I am so proud of you!"

"Thank you," she replied. "It is wonderful – a lot of work though. I am always tired. We work so hard at the business and raising a family. We don't get to bed until late, usually midnight and then start all over again."

"And how are you, Ibrahim? How is the pharmacy coming?" she asked her brother who seemed preoccupied by his own thoughts.

My husband answered her in Arabic. I hated this annoying habit of his. He refused to speak English even when the speaker was fluent in it. The family members who could speak even a little English did so for my benefit so I could be included in the conversation but he didn't. I had brought his attention to this many times – how I felt like a nonperson sitting there while everyone spoke above me, but he wouldn't change. Aisha began to interpret for me but Ibrahim grew annoyed. She respected her brother and took his obvious hint that I was not privy to this discussion. I gave up trying to make sense of their words and picked up a cooking magazine in French, thumbing through the recipes, looking at the pictures. The visit that I had so looked forward to had once again become a familiar rerun of me sitting idly by like a child, staring around the room, letting my mind wander while others conversed in a language I couldn't understand.

After an hour discussion, Ibrahim rose to leave and Aisha apologized for not talking to me as much as she wanted to and we made plans to see each other soon. We drove home in the dark, the girls chatting in the back about their cousins and their plans for visiting them again.

"I heard that there is a class that teaches Arabic for foreigners that is put out by the British embassy," I said hopefully.

"Who told you about this?" he asked.

"Your sister did," I answered. "Maybe you could look into it. I think it is a necessity that I learn to speak the language here in order to survive."

"I have so many things on my mind right now, so many things to take care of," he said seeming disinterested.

"Well, it is really hard for me to sit there with your family and not understand a word you are saying except the very basics," I replied. "I am already feeling isolated and lonely – this could only help me."

"This is the last thing on my mind right now," he replied. "I don't know – maybe Mohammed knows someone who can tutor you and the girls at our house."

I looked over at him as he lit a cigarette knowing that this was just another empty promise. His discussion with Aisha instead of giving him encouragement made him more apprehensive. His family was waiting for him to open a pharmacy and set up roots here. To a man that moved us almost every year since we had been married, the permanence of this decision seemed to weigh heavily on him.

"My family has it all worked out," he said. "They want me to open a pharmacy."

"Yes – isn't that why we are here?" I asked, confused.

"Aisha's husband must have told her to convince me to do this," he said. "He considers himself the doctor in the family. Did you know they call him 'doctor' here instead of dentist? I am supposed to be the doctor in the family."

Pride had reared its ugly head and his brother-in-law now threatened Ibrahim's place in the family.

"You are the one with the medical degree," I said trying to smooth his ego. "You should be proud of what you have accomplished so far. It's not very often a person has two degrees like yours."

My words held no weight with him. I was invisible to him as were my words. I blended into the darkness now enveloping the lightless street as I watched the burning ember on the end of his cigarette.

DATE NIGHT

March arrived and with it no reprieve from the bitter cold. Our belongings still hadn't arrived from America and we were homesick. The girls and I rarely went out and I began to feel trapped. Ibrahim's parents had left for Kuwait and wouldn't be back until summer, so we were the only people left in the family building beside his brother Mohammed and Bassam the chauffeur.

Aisha seemed to sense how lonely I was on the phone and somehow convinced her brother to take me out on a date night while she watched our daughters. He decided on dinner and a movie. I looked forward to getting out of the house. This would be the first time we had gone on a date since Paris.

We drove to the Concorde Cinema in the Hamra area of Beirut, the more upscale part of the city that tourists often visited. High-end stores such as Gucci, Benetton and Dior stood out in stark contrast with the concrete buildings crumbling around it.

American movies were advertised everywhere on brightly lit marquees. We chose "A Beautiful Mind," with Russell Crowe and sat together, alone in an empty theater, watching, while Arabic and French subtitles ran underneath. It was a depressing movie; it did nothing to elevate my mood. I watched the main character deteriorate into paranoid schizophrenia with each delusional episode worse than the other. I felt very alone in the theatre – Ibrahim only acknowledging me when he offered me some stale popcorn or warm soda.

After the film was over, we chose to eat at the Modca Café, which was teeming with people, mostly couples engaged in lively conversation. We sat down and ordered drinks. On the rare occasion we went out in the United States, we would always order a drink before dinner but this time when I ordered a glass of wine, he ordered a coffee, not his usual scotch on the rocks. I noticed a young couple next to us, playfully bantering back and forth. The woman was wearing full hijab, completely covered except for her face, and the man was enjoying a cocktail while she held a beer bottle. They were both leaning toward each other, fully engaged, laughing and talking.

"Is that a beer she is drinking?" I whispered to my husband.

"I don't know. It looks like it," he said, staring at them.

"It just seems so funny to me – to see a woman in hijab drinking a beer," I said. "Is her husband drinking too?"

"I don't think that's her husband," he murmured.

Stunned, I replied, "Of course it's her husband. She's wearing hijab."

"Let's change the subject," he said. "I didn't come here to talk about other people."

Taking my cue I asked, "So, how did you like the movie?"

"Not so much," he replied. "It was confusing and depressing."

He was looking around nervously, obviously not enjoying himself. I reached out across the table and touched his hand. He flinched and pulled his hand back.

"What's wrong?" I asked. "You're acting very strangely and I noticed you wouldn't hold hands with me when we walked. It's like you are embarrassed to be seen with me."

"I feel like I am cheating on my wife," he confessed.

I thought I had heard wrong. "Your wife?" I said. "I am your wife."

"No, I mean here I am, going out with a blonde, blue-eyed foreigner. People are staring at us, probably thinking the worst," he said still looking around.

"Since when do you care what others think?" I asked still stunned. "With that guilty look on your face, you're feeding their suspicions. We know we are married – for over fourteen years I might add – that's all that matters."

"It's different here," he said. "Don't you feel everyone's eyes on you all the time? I hate it when we go out anywhere and everyone is always staring at you. We really stand out and no one can go anywhere in this country without a hundred people watching for lack of anything better to do!"

I could see how upset he was by this and for the first time I looked around the café and caught the glances of others watching us. I suddenly felt very self-conscious. I leaned back in my chair, staring at my husband somberly. I waited for him to start the conversation.

"I think we better get back to the girls," he finally said.

"So you're not hungry?" I asked, disappointed.

"No, not really, but if you want to…" he said half-heartedly standing up to leave.

"No, it's okay. Let's go," I replied putting my coat on by myself. He was already out the door. I walked quickly behind him, trying to catch up but he walked quickly ahead of me as if we weren't together. I gave up trying to keep pace with him and burrowed my face into the folds of my wool coat. An icy tear streamed down my cheek as a cold chill went down my back. Only a few months ago in Europe, we were holding hands and sharing romantic dinners. Here, he was embarrassed to even walk with me.

Part VII Predators

"Lord my God, I take refuge in you;
save and deliver me from all who pursue me,
or they will tear me apart like a lion
and rip me to pieces with no one to rescue me."
Psalm 7:1-2

SANDRA

Now that Layla had begun school, Nadine and I were left alone all day
and my life became a dull routine. I tried to make this empty apartment
a home and maintain some sense of normalcy. Here life revolved
around food and a woman was judged by how well she cooked and
kept her house. I would begin by sorting through the rice, grain by
grain, discarding any tiny black bugs, washing the vegetables in bleach
water as his mother had taught me. Every kind of meat was boiled just
to be safe before cooking. We could not trust the municipal city water
so we had to buy bottled water and consume it sparingly. Lebanese
dishes were time-consuming and elaborate but I did my best to prepare
my husband's favorite dishes and keep a clean home. Nadine would
occupy herself by watching the one channel she could understand and
playing with the few toys we had brought on the airplane. The only
reprieve I had from my daily duties was visiting my sister-in-law Hala.

Hala lived across the street from us, one block down with my
husband's brother and two children. I visited her whenever Ibrahim
would drive us. Her husband, Yusef, had left a month after we had
arrived accepting a job in Kuwait. She never came to visit me because I
found out she was forbidden by our mother-in-law.

144

Hala was a strong-willed, highly educated Lebanese woman who wasn't about to follow passively on the heels of my mother-in-law, like the other daughters-in-law. She was studying to be a lawyer, a role in which I could see her doing well. Her quick wit and intelligence would be an asset to any legal system. She did not wear a scarf or cover like the rest of the women in the family but instead dressed modernly, showing off her slim figure in various European styles, her makeup always understated, yet elegant, complete with tasteful jewelry. Her home reflected the same simple elegance. In fact everything about her seemed to be deliberately chosen to proclaim that she was a modern, independent woman.

My mother-in-law did not like this daughter-in-law who did not follow the cultural tradition of daughters-in-law groveling before her. Hala wouldn't accept any insulting remarks from her mother-in-law and enmity was established quickly between them. I secretly admired her feistiness and strong personality but I feared receiving her wrath. Once when Amu Ali verbally insulted her, Hala slapped her in the face and since then she was barred from visiting the family building.

One day while I was visiting, her maid Sandra brought in a large pile of lentils on a platter that she had evidently sorted through. Hala examined them and with a "tch tch" of her tongue began to sort through them again.

"What are you looking for?" I asked.

Handing me a lentil, she responded with a perfect British accent, "Here, look at this lentil. It looks normal, right?"

I nodded.

"Open it," she commanded.

I cracked open the lentil and found a black bug curled up inside.

"These are baby cockroaches," she said matter-of-factly.

I grimaced. "Well, I am going to just eliminate lentils from our diet," I said. "I already have to sort through the rice."

"What you need is a maid," Hala said. "Here, it is different than America. Housecleaning and cooking can take a woman's whole day. All of us have maids here except Fatima and they are not that expensive." She shooed her maid back into the kitchen and added, "She is really stupid, this one."

Disconcerted by her last comment, I paused and said, "I don't think we can afford it right now and I think I would feel uncomfortable having another woman live with us picking up after us."

"You will become old and worn out without one," she warned me. "Like Fatima – her husband can't afford one so she has ailments of her feet and back." Hala suddenly paused and looked down at the floor next to my feet and asked, "Can I see the bottom of your shoes?" Hala was the only family member that didn't ask visitors to remove their shoes.

"Why?" I asked.

"I see dirt on the floor," she answered. I stood up from the couch and lifted up my heels, embarrassed by her demand. She inspected the soles of my shoes thoroughly.

"No, it isn't you," she muttered. "I had company right before you came. They must have tracked it inside."

I looked down at the miniscule flecks of red dirt she was referring to. "Sandra!" she yelled in a shrill voice.

"Yes Madame?" Sandra appeared immediately at her side, bowing meekly.

"Clean that up," Hala ordered. "And how are you coming with that salad?"

"Fine, Madame," she bowed again, kneeling down to pick up the dirt with her hands.

"Do you want me to take off my shoes?" I asked.

"No, no. I deplore this habit," she answered. "I can't abide a pile of shoes in the foyer. I wasn't raised this way," she sniffed. "But you would assume guests would know how to wipe their feet on the doormat before they came in."

"Not like that!!" Hanna suddenly shrieked at Sandra who shrank from her mistress. "Take the tissues and pick it up. You are smearing it everywhere."

An uncomfortable silence filled the room as we watched Sandra pick up the dirt with a tissue. "It is taking me so long to train this one," Hala moaned shaking her head. "She has been with me two months now and is giving me headaches."

"She looks very young," I offered. "Where is she from?"

"Sierra Leone," Hala said. "And this is her first job."

"Well, that explains it," I answered. "It's her first time away from home. Does she have any family?"

"Yes, she has a husband and two children," Hala said rolling her eyes. "She hasn't stopped crying for them since she's been here and wants to go home."

My heart burned with compassion for this young woman and I

commiserated with her feelings of homesickness. After Sandra returned to the kitchen, Hala leaned forward whispering, "I don't trust her. The other day when I went through her things I found broken glass in my linen napkin. I asked her what this was for and she told me it was for her – that she was going to swallow it and kill herself!"

"Oh Hala, that's terrible," I said, feeling sorry for this poor woman. "What did you do?"

"I threw it in the garbage and I warned her that if she makes trouble for me that I will send her back to the agency again where they will deal with her," she replied, her black eyes clouding over.

"You…um," I began, shocked at this callous reply. "I think she just needs a little compassion. Take it easy on her. I know what it is like being so far from home where you don't speak the language and I can't even imagine being apart from my daughters for so long," I gently advised her.

"No, you don't understand how things work here," Hala said smiling. "What is this favorite saying of mine? Ah yes, if you give them an inch, they will take a mile. If I am easy on her, she will grow lazy and spite me. I am alone now with my husband working in Kuwait and I need to show her who is boss!"

"Yes, but perhaps a more gentle way will work better?" I suggested. "This is her first time – she has never done this before."

"I know. I choose all of my maids this way," Hala said.

When I gave her a puzzled look she continued, "I don't want a maid that has already been ruined by another mistress. I like them fresh, so I can train them correctly. I have a certain way of doing things and I will not accept less."

My eyes widened as she continued. "She thinks that by pretending to be slow and stupid that I will relent on my standards. Well last night I kept her up until 2 a.m. until she cleaned the kitchen properly."

Her eleven-year-old son shuffled into the room, interrupting us. "Mama, don't forget my swimming lessons," he reminded her.

"I haven't forgotten, habebe," she crooned. I will drive you right now. Kelly, do you mind? It will only take me ten minutes." She rose quickly, already grabbing her coat and car keys.

After she left I went to check on my girls who were playing with Hala's oldest daughter and then peeked my head into the kitchen to check up on Sandra. I saw her clumsily trying to cut tomatoes like she never held a knife before. Tears stains ran down her cheeks. She quickly smiled at me bowing when she saw me as she had been trained.

"Hello, Madame," she said weakly avoiding my eyes.

Not knowing how much English she understood, I smiled and said, "Hello Sandra. My name is Kelly." I pointed at my chest and spoke slowly. Her eyes widened when she saw the small cross around my neck.

"You no Muslim?" she asked, pointing to my cross. "I have this too!"

"No, I am Christian," I responded, smiling.

She immediately grabbed my hand leading me to the corner of the kitchen. "My mistress - she take this," she said pointing to my cross. "She throw there," she said pointing to the garbage. "She throw away everything." She ran to her room, no bigger than a closet, off the kitchen balcony and returned with a picture of a young girl around four-years-old who resembled her and a baby no more than a few months.

"These, my children," she explained. "My baby, he needs me. He needs my milk. I need to go home. Please, Madame, I need to go home! My mistress – she hit me. She yell and yell. She bad woman. She very bad woman." She pulled out a roach killing powder from under the sink. "I want to eat this. I want to die."

I instinctively pulled her toward me and held her to my chest, hugging her. Her little body wracked with tears. "Don't do this Sandra. Your children need their mother. She can't treat you like this! I will talk to her," I said, anger rising in my chest, tears filling my eyes.

"No! No!" she whispered loudly. "Please don't tell her you talk to me!" She grasped my arm tightly, her eyes bulging with fear. She will take me to a very bad place. Please, don't tell her!"

Frightened by the look of terror in her eyes, I calmed her down by saying, "I promise. I promise. I won't tell her anything. But I will help you Sandra. I will find a way."

Realizing that Hala would be returning soon, I picked up the knife and hurriedly cut the tomatoes and put them into the bowl. I grabbed the washed leaves of lettuce and cucumber; finely slicing them as perfectly as I thought Hala would want them. I quickly finished the salad and rushed into the living room when I heard the elevator outside ascending.

"I am so sorry I kept you waiting," Hala apologized, leaning her head into the room as Sandra took her coat. "I will be right with you. I told this one to make a salad with dinner. Let me check on her progress."

Hala returned to the living room after a few minutes with a look of consternation on her face. "She finished the salad!" She sat down on the plush, saffron-colored sofa and rearranged the shimmering salmon cushions next to her. "You see! This just proves my point. She is just pretending to be stupid to make my life miserable. She could do it all along!"

I winced inwardly at her words, realizing I had probably done Sandra a disservice by helping her.

"Sandra!" Hala called out. "Take these cups away and bring us some more coffee." Sandra appeared and timidly picked up Hala's cup, avoiding my eyes as I handed her mine.

Anger was welling within me. "Hala, I can't believe that you have outfitted your maid in such a skimpy clothes in this freezing weather," I said, trying to shame her. Sandra was wearing a thin, short-sleeved uniform. Her legs were bare, raised with goose bumps. "I am barely warm enough wearing two layers under this wool sweater."

Hala's face flushed red. "Well, I went through her clothes when she arrived and she had nothing suitable to wear…"

"She should be wearing pants at least, Hala. You should buy her some pants," I interrupted her firmly. "She is a stranger, in a strange land and not used to this weather or lifestyle. She is lonely. She needs tenderness and compassion. I think you will get farther with her if you are gentle with her."

"But I am all alone here while my husband is in Kuwait," she responded. "I am left alone to raise my children and I am trying to finish law school. She acts like a baby, Kelly, a baby! It's disgusting! I had to slap her so she would come to her senses. I finally had to banish her to her room and lock her in there!"

I didn't hold back the shock in my face.

"I had no choice, and because of her theatrics, I failed my exam!" she continued. "I called the agency where I hired her and told them about the trouble I was having with her. They told me to bring her in so I drove her down and the manager was very understanding, telling me he knew how to handle her. He looked at her and threatened to cut off all of her hair if she didn't obey me." A smug look of validation came over her face. "He told me that I had done the right thing and showed me a room where other troublemakers were kept until they came to their senses."

"Send her back home Hala!" I almost shouted, pretending to

149

understand her pain. My real motive was to save Sandra from her. "She is obviously causing you more trouble than it's worth. Send her home before it gets worse."

"I can't do this," Hala shook her head. "I will lose money on her. I still have one more year on her two-year contract."

My thoughts reeled. I feared that Sandra might follow through on her suicidal threats before her sentence was up. I leaned forward earnestly trying to convince her to let Sandra go. "I don't think she's going to make it that long," I said. "You should send her home now and get a maid that's older and has more experience so you can study."

Our conversation was interrupted by the buzz of the intercom. It was Ibrahim. He didn't dare come into the apartment of the sister-in-law that was forbidden to step foot in our building. I thanked Hala and looked one more time at Sandra – we caught each other's eyes – and exchanged more in our silent look than we could with words.

When we returned home, I couldn't wait to tell my husband about Sandra. I conveyed my fears about the abuse that she was under, but he refused to get involved.

"Hala is a strong woman, but she would never do these things you are accusing her of," he said.

"But, Sandra told me herself! I am afraid for her!" I replied. "I am afraid she might hurt herself… I want to help her – please."

He turned sharply towards me, waving his finger in my face. "I don't want you to get involved in this. Do you understand? I want you to stay out of it. That's all I need right now is to stir up trouble with my brother Yusef!"

I looked up at him and nodded my head, disagreeing in my heart. "*I will not stay out of it,*" I thought as I walked away. I wracked my brain trying to come up with a plan to help her. By evening, I realized that all of the regular courses of action I would have taken in America weren't available here. "*Who would I file a complaint with – the agency? They approve of using physical abuse to keep these women in line. If I contacted the U.S. embassy, they couldn't help her because she was not a U.S. citizen. If I confront Hala it will just make more of conflict for my husband and then I will never see Sandra again.*"

I had no resources and knew my husband wouldn't help me and I felt angry at his apathy toward this situation. I felt powerless, unable to help this poor young woman - her face came to me repeatedly that night as I tossed and turned in bed. I wanted to run over there and help her escape – to have the power to send her home, back to her family. I cried angry tears, staring at Ibrahim's back as he slept peacefully, indifferent to her plight. I cried softly for Sandra – for me, for this whole awful mess.

RANDY

As I lay in bed tossing and turning, I couldn't stop thinking about Sandra's situation and mine. My mind carried me back to another time when I couldn't rescue the person I loved the most in this life. I had just turned seven that summer in Great Falls, Montana, and I was still in that unconscious state of childhood where lazy summer days followed each other, stretching out endlessly before me. My mother approached me one morning with news that would change my world forever.

"Kelly," she said. "Guess what? I am going to go back to school to be a nurse!"

I smiled, happy for her. "That's great Mom!" I said matching her enthusiasm, giving her a hug. I was happy to see her smiling again.

It had been awhile since I had seen her in this kind of mood. I felt the heavy sadness that had enveloped her lately, shadowing everything she did. She still kept an immaculate house, cooked and took care of her three children: Randy, myself, and my little brother Corey but it was like she was on autopilot. When I was older she told me that during that phase of her life she had a "death wish" and didn't want to live anymore.

This was about the time she had given up hope of "fixing" my brother Randy. His illness had affected her deeply. Ever since she found out my brother Randy was severely mentally and physically handicapped, she tackled his illness with a vengeance looking for answers. She found hope in the theory of psychomotor patterning invented by Glen Doman who founded the Institute for the Achievement of Human Potential (IAHP). After attending an expensive seminar, my parents paid for an evaluation of Randy hiring expensive special instructors from Canada who taught them how to pattern Randy so he could gain some sense of normalcy.

My parents followed this patterning faithfully, five times a day. It included manipulating him to crawl, creep, roll into somersaults, and other physical feats. They would also stimulate him with certain toys and aids but the worst was something called masking, where they had Randy breathe into a mask to increase the amount of carbon dioxide inhaled which was supposed to increase blood flow to his brain. I watched my brother gasp for air, pushing away this mask as they held it over his face. This intense program altered our family life, dominating all of my mother and father's free time because they were determined to fix Randy.

I watched as they set up the blue mats that took up our whole living room and put up obstacle courses for him to crawl through. Randy did not know how to crawl so they would move his arms and legs for him, "patterning" him to crawl – the first step in the series to teach him how to walk by himself one day. I would crawl through the obstacles myself many times, trying to show my brother how to do it. This daily routine was demanding and after many months, maybe years of patterning and seeing no improvement in her son, my mother had to face the sad truth that Randy was not going to change – that he would never be able to speak or walk on his own- that he would always need to be fed, changed and dressed like an infant the rest of his life. She had placed a lot of confidence in this program and now that her hopes were dashed, she became depressed and even more unavailable to me.

I embraced her happiness now, thinking that these sad days were all behind us and I would have my mother back.

"Your brother Randy is going to go to school too!" she said cheerily.

"Where?" I asked.

"To Boulder River School, in Boulder, Montana!" she said.

What she didn't explain at that moment was that that Randy was leaving us permanently – that school meant an institution in another city. She also took Corey with her to nursing school and put him in a daycare, but I saw him every weekend for the next two years, unlike Randy never came home again except on holidays.

Randy was two years my senior and we spent a lot of time together. As a toddler, I didn't realize there was anything wrong with my brother so we roughhoused like normal siblings. As I got older and realized that there was something different about my brother, it only made me even more protective of him. We would have rocking wars on the couch – seeing who could rock back and forth the fastest – the whole time he would be grinning at me – enjoying every minute. He would give great big bear hugs, squeezing so hard that I couldn't get out of his hold until he let me go.

Randy had seizures everyday without warning and I would stand by and watch helplessly while his body convulsed violently, his eyes rolling back into his head. My mother would run over and put a spoon in his mouth so he wouldn't choke on his own tongue. It would last minutes that felt like eternity and when it was over I would hug my big brother limp from exhaustion. Even though Randy couldn't speak I could understand his nonverbal language and I helped "translate" for him like when I knew he was full or tired or just needed a hug.

But now when I got home from school, it was to an empty, lonely house. I missed him and would go sit on the old brown couch where we would have our rocking wars and just rub my hands on the worn out armrest where he used to sit.

At first we took the two-hour drive to Boulder every month to visit Randy. On the first visit I remember driving up to a large brick building where my brother lived, but my parents decided against visiting him there so my father dropped us off at a local park while he picked up Randy and brought him to us. I was ecstatic to see him. Randy was so happy to see us, and he couldn't stop hugging us, like he didn't want to let go. He wasn't the same though – he was skinnier, paler and had a look of despondency in his eyes that I had never seen before. He wasn't happy and I knew it.

When I asked my parents what was wrong with him, they assured me it was what was best for him but I knew something wasn't quite right when the next time we visited him he had a deep, thick scar from his ear to his lip on his cheek. When I asked my mother what happened she said he fell on a sugar bowl.

"We need to take Randy out of here!" I said, emphatically. "We need to take him back home. I will take care of him."

It was explained to me that this wasn't possible, but to my seven-year old mind, I couldn't understand why. My brother was only nine and I knew that this was an awful place but I couldn't do anything to rescue him. Thankfully, two years later when we moved to Boise, Idaho my parents put him in an institution in Nampa, only an hour from our home, and then eventually a private home, but things were never the same. I missed him and when we would visit him I would spend my time next to my big brother, just hugging him and on the ride home I would cry silently in the backseat. I felt powerless to help him, and I missed him now more than ever. I wondered what he would think of my life choices now as tears streamed down my face.

Somehow I knew he would give me a big bear hug and tell me, "You can do this Kel. Be strong!. God will help you."

I knew that what I was facing was nothing compared to the pain he suffered in this life. I dried my tears and set my mind to make the best of this situation.

BULLIES

Layla had been in school for over a month now. Ibrahim would drive her in the morning and I would sit anxiously by the front door in the afternoon, waiting for her return. At first she seemed happy and came home with good reports but then one morning, after I gently woke her up to get ready for school, she unexpectedly burst into tears.

"What's wrong honey?" I asked, now alarmed.

"I need a hug," she said, reaching her arms out to me.

I crawled into bed with her and held her tight. "What is it baby? Are you sick?"

"Please don't send me to school today Mommy!" she blurted.

"Why? What's going on?" I asked.

"I hate it there. I have no friends. I stand alone at lunch and recess and they make fun of me," she said, sobbing. "They laugh at the way I speak Arabic and call me stupid! During lunch they stand and point at me, laughing!"

"How long has this been going on?" I asked, pulling her closer to me.

"Since the first week," she said truthfully.

My stomach tightened into stiff knots. Guilt washed over me. My brave Layla had been keeping all of this from me because she knew it would cause turmoil between Ibrahim and me. She was doing what she always did – being the good obedient daughter, trying to make the best of a terrible situation. I was angry with these children and even angrier at the teachers who did nothing about it.

"You aren't going to school today," I told her. "I am going to talk to your father."

I told Ibrahim that she was sick and then later told him what was happening his daughter at the school.

"This is normal," he replied, seeming unconcerned. "It will get easier when she learns Arabic."

"Can't you talk to the principal or teachers about this?" I asked.

156

I was surprised by his indifference. This was Layla, his daughter who he claimed to love the most. She resembled him the most and he even called her "Little Ibrahima."

One afternoon after Ibrahim picked Layla up from school, she came in the front door, her hair a mess, tears streaming down her face.

"What wrong?" I asked my husband, running to her.

"I don't know..." he said avoiding my eyes.

"Some boys at school spit on me today!" Layla blurted out looking at her father angrily. "They said that I love America and Israel and that I was an American yahmara (ass)!"

I immediately pulled her to me and embraced her. "What did the teacher do?" I asked her.

"She let me go to the bathroom to wash it out with salt water and it burned my eyes," she answered.

"But what did she do about the boys?" I asked.

"She yelled at them and hit them with a stick," Layla answered.

"Are you going to do something about this now?" I demanded, glaring at my husband.

Empowered by me, Layla continued, "I hate that school Baba. There is nothing to do at lunch or recess – we stand around in the cold, freezing. There are no jump ropes or play equipment like in America. The kids are mean and they are always screaming in the classroom. The teacher is always hitting them and yelling and they just yell back."

"Does the teacher ever hit you?" I asked.

"Yes," Layla whimpered. "She hits me on the head with a book when I don't understand Arabic."

"Are you kidding me!" I exclaimed. "They have no right to hit my daughter! I am going to go down there right now – I will walk!" I was hot and seeing red. No one hits my kid. No one.

I walked toward the front door and Ibrahim grabbed my arm. "Let's just sit down and talk about this."

We sat down at the kitchen table; Layla sat on my lap, wiping away her tears.

"Did you know that when I went to school, worse things happened to me?" Ibrahim began. "The monks would discipline me worse than this! Two of them would hold me down on a desk, take off my shoes and another one would take his long wooden stick and hit my feet as hard as he could over and over!" Ibrahim was standing up now imitating the monk's striking movements as he jumped in the air for effect. "I couldn't walk without pain for a long time!"

157

"Why? What did you do Baba?" Layla asked.

"I don't know – I probably started a fight at recess with some bullies," he replied. "Sometimes they would have us sleep on the cold bathroom floor for punishment. And those sons of bitches were perverts! We knew which ones liked little boys and one time I was called into the office to meet with one of them. He pulled up his chair close to mine until our knees were touching and when he started to put his hands on my thigh I jumped up and kicked the chair at him and screamed, "Don't touch me or I will kill you! He backed off then! That bastard!"

"Good for you Baba!" Layla said. She got up instinctively to give him a hug and sat on his lap.

I watched with a sickening feeling in my stomach as he gathered sympathy from his daughter as if this was a right of passage – a normal part of growing up.

"Are you going to talk to the teacher about this?" I asked bluntly, trying to redirect him.

He glared back at me. "I will handle this," he said.

After I washed Layla's hair and gave her a bath, I went to my husband and asked, "So you are going to talk to them?"

His face furrowed in anger at me. "I will handle this!" he said before slamming the bedroom door in my face.

Layla had gotten the message that compared to her father's troubled school years, she had nothing to complain about so from then on whenever I would ask her about school she would exchange a look with her father and respond, "Fine Mom, everything's fine."

Ibrahim's disregard for his daughter's plight surprised me. His only concern was finding an ideal place to open up his pharmacy.

One day, they were late coming home from school. Four o'clock came, then half past four. I did not have the phone number for the school and no one to call. I knew in my gut that he had forgotten to pick Layla up so I put on Nadine's coat and mine and walked out the front door of our apartment.

"Where are we going Mommy?" Nadine asked, surprised that we were going outside.

"To go get Layla. Come on honey, let's go," I said, swinging her up on my right hip.

We walked down the three flights of stairs and walked up to the gate leading to the courtyard. I turned the doorknob but it was locked. I tried my house key to no avail. I went to the first floor and banged on my college nephews' front door. They weren't home. We walked down to the basement and found no one at the chauffeur's house. Frustrated, I ran back up to the steel bars that held me back and banged on them with my fists.

"Are you kidding me?" I said angrily. "We are locked in here Nadine!"

There was no way to climb over this gate; it ran from the ceiling to the floor. We went back to our apartment and I walked out onto the forbidden balcony, craning my neck over the side to watch the busy main street, hoping to catch a glimpse of Ibrahim's car. As I watched, terrifying thoughts about what might have happened to my daughter raced through my mind. Finally, at 5:30 p.m. a car drove in the driveway. It was Mehde, my nephew, getting home from his classes.

"Mehde! Mehde!," I yelled down. "Up here! I need to go pick up Layla! Ibrahim's not home yet!"

"Hang on Auntie," he yelled back. "I will drive you!"

I skipped down the stairs with Nadine and he unlocked the gates for us. Just as we were pulling out of the driveway, a tan car drove up and I saw Layla in the backseat.

"Stop!" I told Mehde. "There she is!"

We pulled over and a short, bald man with a disgruntled look on his face got out of the car and opened the backdoor. I jumped out of the car and ran to my daughter. Her face was tear-stained and she looked scared.

"Mama, where was Baba?" she asked. "I was waiting and waiting but he never came! The principal finally saw me standing there and drove me home!"

I was relieved to see my daughter again. I walked over to the man and thanked him profusely for bringing my daughter home safely.

He looked me up and down and spat out, "What kind of mother leaves her daughter alone and forgets her like this? You Americans!"

"I didn't – my husband… he," I began, but before I could explain he shook his head and sped off.

After we went back upstairs, I waited impatiently until my husband came home. It was six o'clock.

"Where's Layla?" I asked him when he walked in.

"Oh my God!" he said. "I'll be right back!"

"Wait, wait, she's right here," I said. "The principal had to drive her home. She didn't get home until 5:30. I was going to walk to the school with Nadine but I found out we are locked in! Why in the world are we locked in here?"

"We have to keep that outside door locked up," he answered. "It's for your own protection."

"I want a key!" I demanded. "I will not be locked up like a prisoner!"

"I will have to ask my father before making copies," he said holding up his keys.

I noticed a new keychain dangling from his hands. It was a small rendition of the Twin Towers in New York, before they had been destroyed.

"Where did you get this?" I asked suspiciously.

"From my mother," he replied, avoiding my eyes.

"Why would she give you a keychain of the Twin Towers?" I asked. I took it from him and looked closer, turning it over in my hands.

"She just did," he answered. "She gave them to all of us."

I gasped audibly and my eyes didn't betray my thoughts. I recognized it for what it was: a reminder of what the terrorists did to America – bragging rights if you will. I kept silent.

"I will make a copy for you," he promised, avoiding the obvious, as he grabbed the keys from me and left me standing in the kitchen, my mouth still open in disbelief.

TERMS OF ENDEARMENT

Early one Saturday morning, I found Ibrahim at the kitchen table drinking a cup of coffee, smoking his second cigarette.

"I need you to sign these," he said, pointing to a stack of papers on the table.

"What are they?" I asked.

"Lebanese citizen applications for Layla and Nadine," he said, handing me a pen.

Fear seized me. "Where is mine?" I asked.

"Yours is a much longer process," he answered. "I am not even sure where to apply."

"As long as I get it before my 90-day visa expires," I said. "I don't want to be an illegal in your country."

He avoided my eyes. "Don't worry," he said. "You always worry too much. I will take care of it."

I signed the papers but I didn't believe him anymore. Everything he had promised never materialized. I stared out the window noting that nothing here was what I expected, and he never kept his promises. When we had first arrived, he took me faithfully to a Maronite church but he soon tired of that and made excuses not to take me. It was just as well; no one welcomed me at these churches. The same mass and rituals were familiar but I felt very alone in the pew by myself. I thought I would connect with other Catholics here but I was extremely disappointed. The mass was said in Aramaic, the language that Jesus spoke, and it was beautiful but it was just another language I couldn't understand. Here two types of parishioners attended: Lebanese families who avoided me for some reason, and little maids from the Philippines who were kinder and sat next to me but didn't speak English. I tried to find solace kneeling in front of a statue of Mother Mary and lit candles, asking for her intercession but as I looked up at her face, she stared blankly ahead, oblivious to my requests.

"Oh, and we are invited for tea again with Mohammed and Fatima," Ibrahim said, startling me out of my thoughts. *"Thank God,"* I thought. *"Something to look forward to, anything to get out of this depressing apartment."*

That evening, we sat with Mohammed and his wife, enjoying ourselves over tea and mamoosa cakes. I observed how Fatima and Mohammed always addressed each other, using loving names like habebti (my love) and ya ine (my eyes).

"Honey? Shoo Honey?" Fatima interrupted me after I thanked Ibrahim for passing the cakes.

When I looked at her with a puzzled look, Mohammed explained, "My wife is asking about the name you always call Ibrahim. She wants to know what honey means."

"Oh, it's just a term of endearment," I explained. "Like you call Fatima habebti (my love).

My husband translated the word "honey" into "helloway" (sweet) for Fatima and she nodded her head in understanding.

"Ibrahim has a nickname for me, also," I said.

"Ahhh, he does?" Mohammed asked, smiling at his brother.

"Yes," I said. "It's kas kusa."

Mohammed's face turned crimson. He turned his head, breaking into peals of laughter. Fatima blushed, opened her mouth in shock and then covered it with her hand. She repressed a giggle and gave Ibrahim a coy look. "Ibrahim – ibe a shoom alak! (Shame on you!)"

"What's wrong?" I asked, bewildered, looking from one person to the other. Soon the room resounded with laughter. Even Ibrahim chuckled with a sheepish grin on his face.

"Nothing. It's nothing," Ibrahim said to me repressing a smile.

"Ibe. Ibe (Shame)," Mohammed admonished his brother and quickly changed the subject for my sake, but I noticed Fatima couldn't repress her mirth and kept chuckling to herself.

I couldn't wait to get Ibrahim alone. The minute we left I asked him, "What does kas kusa mean? I thought it was a play on my name Kelly."

"Shh, not in front of the girls," he said. "It doesn't mean anything, just drop it."

"Just drop it?" I repeated, raising my voice. "They were laughing so hard I thought their sides would burst!"

"Just drop it!" he said. "I told you it doesn't mean anything!"

I knew he would never tell me and Mohammed was too embarrassed so that night I pretended to sleep and then snuck into the living room hoping the electricity was on so I could log onto our computer. It took several attempts but I finally found a website translating Arabic slang.

I found what I was looking for: kusa was slang for cunt.

The blood drained from my face. I felt betrayed and humiliated all at once. I didn't want to believe this so I accessed an Arabic chat room and struck up a conversation with a Lebanese female who confirmed that his "term of endearment" meant just what I feared. I lied and told her that Ibrahim was my fiancé.

"You must get rid of him immediately!" she warned me. "Do not marry him!"

"Too late," I thought bitterly. *"Too late."*

GUARDIAN DEVILS

Late one evening the phone rang, startling us out of our sleep. It was Hala and she wanted to speak to Ibrahim. He talked with her for a few minutes and hung up.

"It's Hala's maid, Sandra," he said. "She burned herself badly and Hala doesn't want to take her to a doctor – it's too late."

My heart fell. "How badly?" I asked. "Can I come?"

"No, she's fine," he said. "Hala said it's just a burn. I will be right back."

An hour later, I heard the whirr of the elevator rising. He came in and sat at the kitchen table reaching for a cigarette.

"Well, how is she?" I asked, worried.

"Well, it was quite a burn. I would say a second degree burn," he said calmly lighting his cigarette.

"Where?" I asked anxiously.

"On her forearm – from her elbow to her wrist," he said, pointing to his own arm. "The skin completely came off. I had to cut off the part that was dangling there."

"Oh my God!" I said. "Did you have anything to numb it?"

"No, but I put ointment and gauze on it," he said puffing on his cigarette calmly. "She was in a lot of pain though."

"What happened?" I wanted to know.

"Hala said that Sandra accidentally poured hot boiling water on herself," he answered.

I kept my thoughts to myself but he seemed to know what I was thinking. "That's what Hala said," he continued. "She said that Sandra forgets what she is doing sometimes."

"Do you think Hala did this?" I asked him directly.

He turned and cocked his head for a moment as if he was seriously considering my question. But then he quietly shook his head and sighed, "No, no, I believe it was an accident."

"Well, I don't!" I said. "I don't believe her story – not for a minute and neither do you if you are honest with yourself!"

"I don't believe my brother's wife did this and you have no right to suggest this!" he yelled.

I slumped back into my chair and put my head down on my folded arms. I hoped he was right – that it was just an accident, but something told me it wasn't.

The girls were awake now, alone in the dark, and began calling me, "Mommy, come here, we're scared!"

I went into the bedroom, kissed them and pulled up the covers. I noticed Layla was clasping her throat with her hands, protectively.

"What's wrong, honey?" I asked. "Does your throat hurt?"

"I'm keeping the rope from being put around my neck," she answered.

"What rope?" I asked.

"The rope that the shaytan (devil) puts around our neck every night before we go to sleep," she answered. "He tightens it every time we forget to pray and I didn't pray tonight."[12]

"That is not true!" I told her.

"That's what they taught me at school, Mom," she answered. "And did you know that each of us has a demon always watching us and writing down all the bad things we do?"[13]

"I'm scared, Mommy," she said with frightened eyes. "Why does the devil have so much power over us?"

"He doesn't," I answered. "God has given you authority to trample on snakes and scorpions and to overcome all the power of the enemy; nothing will harm you (John 10:19). The devil has no power over you, unless you give it to him, honey. He has no authority to place ropes around your neck, either."

I continued to reassure her and lay next to both girls until they fell asleep. I didn't let them see my tears in the dark. I knew now that this school he had enrolled my daughter in wasn't an international school as he had said, but a Muslim school that was trying to indoctrinate my daughter into its theology.

The theology was the least of my worries, because the anti-American culture that she had to endure at school began to change Layla. My sweet, compassionate daughter became rebellious toward me and more aggressive with her sister. She began talking back to me and would fly into an unexpected rage for no apparent reason and pick fights with her sister.

Nadine was normally an adventurous three-year-old who was

independent and strong-willed. Now, however, she clung to me all the time, afraid to let me out of her sight. She rejected her father and refused to let him near her.

One day after Nadine pushed him away again, he asked, "Are you telling her not to come to me?"

"Of course not! Why would I do that?" I responded.

"She wants nothing to do with me," he said. "Look!" he said trying to hug her as she pushed him away.

"Mama! Mama!" she cried, running to me.

Ibrahim frowned at her, and then turned his attention to Layla. "Habebti Layla, you are my love. Tell me, who are you going to marry when you grow up?"

"You Baba," she responded. "I'm going to marry you." Ibrahim hugged and kissed her profusely in reward for her answer.

Layla reveled in her favored status and he would often call her "his wife" and try to pit her against me. Layla's contempt for me grew along with his and it broke my heart to see her disrespect me.

One day she talked down to me when I asked for some help and slammed the bedroom door right in my face. I quickly opened the door and said, "You are not allowed to speak to me like that!"

"Everybody else does here. What's the difference?" she responded flippantly.

It was a battle to maintain respect. Even my parenting methods were under attack. Here, Ibrahim followed his culture and would remove his size thirteen shoe to strike Layla and Nadine if they angered him. I would grab them quickly and hide them in the bedroom away from him. My mother-in-law would admonish Nadine when she would cry saying, "Skiiti! Skiiti! (Shut up!), motioning for me to slap her. I was horrified when I watched one sister-in-law smack her one-year-old son over and over in the face when he cried. This repetitive, rough slapping only made him cry harder. I would cringe as I watched older sisters mimic their mothers by hitting and slapping their baby brothers.

When I picked up Nadine to comfort her and kiss her, my mother-in-law would click her tongue at me disapprovingly, shaking her head. I ignored all of their suggestions and continued to comfort my children, stubbornly refusing to apply their abusive parenting methods.

FAILED CONVERSION

We were invited to Mohammed's house again along with my husband's nephews. The smell of lamb shish kabob sizzling on the grill welcomed us when we walked in. We sat down and ate quickly as each skewer came back hot and tender.

Afterwards, the adults retired to the living room where we sat in a circle on the carpet. Fatima set the steaming hot kettle of tea next to her and served all of us, throwing heaping spoons of sugar in our tiny glass teacups. As we sat down, one of my nephews, Mehde, who was sitting next to my husband, pulled out a few papers in his hands that were stapled together. After a nod from my husband, Mehde began to address me.

"Auntie, I am taking a religious class at the university and we are studying Christianity right now and I had a few questions. Can you help me?" he began.

Mehde was a striking young man in his early twenties with wavy black hair that he wore in long layers. He was blessed with winsome good looks and a boyish charm that hadn't yet been spoiled. He reminded me of Ibrahim when I first met him – outgoing, friendly and charming. His uncle Mohammed was a striking contrast sitting on his right – his tight curly hair was severely shaved close to his head and his black eyes quivered from side to side. His demeanor always seemed agitated and nervous. Islam was his passion and he prided himself on being the most knowledgeable about his faith within the family. He spent countless hours pouring over the Quran and spent every Friday at the mosque listening to radical Shiite clerics supportive of Hezbollah.

Although I questioned Mehde's sudden need for my help with his studies I answered, "Sure. How can I help?"

"Well, maybe you can help explain a few things I don't understand," he said shyly, looking down at the papers in his hands. "Like, for instance, I don't understand how Christians believe that

167

Nebi Issa (the prophet Jesus) or as you say, "the Christ" was the Son of God? I mean… how can something infinite, Allah, be contained in something finite, the body of Jesus?"

All eyes turned to me waiting for a response.

"Can I look at those?" I asked suspiciously, holding out my hands for the papers he held. I skimmed through them. These were not from a class at the university but questions and answers taken from a popular Islamic website rebutting Christian beliefs.

I sighed, knowing that my husband and his brother were behind this. "Well, this is a miracle that is taking place right now in all of us," I began.

"What do you mean?" he asked, puzzled.

"Well, if you believe that we all have souls that will live on after we die, then you believe our finite bodies contain infinite souls that will live forever. If this is possible with us, why not with Jesus?" I answered softly.

Mehde looked over at his uncle Mohammed who was frowning. My husband just sighed, his face turning red with embarrassment.

Mehde moved onto the next question and asked, "Why do you believe that Jesus died on the cross?"

"Because the Bible says it happened and because of historical eyewitness accounts from other sources," I answered.

"Aha, but you guys don't have the real Bible!" Mehde repeated the familiar refrain I had heard so many times before. "It has been corrupted! The real one was given to Jesus and is lost and the one you Christians have now is full of errors, " he stated with certitude. "We believe that Jesus did not die on the cross. He was rescued by his disciples and someone else died there for him."

Mohammed was smiling eagerly at me now waiting for my response.

"I don't understand why Muslims don't want to acknowledge even the possibility that Jesus died on the cross." I began. "What does it matter to you, if you think he was just a prophet and not the Son of God anyway? We don't believe that a Bible was magically handed down from heaven to Jesus. It is a series of books divinely inspired by God, written by ordinary men living at different times over many years. It is the story of how God created us, our fall from Heaven, how God began his covenant with Abraham and promised that a Savior would come to offer the ultimate sacrifice to die for us so we can reunite with

Him in Heaven. You know as well as I that this life is not what we were created for. We yearn for more and were made for more than this. This is not our home and this life is full of sin and pain because God does not violate our free will. We needed a Savior who was without sin to offer His life for us - even Muslims believe that Jesus was without sin. And as far as being corrupt – this is another lie - the discovery of the Dead Sea Scrolls confirmed this."

Mehde looked confused and Ibrahim tried to explain what I said in Arabic to his brother Mohammed. Soon a heated discussion in Arabic broke out. Mehde tried to interject his opinion, but in vain. He gave up on his uncles and turned to ask me about the Dead Sea Scrolls. In the midst of explaining it to him, I was interrupted by Mohammed grabbing the pages from Mehde's hand and pointing to another page. Mehde looked at me sheepishly and asked the next question.

"Well, why do you believe in three gods?" he asked dutifully. Mohammed shot me an "aha!" look when I paused. Ibrahim just looked up at the ceiling, already knowing my response.

"We don't. We believe in one God," I sighed, trying to catch my husband's eyes for some support.

"There is only one God and Mohammed is his prophet," Mohammed said with conviction. "Islam is the final religion and we brought monotheism to the world."

"No, that would be the Jews who did that," I responded.

"There are scholars who sit for years studying just one verse from the Quran. Who are you to think you understand Islam?" Ibrahim responded. "Why can't you defend Islam and understand the errors in your faith?"

"Because I know Jesus," I answered truthfully. "I know Him personally and He is my Lord and my Savior. He is as real to me as you are."

As Ibrahim and I continued to debate each other Mehde watched, open-mouthed. He seemed startled by my strong convictions and said, "I am sorry Amo (Uncle); I didn't mean to make you two fight."

"We're not fighting. We are just debating," I told Mehde.

"Do you two do this often?" he asked. "Discuss religion like this?"

"Yes, many times," I answered.

He turned to my husband and asked, "And you still haven't converted her?"

A dark shadow passed over Ibrahim's face as he pursed his lips together. He took Mehde's words as an insult.

"Tfaddal!" (Please, after you!), he said to Mehde, motioning with his arms in my direction.

I winced. "I think we should stop this," I said. "Let's talk about something else."

"No, no, no," Mohammed interjected. "We are family here. Eh?"

I felt uncomfortable and looked at the floor avoiding my husband's irate face.

"I have just one question, Auntie," Mehde asked me softly. "Why don't you become Muslim?"

I looked over at Ibrahim who hesitantly motioned for me to answer.

"Well, I just find Islam to be...so violent," I responded.

"So violent?" Mehde seemed shocked. "What do you mean?"

I hesitated. "Well, some of the ways in which your prophet had people killed who disagreed with him – seemed a little ... harsh."

"We went to war against enemy tribes, just like in your Old Testament," Ibrahim was quick to point out.

"I understand defending yourself," I said. "But I am talking about the way in which those who just criticized Islam or his prophet were murdered. Like the Quraiza fort – the Jewish fort that resisted Islam where over a thousand people surrendered to Mohammed and were taken prisoners. They begged for mercy but in the morning Mohammed commanded that all the men's heads be cut off and their bodies thrown into massive graves. The women were given the choice to convert and become wives or refuse and become slaves."[14]

"These Jews obviously couldn't be trusted," Ibrahim said.

"But there are many verses in the Quran that tell Muslims to fight and kill disbelievers and this is so different from Jesus, who told us to love our enemies and pray for those who persecute us."

"Aha! But what about in the Old Testament, when God commanded the Jews to kill the Canaanites?" Ibrahim asked, knowing this caused the most angst with me.

"Well, I have researched this and God actually gave the Canaanites over 400 years to change their ways. He was very patient with them (Genesis 15:13-16). God hated the religion of the Canaanites. They engaged in bestiality, incest and even child sacrifice to their gods. It wasn't ethnic hatred. God wants all to turn from their sin like Rahab, the Canaanite prostitute in Jericho who repented and is now given honor in the bible." (Joshua 2)

"Allah is merciful!" Ibrahim responded.

"Okay, well if you mean God is merciful, but I honestly don't believe the God of the bible and the Allah of Islam are one and the same," I answered.

"Oh! You are wrong about… what is this word? Ah! The Trinity!" Mohammed interjected. "God is one! He is not Father, Mother and Son."

"We don't believe that it is Father, Mother and Son," I replied. "The Quran is wrong when it describes the Trinity like this (Quran 5:119). It is the Father, the Son and the Holy Spirit."

Mohammed looked completely confused. I sighed. "But one of the biggest stumbling blocks I have, as a woman, is the inequality between men and women in Islam."

"Such as?" Mohammed asked looking perplexed.

"Such as men are allowed to marry four women, that when men die one of the rewards is perpetual virgins, that men are allowed to beat their wives if they disobey them…"

"Enough!" my husband interjected, now completely embarrassed by his disobedient wife. "Even your own prophet, Isa, says in the bible that women are to be obedient to their husbands!" Ibrahim retorted.

"Yes, but not when the husbands are being abusive or telling them to do something wrong. A husband is supposed to love their wife like Christ loves the church, which means they should lay down their own life for their wife." I exclaimed. "And Jesus is not my prophet, He is my Lord and Savior."

Ibrahim stood up. "Enough!" he exclaimed, his face turning red.

I flinched and realized I went too far. Ibrahim was seething. Mehde and Mohammed stood up and they began arguing in Arabic around me. I caught my husband's eye and saw nothing but revulsion and disgust toward me. I felt naked and completely alone in this hostile room. I bowed my head, watching my tears splash on the cardamom seed left behind in my teacup. I rose to my feet and walked to the hallway in a daze, a blur of colors swirling past me. I stood there a long time, trying to bring myself together and put on a brave face, but my body betrayed me and began heaving in convulsions, forcing me to take rapid gasps of air.

At that moment, Nadine came running up to me holding an armful of stuffed animals. "Mommy! Mommy, look at this!" she wailed.

"What is it Honey?" I asked, wiping my face.

"My animals!" she said. "I found my animals here! They stole my toys!"

"Well, let's just take them back upstairs where they belong," I whispered.

I opened the front door and we snuck upstairs. "Those sneaky cousins!" Nadine pouted as she placed her toys back where they belonged on her bed. I dreaded going back in the lion's den again so I went to my bed and began weeping uncontrollably.

My husband came upstairs an hour later with Layla and joined me in bed. We lay next to each other, back to back, both wide awake, only a deafening silence between us. Eventually, he began to snore and I let loose another wave of tears, soaking my pillow once again.

Part VIII Behind Bars

"I am like a desert owl, like an owl among the ruins.
I lie awake; I have become like a bird alone on a roof.
All day long my enemies taunt me;
those who rail against me use my name as a curse."
Psalm 102:6-8

AMU ALI

It was May 2002 and our belongings had finally arrived from America. All we had to do was wait for the port authorities to call us to come pick them up, after the inspectors opened every box and looked for contraband. It wasn't long before Ibrahim was called in for questioning. He was asked to explain why he had in his possession two forbidden musical CD's: Frank Sinatra's Greatest Hits and the movie soundtrack from the children's animated film, "Moses." For supporting these "known Zionist supporters," he was charged forty American dollars.

It was like Christmas when we opened these boxes. Long forgotten toys and dolls greeted the girls who squealed with happiness. I embraced my books and music like long lost friends. I was so thankful for dishes and silverware, pots and pans and the girls' bunk bed, books and clothes. Under the constant uncertainty of our lives here, I filled my days unpacking, trying to make this sparse apartment a home.

The girls were especially thrilled to have their bikes and rollerblades but they were not allowed to ride them in the courtyard or outside on the street because it was too dangerous; so I went against all protocol and let them ride their bikes in the house and rollerblade on the marble floors as much as they wanted.

We had other news: his parents were returning for the summer and everyone began preparing for their arrival. Mohammed cleaned the stairwell with his sons; Fatima cleaned her mother-in-law's house with her ever-present cigarette dangling from her mouth. Basaam, the chauffeur suddenly found the energy to clean the debris-ridden courtyard and wash his employer's dusty cars.

The day of their arrival, all of us lined up in the courtyard waiting for them. My mother-in-law exited the silver Mercedes first, dressed in a bright yellow jacket and floor-length skirt; Abu Ali followed behind her dressed in a gray silk business suit with a black trench coat draped over his shoulder. His posture was stiff and his face serious behind his dark glasses. He looked all the part of the godfather.

After the traditional greetings, my mother-in-law looked at me and loudly asked in Arabic in front of all present, "So, are you happy in Lebanon?"

Not wanting to insult her I nodded in affirmation and she threw her hands into the air proclaiming, "IlhamdilAllah!" thanking God for this miracle.

The chauffeur's wife had made dinner for their return and after a meal of shish kebob with tabooli, she served us thick Arabic coffee with sweet, sticky baklava. Abu Ali and my husband lit up cigarettes and soon the room was filled with a swirling fog of smoke. The smoke caused my eyes to sting. Abu Ali leaned back importantly in a high-backed chair, resting his large arm on the armrest, while his favorite son, my husband, sat to his right, leaning forward, laughing at his father's every word. I had never seen my husband in this light, so ingratiating and subservient to anyone.

Bored with a conversation I couldn't understand, I glanced around the room and watched his mother open a cigar box. She pulled out cigarette paper and loose tobacco, carefully placing pinches of the snuff in the middle of white transparent paper. Her trembling hands brought the concoction to her lips whereupon she licked the edges sealing the contents. She rolled the paper into a thin flute, twisting the ends tightly. My eyes widened as I watched her light the end like a pro and begin to inhale deeply, slowly, while she expounded upon a tale that my husband translated at my insistence.

"She is talking about how rolling these homemade cigarettes reminds her of her youth. She was young when her father died and she and her sisters used to help her mother cut and dry tobacco from their gardens and roll cigarettes like this to sell," he explained.

As she spoke, Amu Ali's eyes lit up and a girlish charm displayed itself in her gestures. She laughed confidently, throwing her head back in a way I had never seen before. Her husband ignored her and talked to the chauffeur but I listened to her as though I understood the girl before the woman, the independent free spirit, someone separate and unique from the servant she became in marriage. She was relaying how her mother and sisters would work together eking out a living in a tiny southern village of Lebanon.

I imagined her then as she described herself, the most sought after maiden in her village with her haunting eyes and curvaceous figure. I could see a hint of this fiery young girl now and it saddened me to see how over the years her husband had tried to break her spirit and tame her to his own liking. She had 13 children – 3 died in childbirth and one as a toddler. She faithfully took care of her children, kept an immaculate home and was a wonderful cook. But her husband had a wandering eye and was not faithful to her, and I knew the anger that welled up in her sometimes was because of his infidelity. I knew from stories from my husband how often she was struck by that giant arm, how she was ridiculed and persecuted by his family because she was not from his village and how even now he flaunted his affairs with younger women in front of her. He treated her like she was merely his possession, his cook, and his maid.

In the middle of her story, Abu Ali, who wasn't listening to her anyway, stood up and declared it was time to go and we, like obedient dogs, followed him upstairs. He led the way as his wife grasped the handrail tightly while lifting her legs one at a time, wincing with each step. Every so often she stopped to catch her breath. Her husband walked in front of her, oblivious to her struggle and didn't offer to help.

I knew she had no choice; She only had an eighth grade education and no resources of her own. She could not leave him and survive on her own and he knew this. I began to see an eerie parallel between her and myself and I didn't like it. Her son, my husband, was like his father and I did not want to end up like her. The difference, however, was that I could leave at any moment but I would not do this without my daughters. I had long ago resigned myself to the fact that I was miserable in this marriage but the stakes were too high to leave him in America. I knew without a shadow of a doubt that he would have taken them back here without me to be raised by his family and I would never see them again. My love for my daughters held me captive

there but I knew that God still had a plan for us – that despite
the darkness that surrounded us, we were still in the palm of His hand
and He would take care of us.

HEZBOLLAH

The next morning my husband announced that we were taking his mother to her home village in southern Lebanon where her sister lived. Ibrahim drove with his mother in front, the girls and I in the back. We drove on the highway bordering the coastline; the cerulean blue Mediterranean Sea loomed on our right, seeming to rise higher than the rust-colored earth that bordered it. At several places along the road we were stopped by Syrian and Lebanese military checkpoints, guarded by men in black berets and sunglasses with AK-47s slung over their shoulders. After showing our paperwork, we were waved on.

We passed the ancient Phoenician city, Sidon, once known for murex, a highly valued purple dye extracted from mollusks that now are extinct. This was the birthplace of the Prime Minister, Rafiq Hariri, who was channeling huge amounts of money into reconstruction. As ancient churches crumbled, several new mosques were constructed to replace them. Large billboards displayed the face of this generous benefactor.

We turned east, away from the Mediterranean, ascending the backbone that split this country, the Mt. Lebanon range, driving past scattered orchards of banana, apple, orange and olive trees. The roads began to twist now, winding around hairpin turns until it branched off to an old country road. It was beautiful. Hillsides scattered with pine, juniper and cypress trees and wildflowers of many colors that were just beginning to blossom, but the countryside was scarred from widespread deforestation that took place during fifteen years of civil war.

Nadine and Layla saw the flowers and asked if they could stop and pick some so we pulled over to the side of the road to stretch our legs. After being cooped up in the concrete building for months, they were happy to be running out in the meadow picking flowers. I watched them, smiling, as they gathered their treasures, but as they skipped off further up a hill to collect more, Ibrahim suddenly shouted, "Don't go so far! Get back here! Hurry!"

Layla, noticing the warning in his voice, quickly ran to her father. "What's wrong Baba?"

"Nothing," he answered. "It's just that there are many snakes around and I don't want you to get bitten."

"What kind of snakes?" I asked him.

"It's not the snakes I am worried about," he whispered to me. "There are many land mines left over from the war that are all over southern Lebanon's countryside and we have to be careful."

I immediately panicked, and sped off after Nadine who was slowly wandering farther away, oblivious to the dangers that lurked beneath her. I shouted at Layla to get back to the road. My legs couldn't move fast enough after Nadine, who saw me coming after her. She thought I was playing and started to run away from me. It was like I was dreaming - running in slow motion. I quickly overtook her and scooped her up in my arms bringing her back to the road safely.

"What were you thinking?" I asked Ibrahim. "You should have told us!"

"Never mind," he answered. "You always worry too much!"

I turned to my daughters and said, "Don't go out in the field again – it is littered with landmines!"

As we got back in the car I explained to my daughters what a landmine was and they listened.

We arrived in his father's village first - a tiny hamlet of ashen-colored homes made of pale sandstone blocks with red Spanish tiles. We parked and took in the mountain air. It was cooler up here and quiet, far away from the traffic noise in Beirut. I looked around and noticed a white outpost on the hillside a few hundred feet from us.

"What is that?" I asked, pointing.

"That is an Israeli outpost. The border between Lebanon and Israel runs right there, where that wire fence is," Ibrahim answered.

"Isn't this dangerous to be so close to the border?" I asked, remembering the fighting I had heard a month earlier.

Ibrahim laughed and then translated for his mother who chuckled and told me through translation, "Come, let me show you where we kicked the Jews out of southern Lebanon. They are too afraid of us!"

We walked a short distance to a cliff overhanging over a green valley below. I approached the edge and looked down. A few feet away I saw charming white farmhouses, neatly arrayed in an orderly subdivision. Paved roads lead up to the houses with white picket fences and green yards surrounded by neatly planted crops in rectangular patterned fields.

Amu Ali picked up a big rock and yelled out some expletive in Arabic and threw a stone over the border. Nadine saw her and picked up her own rock and imitated her. Ibrahim followed suit throwing a large rock full-force landing it on their fields.

His mother held out a rock for me to throw. "Throw it," my husband said.

"No," I said. I backed away glancing warily at the Israeli outpost overlooking us. "Come on girls, let's go."

We drove now on the dirt road, next to a barbed wire fence that represented the border between Israel and Lebanon until we arrived in Amu Ali's village. We were greeted with yellow Hezbollah flags fluttering in the wind. On each flag, below the emblem of a fist clenching a Kalashnikov rifle, a verse from the Koran declared: "Surely the party of God are they that shall be triumphant." We pulled up to a small, gray home where an elderly woman in a white scarf was pulling lemons off her tree. This was Amu Ali's sister.

Her fair green eyes illuminated against her tanned, worn skin lit up when she saw her sister and she welcomed us into her humble home. We took a seat on a worn couch in the living room right under a window – an open hole cut out of the gray stone with no glass. She brought out a bowl of sweet candies and offered them to the girls

Through translation she kindly said, "I also have a blonde blue-eyed daughter-in-law who lives in Germany with my son. She calls me Mama now."

As they began to talk in Arabic, I noticed a huge, poster-sized framed picture of a somber young man on the wall. Plastic flowers had lovingly been placed around it.

"Who is that?" I asked my husband.

"That is her other son who was murdered," he answered.

"Murdered, by who?" I asked.

"Well he was taken by the Israelis and put in prison during the occupation," he said. "They kept him there for a few years and then released him."

"Oh, so he died after that?" I asked thinking he died from an illness.

"No, he was shot one day here by the people in the village," he answered. "They gunned him down in front of the bank."

"What?" I asked, not understanding.

"They thought he was a traitor and that he talked while he was in prison," Ibrahim explained. "They thought it was suspicious that he was released so soon. He didn't talk though – he was innocent and his mother honors him as a martyr."

Ibrahim looked at his cousin's picture sadly and said, "He was a good guy – Allah be with him."

It suddenly struck me how similar this picture mimicked the other men's faces who were posted around these southern Shiite villages by Hezbollah. Ironically, his picture was not to be hung among them. He had been found guilty and served his sentence without a trial by those who were his comrades in arms, his brothers and fellow Muslims.

The two sisters talked until the shadows outside lengthened. Before we left, Ibrahim's Aunt pulled some herbs from her garden and placed them in a sack for us. Her humble gifts in tow, we waved goodbye and started back toward Beirut. As we approached the suburbs of Beirut, huge billboards with willowy, Arabian models shaking their long black hair promoting hair products loomed above. Consistently, angry Muslim citizens had torn off the offensive bare legs and plunging necklines and modified every picture. A Marlboro cowboy outfitted in a Stetson hat, riding the open range, clasping a cigarette in his gloved hand, stood out of place in this backdrop and I felt just as lost as he looked.

THE GREAT SATAN

It was Friday, May 10, 2002 and the standoff at the Church of the
Nativity in Bethlehem that we had been watching every day for the past
thirty-eight days had come to an end. The month of March had
brought a wave of Islamic extremist groups' suicide attacks that had
killed nearly one hundred Israeli civilians and soldiers. So in response
to this, Israeli tanks rolled into Bethlehem, as well as Nablu, Jenin and
Ramallah. Forty guerillas, seeing that they were cornered, retreated to
the Church of the Nativity on April 2, 2002, Christianity's holiest site -
the place where Jesus was born.[15]

For weeks, my husband and family had been watching this
ordeal and the news channels from Lebanon portrayed these gunmen
as innocent Palestinian citizens who were unarmed. Yassar Arafat
loudly condemned Israel for desecrating this holy site.

However, the truth did prevail and later new accounts by the
Washington Times and other newspapers identified the forty men as
wanted terrorist and prominent members of Hamas, a Palestinian
terrorist organization. The desecration of this holy site was not
committed by the Israelis, as the Arab news sources would have the
world believe, but by these Palestinian gunmen armed with AK-47s
who fired their weapons from within the Church. They deliberately
commandeered this holy structure to avoid capture. During the 39-day
siege, they hoarded food stores for themselves while more than 150
civilians inside went hungry. They guzzled beer, wine and Johnnie
Walker scotch, ignoring their Islamic restriction from drinking alcohol.
They looted the premises, stealing whatever was of value and tore up
bibles to use for toilet paper.[16]

Even in the face of the truth, my husband's family believed that
this was an Israeli conspiracy. I reminded Ibrahim that if Christians
went into a mosque and did this, it would be enough to start another
war. Just the presence of infidels in a mosque is enough to start a riot,
as was the case when Ariel Sharon tried to visit the Dome of the Rock,
located on the temple mount in the old city of Jerusalem. He had the

right as an Israeli citizen but he didn't get very far because angry crowds of Muslims blocked his way, shoving him and his security guards away. My husband defended these men however, and accused me of sympathizing with the enemy.

Hatred for Israel ran very deep here in Lebanon, as it did in Ibrahim's family. What was considered a terrorist organization by Western nations was simply another political party here and this indoctrination started at an early age. I didn't realize how close to home this was until one day when I noticed a poster on our kitchen counter depicting very young boys marching in army fatigues and black berets, holding the now-familiar Hezbollah yellow flag. In the lower left-hand corner were large letters spelling Al-Mehdi (Hezbollah boy scouts) and a picture of a somber man in a black turban whom I recognized as Nasrallah, the spiritual leader of Hezbollah.

Beneath the poster was a comic book showing an evil king and queen, caricatures of Sharon, the Prime Minister of Israel, and his wife. Oppressed people were depicted crying and hungry while Sharon and his wife sat in luxury ignoring the plight of their subjects. The happy ending showed children pelting rocks at the queen and king, kneeling on the ground, bloodied from the assault.

I was shocked by how violent these were. I showed them to Ibrahim and asked him, "What are these?" hoping Mohammed had left them behind.

"They are for Layla," he answered.

"For Layla!?" I asked.

"Yes, my mother gave them to her," he answered. I didn't say a word but later hid them out of sight.

Hezbollah had its own television station, Al-Manar, which my husband and his family watched often. Between stories, they repeatedly showed a four-minute clip of Israeli soldiers brutally beating a Palestinian man in some deserted foothills. The soldiers' faces were blurred – only the Israeli uniforms were clear. They took turns kicking their prisoner and cutting him with knives.

The first time I had seen this I couldn't stop crying. My husband at the time told me, "Yes, you should cry. That is the real face of Israel. This is the real news, the news that America will never show you!"

However, after seeing this same scene played out several times a day, against the backdrop of chanting soldiers calling Muslims to jihad, it became obvious to me that it was a propaganda tool used to incite them to arms. I began to question how the cameraman remained undetected in the middle of this barren landscape and why the solders' faces were blurred. This same station always portrayed America as the "Great Satan" showing images of the Statue of Liberty, a skull for her face, wearing a gown dripping with blood.

SHARIA LAW

The next evening, we met Aisha and her husband Khalil for dinner at the Yucca Café. The children played on the playground, while we adults sat alone. Aisha was completely covered in a black hijab with a white scarf tightly clasped under her chin. She looked exhausted; the dark shadows under her eyes were heavier than usual.

Ibrahim and Khalil ignored us and began to discuss business while Aisha and I caught up with each other. On the way home I asked Ibrahim what he had talked about.

"Business," Ibrahim answered. "Khalil said that Family Practice doctors are only considered General Practice doctors here and that I won't make a decent salary. He is trying to convince me to just settle and open a pharmacy. I am going to take my medical boards in July even though no one in my family supports me."

"I think it is worth a try," I added.

"Yes, of course... oh, and by the way, Khalil also brought up the student loans I still owe in America," he continued. "He said that according to Islam, any action against America is considered "halal" (that which Allah and his prophet have allowed to be done in a lawful manner), so I don't have to pay back those loans – or the credit cards either!"

"Are you serious?" I asked. "You can't do that. That will ruin our credit and besides ....it isn't right!"

"Yes, I am serious," he replied. "In fact I want you to write a letter to the medical board that denied me my license. I want you to tell them that they are now responsible for my loans since they are not allowing me to work as a doctor."

"No, I am not going to write a letter!" I responded. "That would mean career suicide! Those loan people will work with you. They can consolidate them and we will only have one monthly payment." I softened my tone trying to convince him.

Ibrahim turned to look at me for the first time. "No! I am not paying back those loans!" he said. "They screwed me up! Them and that damned lawyer I hired to clean my record – they were all in on it to ruin my life!" Purple veins were protruding from his neck as he shouted.

"Well, I know your parents won't agree to this," I said softly.

"They have already told me that it is between me and Allah and that I have been wronged. Allah sees all and knows all. He knows what happened to me," he said pointing his forefinger upward.

I felt like I was going to get sick. I tried to close my ears and mind to what he was saying as he continued to rant and rave about America and the evildoers who had betrayed him.

When we reached the house it was dark and one of Mohammed's sons came running up to us in the driveway. Mohammed's wife Fatima was extremely sick. I followed my husband to their apartment and found Fatima in her bed writhing in pain. Without her housecoat, she was skin and bones and I felt her ribs when I embraced her. Ibrahim examined her and left to pick up some pain medication for her at the local pharmacy. I went upstairs after he returned and while I was getting ready for bed I heard my mother-in-law and Mohammed's voice shouting at each other from upstairs.

Later, that night in bed I asked, "What was wrong with Fatima?"

"It seems to be her back," he answered.

"Maybe it's her shoes," I offered. "She is the only one here besides me who doesn't have a maid and those cheap plastic sandals aren't great for her back on this hard marble floor."

My husband sighed. "Fatima is always sick and I don't think it's the footwear."

"What was all the shouting about upstairs?" I asked.

"It was Mohammed," he answered. "He was complaining about his wife, that he works hard all day and Fatima is not doing her duties like she should. He has to help her out with some chores lately and he is very upset about it."

"So what did everyone suggest?" I asked. "Perhaps your parents could hire a part-time maid for her or something until she is better?"

"Well, I put forth the suggestion that maybe it was time for Mohammed to take another wife," he answered. "She doesn't seem to be capable of performing her duties."

Anger boiled up within me. "You said what?" I began. "What did your parents say?"

"My mother agreed with me and thought it might be a good idea," he answered.

"So this is the answer to poor Fatima?" I asked. "To get another wife? This poor woman stays home all day, isn't allowed to drive, never goes out, has no friends but the chauffeur's wife. She cooks, cleans and takes care of his sons and now that she has a back problem he wants a new wife? This poor woman needs to be helped, not thrown out for a new model!" I was angry. "I can't believe you even offered that! Is that what you are going to do to me when I can't cook or clean?"

"Oh, go to sleep!" he snapped back. "You don't understand anything here!" He shoved me over roughly and turned angrily away from me on his side.

I lay there fuming, staring at his back wondering how I could ever have loved such a hateful man. He was not my husband. He was a stranger to me.

The next day Aisha came for a visit after lunch with her daughters. But too soon, her husband called her home to fix his dinner. Layla and Nadine drew Farah and Jasmine into a huddle and they were busy whispering to each other.

"We have decided that we want Farah and Jasmine to spend the night," Layla said, speaking for all of them.

"No!" Aisha admonished them, frowning. "Now, get in the car or I will tell your father."

All four girls burst into tears begging her to let them.

"It's okay, Aisha," I said. "I would love for them to spend the night."

"But I don't have their pajamas with me or anything else," she said.

"We have extras," I answered. "It's no problem." I put my hand on her arm. "Let me do something for you, for once."

Her girls broke in whining, "Please Mama, please can we stay?"

Aisha looked extremely worried but then finally gave in and agreed. Ibrahim drove up the driveway just as she was about to leave and finding out what our plan was said, "No, Aisha, we can't do this. Not tonight, but maybe another time."

The girls heard him and burst into tears again begging their uncle to let them stay. I took him aside and said, "It's not a problem. I can watch them. It would be great for the girls."

"It's on you then," Ibrahim said frowning. "I will have nothing to do with it."

I ran over to Aisha and told her the good news and the girls jumped up and down hugging each other, their tears now turned into laughter. They played together well into the night and when it was time for bed I read each of them a book, sitting in between them on the bed while they snuggled around me.

After reading my fifth book to them, Jasmine looked up at me and said, "I wish you were our mother. I hate my mother."

"Honey, don't ever say that," I said gently to her. "Your mother loves you so much that she would die for you."

"But you don't get angry like my parents," she said.

"Oh, I get angry," I said smiling at her. "Everyone does."

"Not like my parents," she said and then turned to ask Layla, "Does your father hit you with a stick?"

"No, just a few times with his shoe," admitted Layla while I cringed.

"Well my father gets so angry he hits us with this big stick and he hits my mother with it too!" Jasmine exclaimed.

Farah chimed in, "Yes and he didn't want us to ever spend the night here and now he is going to be so angry with us when we go back in the morning. He will hit my mother, and it is all our fault!" She started weeping putting her face in her hands.

"No, no," I said. "It's not you fault and he won't be angry. I will have your Uncle Ibrahim talk to him. I am sure it will be okay." I pulled them closer. "It is never your fault when he hits your Mama."

I continued reading and after I finished each one they broke into a chorus of "More! More!"

After I tucked them in I lingered over them, watching them in the moonlight shining in the window. "Sweet, little girls," I said softly. "Please dear God watch over them and protect them from any harm."

Later that night when my husband came to bed I brought up what his nieces had told me regarding his sister's husband. Ibrahim paused, and said, "That's serious, if it's true, and as her brother, my duty would be to confront Khalil, but you know how kids exaggerate. I just don't believe them."

"Why did I bother to even tell him?" I thought, lying there next to him. Maybe I thought he would be compelled to defend his little sister. *"If he wouldn't defend his own daughter, why did I think he would help his sister?"* I thought angrily.

BROKEN PROMISES

An oppressive sticky heat heralded the entrance of June. It enveloped Beirut and we battled it by locking every window and pulling every blind. We had a small air conditioning unit in the kitchen but the daily power outages meant that it was sporadic at best. The outages would last four hours at a time and the days were long and miserable. I would let Nadine play in the bathtub in cold water to cool off while Layla had to endure the heat at school in classrooms that had no fans or air conditioning.

Ibrahim left Nadine and me alone for most of the day now that his parents were back. We would see him only when he brought Layla home from school and for dinner. I assumed he was upstairs with his parents but I had no idea where he went everyday. Loneliness and isolation started to wear me down. The heat sapped my energy and I quickly fell into a deep depression. The hope that life was going to get better here was dissipating fast. Day after day we were stuck in this apartment, not allowed to even enjoy our balcony, much less be allowed to drive anywhere or even go for a walk outside. The walls started to close in on me and I felt suffocated and forgotten, trapped in this building, not knowing where he went all day or whom he was talking to. My appetite was gone. I lost weight and my clothes hung loosely on me. Days consisted of cleaning, cooking and laundry. Friday was my worst day: the sermon from the local mosque would blare over loudspeakers in the neighborhood and I had no choice but to listen to a man preach at me in a language I didn't understand.

My daughters began to hate it here.

"Mama, it is time to go back to English land!" Nadine declared, summing up how I felt. "I am tired of this Arabic play home – we need to go back to our real home now!"

She refused to speak Arabic even when prompted to just repeat words by Ibrahim's relatives.

"Shoo ismak ya Nadine? (What is your name, Nadine?)", people would ask.

"My name is Nadine!" she would say stubbornly in English stamping her foot.

"What is your Arabic name?" they would ask in English wanting her to say her last name.

"I am Nadine and I speak English!" she would respond.

Layla also vented openly now. One day she came home, her heavy cotton uniform dripping with sweat. "I hate my school!" she said to me after her father left us. "I hate living here! The only fun time we have is when we play with Farah and Jasmine, which is hardly ever! There is nothing to do here! We can't even ride our bikes or go for a walk outside like normal people!"

I tried to give her some hope. "When Baba is finished with his exam, he's going to take us out to more places and we will find you a better school."

"You are a dreamer!" she said, repeating what her father often said about me.

Tears filled my eyes and I held out my arms to her. "I am so sorry, baby. If I could change things I would." Her face softened and she broke down, crying in my arms.

"It's not your fault, Mama," she whispered. "It's not your fault. School is almost over and guess what? I was chosen by the Principal to be the scissor bearer for the visit from the Minister of Education!"

"Of course you were," I said. "You are the prettiest girl in the whole school I bet."

Ibrahim was proud that his daughter was chosen for such an honor and the last day of school we dressed up and attended the year-end ceremony. We sat inside a tent set up on the playground as we watched the Minister of Education stand in front of a long red ribbon. Layla stood next to him dressed in a pale lilac colored dress, holding a pair of scissors on a satin pillow. After cutting the ribbon, he walked down the aisle smiling and shaking hands with his entourage shadowing right behind him.

I went up to Layla, hugged her, telling her how beautiful she was.

"Hey Mom, come with me and see my classroom," she said, taking my hand.

She led me to a second building located right behind the main one. We walked through an iron gate and upstairs to the second floor. As we walked into her classroom, my face fell. It was a small, dark concrete sweatbox; the walls were filthy with years of soot smeared all over. Decrepit desks defaced with graffiti wobbled on rusty metal supports standing on a cracked concrete floor. A timeworn blackboard hung crookedly on a wall with peeling paint; a shoddy metal bookcase in a dusty corner held a few tattered books. I stood there in disbelief.

"This…this was your classroom?" I asked, starting to cry.

Layla took my hand and said, "It's okay Mommy."

"I had no idea it was this bad," I said. "I just can't believe this! No wonder they didn't show us these classrooms. I am so sorry, baby."

"I showed it to Baba," Layla said softly.

"What did he say?" I asked.

"He said, "I can't believe that I am in my daughter's classroom. Now I will always remember what it looked like!"" She put her hand over her heart mimicking him.

"Did it look like this?" I asked, incredulously.

"Yes," she nodded.

"You are not coming back here!" I said, indignation rising in my chest. "You hear me? Never!"

We returned to the schoolyard and joined Ibrahim who was ready to leave.

"Did you see Layla's classroom?" I asked him immediately.

"Yes…" he paused.

"It's filthy!" I began. "Did you see the walls? It was something I would expect in the slums… surely the money they receive in tuition could afford them some paint!"

Ibrahim frowned. "Always complaining!" he whispered. "It wasn't that bad!"

"She is not coming back to this school!" I said.

When we returned home Ibrahim said gently, " Let's go in the living room and talk."

I felt a sliver of hope that he might have some compassion, maybe not for me, but for his daughter. He sat down opposite me, stretching his arms on top of the sofa with one leg crossed over the other like a gentle benefactor, willing to listen to his subject's concerns. I sat uneasily, eyeing him warily.

"I can see that you are not happy here," he began cordially. "Can you tell me why?"

I proceeded cautiously. "Well, I feel like I have lost all of my freedoms," I began.

"What are you talking about?" he laughed. "I have never felt so free in all my life!" He paused then said softly, "I am tired of hearing you complain about something everyday. I can't fix everything but I can do one thing. Just pick one thing that I can do for you and I will do it."

He seemed different tonight. Maybe it was because he was proud of his daughter and the compliments he received from others about his beautiful family tonight. I wasn't sure but I mentally raced through my list of things that I wanted: to be able to drive, to take Arabic lessons, to go to church more often, but the most important concern to me prevailed.

"I want a good school for our daughters," I finally said.

Ibrahim sighed loudly and said, "You know my financial situation. I can't pay for school this fall. My father will have to help me and beggars can't be choosers. My family wants us to put them in the school Aisha's girls go to."

My heart fell. The school Jasmine and Farah went to was a Muslim school even more strict than the one Layla went to.

"I think there has to be other options," I said, softly.

"You always find fault in everything here!" he exploded. "I am beginning to understand you Americans and how you think!" He stood up now tapping his forehead. "You complain about the schools, about not speaking Arabic, about how you can't drive! You are not even one percent Christian!"

I sat there, shocked. "What do you mean?"

"Look at your Mother Theresa!" he shouted now. "Look at how she lived in the slums of India! Did she ever complain or ask to drive a car?" He looked down at me.

"That is not fair," I said. "She chose that way of life. I have been driving since I was fourteen, and to have that taken away from me is really hard. I have chosen to sacrifice a lot of things in this marriage. I have given up my family, my country, and a lot of my freedoms, and you don't seem to appreciate any of it."

"You don't even know what it means to be Christian!" he mocked me. "Your saints put up with worse things than this!"

I buried the anger building within me and slowly rose from the couch, walking toward the bedroom. He followed me, trying to provoke me by still screaming at me. I kept my head down and kept walking. He followed right behind me, telling me that I was a terrible Christian. I hurried to the bathroom and locked the door. He banged on it hard, yelling, "You are no Christian!"

I heard him leave the bedroom and slam the front door. I fell in a terrified puddle on the bathroom floor and started sobbing, my body jerking uncontrollably as I tried to stop the pain of his words. The only thing I clung to through all of this was my faith and he was now making a mockery of my years of sacrifice and patience and it was too much to bear. I looked down at my hands, now shaking, and noticed the 1 carat zirconium ring I had bought myself for fifty dollars a few years ago because I was embarrassed that I didn't have a real wedding ring after all this time with him. It was just another reminder that I meant nothing to him.

I remembered the three things he promised me years ago when I agreed to come back to him: 1) that he would never cheat on me 2) that he would never hit me again and 3) that he would buy me a real wedding ring. He had kept none of his promises.

SALAM

A ray of hope came my way. Ibrahim's older sister, Salam, was coming to stay for the summer in her house in Beirut. Shortly after her arrival to Lebanon, she invited us to lunch. When I saw her again, I remembered why I loved her so much.

"Hello, habebti," she said. "So good to see you again!" She embraced all of us with firm hugs and generous kisses.

Salam was a tall, handsome woman in her late thirties, a full-figured woman, comfortable in her own skin and confident. When she walked into a room, she demanded attention. She was blessed with flawless, porcelain skin, and arresting dark eyes lined with thick black kohl liner. She always wore bright red lipstick and a stylish scarf.

"Come! Come! Sit down," she said, ushering us into her living room. Ibrahim's nephews were there, looking relieved to leave their bachelor pad and live with their mother for the summer. They looked forward to her home-cooking and loving attention.

After serving us a feast, she offered us homemade cherry cheesecake and we enjoyed it with tea. Then she lit up a cigarette and leaned back in her chair ready for conversation. "So how are you Kelly?" she asked.

I looked over at my husband and then said, "Fine, I guess. I am still trying to adapt."

"Don't worry, habebti," she said with sympathy. "Lebanon is a hard country to adapt to – even for me. I prefer to live in Kuwait and I think you would too. The life there is, how do you say... convenient? There are no electricity problems and they have beautiful highways and nice shopping malls like America. Here, it is very stressful – the driving, the people, the problems, the heat. I wouldn't come here every summer if it wasn't for our families," she confided and then added, "Why don't you get a job here?"

"Ibrahim tried to get me a job as an English teacher at one of the schools but they didn't hire me," I answered.

"It's probably because you didn't have any connections to help smooth things out for you," she offered.

"What about you?" I asked. "I hear that you have your Master's degree now in History!"

"Yes, yes I did," she answered smiling. "I only have to submit a dissertation to obtain my doctorate."

"Congratulations!" I said. "So are you going to teach now?"

Salam frowned, putting out her cigarette in the ashtray. "No, my husband won't let me work. I begged him to let me work part time now that our youngest is in high school but he won't change his mind."

Salam, with her tireless energy, high intelligence and personality could do anything she set her mind to. She was a natural born leader and I could easily see her running her own business.

I remembered her story about how she chose her husband. She was born the oldest daughter, and after graduating from high school, watched as brother after brother left for college. Her father refused to send her to college even though she begged him, so she decided to marry and escape her situation. She said she would only marry the man who signed a prenuptial agreement allowing her to get a college education. I sadly noted that she had traded one prison for another, however, when now she realized, years later, that her degree would sit useless because of her husband's refusal to let her work. His religion and culture supported his right to dictate what he did and didn't want for her. She had no choice.

I changed the subject, hoping Salam could help me. I was worried that my visa was about to expire. Ibrahim had still not obtained residency papers for me.

"Salam, can you help me understand something?" I asked.

"Yes, anything," she replied kindly.

"My visa to this country is about to expire and I am worried," I said softly. "I am worried that I am about to become an illegal alien that could be deported."

"What?" What do you mean?" Salam asked, her eyes widening. "You haven't obtained a Lebanese passport for your wife yet?" she asked Ibrahim.

Ibrahim's face flushed red. "I have been too busy," he said.

"What about Layla and Nadine?" she asked.

"Yes, I took care of that," he answered.

"And not your wife?" she asked, furrowing her brow. "Shame on you!" She began to berate her younger brother harshly in front of me and they began a lengthy discussion in Arabic.

"Fine, fine. I promise I will take care of this," he said sheepishly, with his nephews looking on.

"So have you joined the American Wives Club?" she asked me.

"No, Ibrahim has been much too busy to help me with this," I said, excusing my husband.

Salam shot Ibrahim another look of consternation. "I don't understand," she said to him. "Your wife – she needs help and this group will help her adjust to your country. She needs friends like this!"

"I have just been too busy," he said using the same excuse. Another conversation swirled around me in Arabic as Salam defended me and I watched her, grateful for her words, for her concern. She was truly my sister. By the time we left, Ibrahim promised her that he would obtain a Lebanese passport for me and call about the American Wives Club. I could only hope that he would honor his word to her.

MIRIAM

Salam called us later that week to invite us to dinner at the recently remodeled downtown part of Beirut. It was the place where tourists visited and it was purposely constructed to resemble a scene out of Paris: restaurants lined the cobblestone streets where elegantly attired men and women in European fashion sat eating dinner. Local artists displayed their works under the warm glow of Parisian-styled streetlights.

We found Salam at one of the tables surrounded by her children. Her daughter, Miriam rose to greet us. I had met her when she was just a child, but now before me stood a beautiful young woman of twenty. She was completely covered, wearing a pink pastel colored scarf and an ankle length skirt with a long sleeved shirt underneath. Her dark Arabian eyes stood out strongly as if in opposition to her soft covering. These beautiful eyes seemed clouded with dark storms and there was an edge to her I had never seen before.

"Habebti Miriam!" I cried out. "You are absolutely beautiful! And look at how tall you are!"

We exchanged kisses and I introduced my daughters to her and the conversation quickly turned to Miriam's dilemma- her recent marriage proposals.

"Uncle," she asked my husband. "What should I be looking for in a husband?"

"You need someone who can take care of you, who doesn't drink and who is a good Muslim," he answered ironically.

"You want a husband who will love you and only you," I interjected boldly. "Someone who will let you pursue your dreams and goals also,"

"Oh Aunti, it is so hard though," she began. "Don't you realize that I have to please my father, my mother, my grandmother, and my father's sisters first? There are so many people I have to consider when choosing a husband. I am the last one I should think about."

"The last person?" I asked. "You should be the first person to please. After all, you are the one who is going to be married to him for the rest of your life."

"I do not have this luxury, Aunti," she replied sadly. "I am not in control over my own life. Even my father prefers my brothers to me. I cannot go to the university in my own country, Lebanon. I have to go to U.A.E. because he thinks it is too open here, yet my brothers can go wherever they please."

She continued to pour out her frustrations. Despite everything she had learned and was told to believe, something inside her was screaming that this control over her life was wrong and that she had an inherent right to make her own choices about her life.

As she talked I looked at my own choices. I could choose to stay and submit myself to my husband and look the other way as he clipped my daughters' wings one by one, placing a black veil of oppression over their precious spirits before they even discovered who they were. I could convert to this religion to just make him happy and look forward to the same life as my mother-in-law and sister-in-laws - a miserable existence where their happiness was dependent on how well they pleased their husbands, but I could never deny my Lord.

Or I could flee. Flee now, while I still could, before he tired of me and took another wife. Flee before he orchestrated my untimely death as many husbands did here. Or something worse than death: send me home alone without my daughters, to mourn them for the rest of my life.

I could fool myself into thinking I had another choice: to stay and maintain my identity, what shell was left of it, and work things out with my husband. But this would be a fantasy to believe that I could convince him to revolt against the societal pressures, religious laws and family influences.

Suddenly, my thoughts were interrupted by a loud commotion in the crowd. A young boy, dressed in tan shorts and white cotton polo was walking with a small dog on a leash. It was a common terrier, but by the stares it was receiving, you would have thought it was an exotic leopard. As the boy walked, the crowd parted in front of the dog like Noah parting the Red Sea. The crowd's response was a mixture of ridicule, laughter, anger and condemnation.

Nadine saw the dog and ran toward it screaming, "Puppy! Puppy!"

She wanted to pet the dog. Ibrahim ran after her and lifted her away from the offensive animal.

"Nadine, don't touch that dog, it's haram!" (Islam's prophet had a great dislike for dogs so they are considered unclean in this religion.)

Layla kept her distance but Nadine kept screaming, "Puppy! Puppy!" trying to squirm away from her father.

Ibrahim's face became beet red as other people watched him struggle with his daughter. He swung her up over his shoulders but she only screamed louder, drawing more unwanted attention. Frustrated, he said, "Yallah, let's go!" as he headed for the car with Nadine still kicking and screaming.

That night after I put the girls to bed, I came into the kitchen where Ibrahim was watching TV.

"I have a question for you," I began softly. He nodded and I continued. "What is going to happen to Layla and Nadine when they get older and want to marry a Christian or Jewish man for that matter?"

"They won't," he answered confidently. "Because I won't let them."

"But surely they have a choice – to choose the man they love and want to be with the rest of their life!" I exclaimed.

"You know, if anyone has the right to take another wife, it is me!" he yelled slamming his cigarette pack on the table. "You do not understand our ways because you are stupid!"

He stormed out the door and went upstairs to his parents.

"No, there is no other option," I thought. Because I knew for him to stand up for me would require that he at the very least loved me, but I knew he didn't and I doubt he ever did.

A DAY AT THE BEACH

Aisha and Umm Ali invited me and the girls to the Costa Bravo beach, one of the few beaches set aside for covered women. Here, women could shed their hijabs, along with the responsibility of protecting men from impure thoughts for an afternoon. They could wear anything they wanted because it was completely sequestered by a tall fence laden with billboards, keeping them safe from prying eyes.

We walked down concrete steps and entered a forbidden world, where female guards patrolled the fence, watching for peeping Toms. Beyond this was the beach, shaped like a crescent moon, where hundreds of women and children gathered.

The girls squealed when they saw the beach, and quickly undressed down to their swimsuits and rushed to the sea with their cousins.

Aisha shed her abaya and sported a chic new black bathing suit with red trim, a snug tankini - the same suit I wore. We had picked them out together a week before when I was visiting her. We were like sisters, donning our new outfits, proudly showing off our trim waistlines. Umm Ali wore a modest black one-piece swimsuit under a long, black pleated skirt.

I sat down, dug my feet into the silky soft sand, enjoying its warmth when I felt something sharp stab my toe. I reached down to pick up a plastic fork embedded in my skin. I looked more closely and noticed the beach was littered with cans, dirty diapers, paper wrappers and rotten fruit. Garbage cans were placed every few feet, but the beach held more refuse than the hardly used cans.

As I looked around, I noticed I was being stared at even here amongst other women. I was obviously a foreigner here and I felt self-conscious. Foreigners were welcome, in general, but a foreign woman married to one of their own was seen as a threat. A group of young women sitting adjacent to us darted deadly looks my way and when I smiled back, they broke into peals of laughter and whispering. I chose to ignore them.

Women and children strolled by, skipping and laughing. They seemed to revel in their emancipation. The veil had been lifted personally from women here, but only broadened to confine them collectively behind the barriers of this small space of beach.

I joined the girls in the water and enjoyed the cool water washing away the heat. Layla was teaching some girls how to swim and Nadine was bobbing around on her pink inflatable trying to keep up with the older girls. Nadine wanted to make a sand castle so I helped her make a poor rendition of one and dug a moat around it. Nadine kept trying to fill it by running back and forth, filling her bucket with water and dumping it in the moat only to see it sink in the sand.

In the midst of our play, a disgruntled, middle-aged woman began yelling loudly in Arabic. She was pointing her finger at me. Suddenly she was standing over me, yelling. I looked up at her and took off my sunglasses shading my eyes with my hand.

Her hands gestured at the sand around us and at first I thought she had lost something but I listened to her words carefully.

"Shoo am tamle? Hada haram! Shoof!" (What are you doing? This is forbidden! Look!)

"Quickly," I thought. *"What am I doing that is forbidden?"*

Then I realized that she was upset that we were using up the sand so close to the water. She wanted us to move farther back. I looked around and observed scores of other children working on castles and even digging deep pits closer to the water than we were. I became angry that she was singling me out for no good reason, making a scene in front of everyone. I searched the crowd looking for Aisha to help me but she was nowhere to be seen but Umm Ali sat in her chair watching the scenario, never rising to my defense.

I slowly stood up and faced this self-appointed spokesperson for sand preservation and smiled. I looked her directly in the eyes and in my best fake British accent said, "I am so sorry Madame, but I don't understand a single word you're saying so you may as well sit yourself back down and try to have a nice day."

The woman stared back at me, open-mouthed, with a look of consternation on her face. Frustrated by the language barrier and unable to have me do her bidding, she turned and walked off angrily. I purposely put my back to her and returned playing with my daughters as though nothing had happened.

The sun began to move slowly westward the tide rolled in gently, lapping up on the shore. Airplane thundered overhead, flying so low we could read the airlines' names: Air France, KLM, Lufthansa. I looked up, wondering when we would be on one of those planes again, heading for home.

I turned my attention back to the children, watching them splashing each other in the water, laughing, running around, exuding pure innocent joy - boys and girls playing together side by side equally, one not the master over the other.

"Yes, there is a loving Heavenly Father," I thought. *"And He created us to be His sons and daughters and He loves us equally."*

The long day was ending, and the waves rose higher. We rinsed off and joined a crowd of women donning their dark abayas. Scarves were adjusted to cover any offending hair before entering back into the world of men.

AMERICAN WIVES CLUB

It was July, time for Ibrahim's medical boards. We waited patiently for the results, only to find that he had failed. And in his mind everyone but he was to blame.

"It was the stupidest exam I have ever taken!" he lamented. "This exam is beneath me and this country doesn't deserve me!"

During the next few weeks, he was a raging storm. His temper flared at the slightest provocation, so we tiptoed around him, trying not to incur his wrath.

"That son of a bitch lawyer!" he repeated often. "This is all his fault! I am going to fly back to America and take care of him! I wouldn't be here if it wasn't for him! I am going to go back and kill him – just us two – face to face. It will be either him or me!"

When he would rave like this in front of the girls I would tell the girls, "Baba is just kidding. He is just really angry. He wouldn't kill anyone."

"By God, I will do it!" he would scream. "My daughters need to learn that there is no such thing as justice in America! They need to know it is full of liars and evil people!"

I stayed out of his way and tried to smooth his hurt ego as best I could. Soon, he asked me to look up jobs in Australia, New Zealand, Canada, and even Sweden. I spent hours gathering information for him, but I soon found that D.O.'s were not recognized in these countries. Pharmacy jobs abounded, but hurdles had to be passed, such as a year of internship and more exams. I searched furiously on the Internet, hoping that we would leave this God forsaken place and find something in the western world, but to no avail.

One day, he approached me, "I talked to my father and I am going to take the boards again in December."

"You mean you decided to stay?" I asked.

"I know you hate it here, but my father said it would be a waste of my degree not to take this exam and reciprocate my license. He is

202

willing to help me with my dream," he said. "It's going to be okay," he said, showing me a rare moment of sympathy.

I took advantage of that moment and begged him, "Please then, listen to your sister and call the American Wives Club. I know this group will help me adjust to this country."

"Okay, fine," he sighed. "The phone number is in the bedroom in my top dresser."

"Oh, thank you, thank you!" I said, hugging him.

"Just don't get too close to them," he warned, "and don't tell them anything about our personal business!"

Before he changed his mind I found the phone number and dialed it. The phone rang twice.

"Hello?" a female with an American accent answered. I was elated.

"Hello?" I replied. "How are you? My name is Kelly and I am an American married to a Lebanese, and I was given this number so I could join the American Wives Club!" I couldn't hold back my enthusiasm.

"Well hello Kelly," she responded. "My name is Marti. Did you just arrive?"

"No, we came here in early February," I said.

"February!" she exclaimed. "How did you survive this long without calling us?"

"Well, it took this long for us to finally settle in," I lied.

"How many children do you have?" she asked.

I have two daughters, nine and four. What about you?" I asked.

It was wonderful chatting like this with another American woman and I wanted to talk all night, but I kept it simple. I found out the club met once a week at a beach club during the summer. It was an open beach, meaning men and women were allowed, but they only went on Family Day. I made plans to meet them there next week.

I immediately told Ibrahim all about Marti and the beach club after we hung up.

"Family Day?" he asked. "Will there be men there?"

"No, it's just mothers and children," I lied, knowing he would say no otherwise.

"I will drive you and the girls there next week and check it out for myself," he said.

The following Wednesday, before Ibrahim drove us to the beach club, he had me model the only one-piece swimsuit I owned. He insisted that I wear black shorts over it. I didn't care. When we drove up to the beach parking lot I immediately spotted Marti, a tan blonde with hazel-green eyes. She shook hands with Ibrahim and gave him her cell phone number.

We walked into the club where children played in three sparkling blue pools surrounded by palm trees. I walked up to two women under an umbrella sitting on lounge chairs. The women greeted me kindly and then the questions began.

"So how do you find Lebanon?" they asked, staring curiously at me.

"It is beautiful," I edited warily.

"It's okay," Marti said. "You can speak freely with us. We understand. Our first year we hated it here."

"Correction. Some of us still hate it here," one lady spoke up.

"Can I see that?" one woman asked, reaching for the Catholic medals around my neck. "I see you haven't converted yet," she smiled.

"So all of you are Muslims?" I asked.

"Well we weren't when we moved here, but we are now," one woman remarked. "It's just easier for the children and the in-laws and everything else."

"I am just so happy to be talking to American women like myself!" I said happily. "I have really been looking forward to this!"

"Yeah, we understand," Marti said. "The first time I saw another foreigner in the grocery store speaking English I ran over to her and asked for her name and number – something I would never do in the States."

"Where are the rest of the women?" I asked. "My husband told me that there are over a hundred American woman in this group."

"Well, most of them are expatriates –Lebanese Americans who lived awhile in the States and have just returned here to live," said one lady.

"Well, how many are like us – born and raised?" I asked.

"You're pretty much looking at it: the three of us, and you, a couple of Brits, and one Brazilian," she answered. "There are others, but their husbands won't allow them to join."

Since I was the newcomer, most of the questions were fired at me: how long we had been married, how many children, etc.

"Is your husband Shiite or Sunni?" one asked.

"Shiite," I replied.

"Mine is too," she said.

"I feel sorry for you guys," another woman said. "I don't know how you handle that."

"Handle what?" I asked.

"You know, the temporary marriage thing," she responded. "My husband is Sunni, and they don't believe in that, thank God."

I stared at her blankly, and another lady changed the subject.

"So do all of your husbands own businesses here then?" I asked.

Everyone nodded except one lady who said, "My husband owns a few gas stations in the States. He lives there and I live here, raising our six children."

My eyes widened in shock. "He lives in the States and you live here, alone?"

"Yes, he wants his children raised in his country," she explained. "We see each other once a year, either he comes to visit or I go there to visit. We have a home in the States too."

I later discovered that this wasn't an unusual situation. The Lebanese husbands would live and work in America, enjoying their wife's country and send their wives to live in this third world, just so their children could learn Arabic and Islam. Their grown sons usually joined their fathers in America later, but their daughters stayed in Lebanon and were married off to Muslim men that the family agreed on.

After an hour of conversation, we plunged into the pool. I watched my daughters happily playing with the other children.

"Mommy! Mommy!" Nadine said, splashing up to me. "They speak English! They are from English land too!"

We talked and the children played all afternoon enjoying each other's company. Later that afternoon, all of the women lifted cups of homemade iced tea and clanged their rims together.

"Here's to Maria!" they said in unison. "To Maria!"

"Who is Maria?" I asked.

"A friend of ours," one said. "She got out last week."

"She got out?" I asked.

"She escaped, with her kids," one explained. "She had been trying to get out of here for over a year now."

"What happened?" I asked.

"Oh, the usual," she explained. Her husband reverted back to a domineering Arab male, and his family pressured him to divorce her and take another wife. We have all watched this many times. The first year of moving here is critical. If the husband starts to change his attitude toward his foreign wife, then things only get worse. The marriage doesn't stand a chance."

Her words struck me hard. She could have been talking about Ibrahim. "What about your husband?" I asked her.

"I am very fortunate," she said. "When we first moved here his family started stirring up trouble and weren't accepting me. Finally, my husband stood with me in front of them and said, 'This is my wife, the one I have chosen, and if you don't accept her then we will go back to America.'"

"Oh, how wonderful," I said, jealous of her husband's loyalty to her. "He defended you. He must really love you. So how did Maria escape?" I asked.

"She waited until this summer, never letting anyone in on her true intentions," she replied. "He let her visit her family in America every summer with the children. So this time, she just never returned and filed for divorce. But it's never quite that easy."

I wanted to hear more but it was time to leave. On our way home Marti told me, "I am so glad to have met you. We also meet every Saturday with our husbands. It's kind of a mixed-marriage club. The men get together and chat and we catch up. Sometimes we go dancing together at clubs too. Invite your husband – I know he would love it."

"Great! I will," I said.

Marti drove us home and dropped us off in our driveway. I couldn't wait to tell my husband.

"We had a fantastic time!" I said. "The women are so nice, and this beach was so clean and beautiful! The girls got along wonderfully, and the club meets every Wednesday! And the best thing is that their husbands are all Muslim like you. They asked me see if you would like to join them this Saturday. They would love to meet you!"

"No, no, no," he said firmly. "I am not interested."

"But I am sure you will have a lot in common with their husbands," I began, "It would be a great way to integrate ourselves here and make friends."

"No!" he said louder. "I am not established yet. I knew you would rush into things. I don't want them knowing about my personal business and life!"

I didn't push it, and was just thankful for the opportunity to see them as often as he would let me go. These women were my lifelines now, and during our time together I learned a great deal about other American women who had followed their husbands to Lebanon.

"I heard that Maria's husband is going after her in the States, to try and convince her to come back," I heard one lady say.

"Do you think she will come back?" another asked.

"No, I think we have all learned from Angela's mistake." They all nodded somberly.

"What happened to Angela?" I asked.

One of the women paused and offered me a cigarette. When I refused she said, "Just wait. Pretty soon, you'll be smoking like the rest of us."

She began, "Angela visited the States one summer with her children just like Maria, and called to tell her husband that she wasn't coming back. They had a terrible marriage. He started slapping her around and called her an American whore in front of their children." She paused and continued, "Her husband immediately got on the plane, followed her, and begged her to come back. He promised that things would get better. So, she came back and things just got worse. Now of course, he didn't trust her to go home and visit like before so she was stuck here."

"He can't do that," I interjected. "She's an American citizen. She can go back home whenever she wants."

All of the women raised their eyebrows at me and gave each other a knowing look.

"Yes he can Kelly," one woman said. "He can place a hold on his wife and children without a court order. If you are trying to leave the country without your husband's permission, the police can stop you before you even enter the airplane."

I gasped. My heart beat faster. "What happened to her?"

"Well, since she couldn't get out on her own, she contacted the U.S. Embassy here through email, and tried to obtain their help to get her and her kids out," the speaker continued.

"I warned her to be careful," a woman lamented. "I told her to cover her tracks.

"I know," the first woman continued. "It was just stupid the way it happened. She didn't erase her emails and her husband checked it one day and saw these letters to and from the Embassy."

"Oh no!" I exclaimed. "What did he do?"

"I'll tell you what he did," she continued, "he and his whole family took her to the airport with their children, bought her a one-way ticket home, and told her that this was the last time she would see her children. They all waved goodbye to her."

"Can't the U.S. embassy get the children back for her?" I asked.

"They can't do anything," one answered. "Her only hope is to hire mercenaries to kidnap them back."

"But the children are American citizens," I said.

"Look, Kelly, things are different here," one lady told me. "You probably didn't know that any child born to a Muslim man is automatically considered a Muslim, regardless of what faith the mother is. And in Islam your husband can divorce you without your knowledge and take your children from you. Because in his faith, the children belong to him."

"But this isn't Iran or Saudi Arabia!" I said. "Isn't Lebanon a democratic country?"

"It is a republic," one answered. "But personal laws, like marriage, divorce, and custody issues are governed by religious tribunals. This means a sheik will decide custody issues for Muslims, a priest or pastor for Christians."[17]

I felt more and more uneasy as they continued to converse. I couldn't believe how naïve I was about living in this country. Despite the noonday sun beating down, I shivered uncontrollably. When three o'clock came, I was ready to leave.

YOUNG VIRGINS

I watched my husband warily now, my friends' warnings about the first year ringing in my ears. My husband's attitude was changing toward me rapidly. Not even a year ago we were in Paris, and he was full of charm and romance. Now he seemed embarrassed to even be seen with me. His wrath turned on me quickly for any small infraction, and I learned to quickly appease him to avoid any repercussions, but it did no good. To him, I represented all that America stood for in his mind. I watched every comment, every expression, tiptoeing over landmines in my own home that I hoped wouldn't explode.

One day Layla complained to her father that she wanted to go back to America. He pulled her into our bedroom where I was and screamed, "I know your mother has been talking to you!" He pointed his finger at me. "We are never going back to America! We are here now in my country, and your mother has to do whatever I tell her to do and go wherever I tell her to go!"

He cursed America on a daily basis. "America is evil!" he would tell the girls in front of me. "America is the big Satan, and Israel is the little Satan and they work together!"

"All of them Baba?" Layla asked, doubtfully.

"All of them!" he answered. "Every single one of them! They are liars upon liars upon liars!"

"But I'm American Baba," she said.

"You are not American!" he told her. "You are 100 percent Lebanese! I am your father and you always take from the father's side!"

Under these conditions I avoided him when I could and made sure dinner was on time, and the house was immaculate. No longer were we partners raising our daughters together. He was the master of the house, and I was his servant. My nerves were frayed searching for any sign that he was planning on getting rid of me. His sisters were my advocates, and I visited them or had them over whenever I could.

One morning he came home with more paperwork in Arabic

for me to sign.

"Didn't we already obtained Lebanese passports for the girls?" I asked.

"Sign it," he said, threatening me with his eyes.

After I signed my name he said, "This is just a legal paper saying the girls belong to my family now."

"What do you mean?" I cried out. "Layla and Nadine are our children, not your parents'!"

"You don't understand anything!" he retorted.

That week he drove me to a local government office to sign more papers. Ibrahim motioned for me to sit down on a bench while he talked to some man in Arabic behind the counter. He stared at me and motioned for me to sign some more paperwork, which I did. Ibrahim gave the man some money and he handed him an 8x5-laminated card.

When we got back in the car I asked him, "What did I sign? I want to know now!"

"You are too suspicious," he said. "It was just to get you a temporary residency. I thought that's what you wanted. You have been complaining about it or months to my sister!"

He threw an 8x5-laminated card at me, with my picture stamped on it. "You can thank my sister Salam for that," he said.

I looked closely at the card. "This is a one-year residency permit. Why didn't you get me a Lebanese passport like all my friends' husbands did?" I asked. "Don't you want me to become a citizen?"

"I just didn't," he shouted. "You know, you are really beginning to disgust me! I am feeling nothing but disgust for you lately! If anyone deserves to get a new wife, it is me!" He pursed his lips angrily and glared darkly at me.

I shriveled under his stare. My lower lip started trembling uncontrollably as I tried to hold back my tears. I avoided his hateful look by staring out the side window, everything blurring together behind the pools filling my eyes.

When we arrived home, we found the electricity was off, and I prepared myself for another sweltering afternoon while he went upstairs with his parents. Suddenly Layla came running through the front door, Ibrahim following behind her. "Mommy, are you coming upstairs to visit too?"

"Visit who?" I asked Ibrahim.

"My parents want you to come up and meet some people –

they are curious to meet the American wife," my husband said.

"I can't visit anyone right now," I said. My eyes were red from crying and I had no makeup on.

"They insisted, and it would be rude," he demanded. "You will make me look bad in front of them."

"Come on Mommy," Layla pleaded.

"Give me a few minutes," I said. I went into the bathroom and sighed, looking at my face in the mirror. My eyes were red and I looked horrible. I did the best I could, putting on makeup and fixing my hair. I chose one of my better outfits and put on high-heeled sandals and sprayed myself with perfume.

When I walked into the kitchen Layla exclaimed, "Wow! You look beautiful Mama! "

Ibrahim just laughed. "What's wrong?" I asked him.

"You don't have to dress up so much," he said. "Let's go."

"Just a minute," I said. I took the girls into their bedrooms and did their hair up and changed them into summer dresses. I still had my pride, and I wanted to put on a favorable presentation to these curious visitors. We left to go upstairs, but before we walked through his parents' door I asked him, "Please do me one favor? Will you sit next to me and translate for me? I hate sitting alone while everyone is speaking Arabic around me."

"Just sit right next to me and I will," he promised.

The guests were in the parlor. An elderly man of about sixty and his plump wife dressed in hijab sat surrounded by their four young daughters. We politely exchanged greetings. The daughters were young, between the ages of sixteen and twenty, wearing colorful scarves in soft blues and purples, wearing makeup and perfume. I walked in and sat on one of the empty loveseats and left room for Ibrahim to set next to me. My heart fell as I saw him sit on the opposite side of the room from me, as far away as possible next to his mother.

The elderly gentleman asked me in English, "So how do you find Lebanon?"

"It is a beautiful country," I responded politely.

"Yes, yes it is," he agreed. "So how long have you two been married?"

"Fourteen years now," I said, looking at my husband.

"Fourteen years!" he exclaimed. "And you still don't speak Arabic? Shame on you!"

"I tried to take Arabic lessons…" I began looking at my

husband for help.

"You should pay more attention and listen to your husband when he speaks Arabic," he admonished me.

My husband did not defend me but everyone stared at me like I was a terrible wife for not speaking Arabic. No one mentioned how brave I was to come to this country, following my husband. No one chided my husband for not giving me Arabic lessons. I felt ashamed.

They stopped speaking to me at this point as if in punishment and everyone began conversing in Arabic. My husband became the center of attention and I watched as the four daughters leaned forward, nodding at every word he said and laughing playfully. He was a catch in this country – a pharmacist and a doctor and they made no pretense that they weren't interested. My husband enjoyed this attention from the young girls and turned on the charm. I sat there alone until Layla came over and sat next to me putting her arms around me.

"Yallla! (Let's go!)," his mother said motioning for everyone to get up. We walked into the entrance way and my mother-in-law directed the family into the smaller sitting room.

My husband stopped me from going in there. "Why don't you go downstairs and take the girls," he said, talking to me but staring at the young girls.

"You're not coming?" I asked.

"No, I can't be rude," he answered. "I'll be down later."

I took my daughters' hands and we went back to our apartment.

"Who were those girls staring at Baba?" Layla asked.

"Oh, you noticed it too?" I smiled at her.

"Is Baba going to marry again?" she asked with a worried look on her face.

"No, honey," I said.

"But he can marry four wives in Islam," she said seriously.

"Yes, but he said he would never do that when we first got married," I answered. "It's against the law anyway."

"But he can here, right?" she asked maybe realizing he was not a man of his word.

I paused. "Yes, there is nothing to prevent him in this country from marrying another woman."

"I hate it here!" she suddenly burst out. "A man should not marry more than one wife! It isn't right!"

Layla understood at nine years old that the idea of more than one wife or husband for that matter was wrong.

"Why don't we just go back to America where everything is normal?" she asked. "I hate it here! I want to go back!" She buried her face into my chest and I held her while she cried.

"Don't worry, baby," I answered. "I am working on it. "Come on, what do you want for dinner? I'll cook your favorite tonight."

Much later, he returned from his parents' place and walked through the kitchen where I was cleaning dishes.

"Can I fix you a plate?" I offered.

"No, I ate too much of my mother's food," he answered.

"Layla, why don't you take your sister and go play with her in your bedroom," he said to her. "I need to talk to your mother about something."

My stomach clenched. *"What now?"* I thought.

"Let's talk in here," he said motioning toward the living room.

I walked over to the loveseat and sat down. He sat opposite me in a chair and possessed it confidently as he lit up a cigarette.

"Well, it looks like my parents are not accepting you," he said, not even looking at me but at the end of his cigarette.

Panic gripped me as I quickly defended myself. "What do you mean ….not accepting me? I…I don't understand!"

"As a wife," he clarified.

"But I am your wife," I stammered. "We've been married fourteen years and I am the mother of your children…"

"You don't understand how embarrassing this is for them!" he shouted. "Do you think it's easy for them to see me driving you to church?"

"You haven't taken me to church for over two months," I said. "I've only gone a few times since I've been here. How does that offend them? I don't understand – I leave my homeland and family to move to their country. I never argue with them. I obediently do whatever anyone asks me. I have been a faithful wife and mother for all of these years. What else do they want from me?"

"You have three things wrong with you!" he said loudly. "Number one: You are not Arabic! Number two: You are an American! and Number three: You are a Christian who refuses to convert!"

"But you knew that when you married me," I lamented.

"You just don't understand anything," he said, exasperated with me. "All of my brothers married women who are Muslim and Arabic. My family just isn't accepting you anymore."

"So what is their solution?" I asked fearfully. "To throw me out?" I began to cry and kneeled on the floor in front of him.

"I don't know. I don't know," he responded putting his face in his hands rubbing his eyes.

He rose wearily from the couch, slammed the front door, and ran upstairs to his parents, leaving me all alone again. My heart felt like it had been ripped from my chest and torn into pieces. I heard the familiar chirping from Tweety and found her in the corner. She was still acting like a wild bird, jumping from side to side, trying to break free from her cage.

"I know how you feel little one," I said inching closer to her. I kneeled close to her cage, trying to comfort this little bird as tears streamed down my face.

Part IX Songs of Freedom

A MOTHER'S FURY

If I could choose the national flower for Lebanon I would choose the gardenia. It blooms everywhere in the summer. People thread it into leis and hang it on their rearview mirrors or float the flowers in bowls of water throughout their homes. It has a strong, heady aroma; its thick velvety petals look strong and sturdy, but the slightest touch crushes the tender petals. It withers quickly, until nothing remains but a dark heap of dismal brown.

As I held this flower in my hands, I felt my own bruises - deep wounds that had been inflicted by the hands of the man I had loved and given up my life for. My own spirit was crushed, like this soft delicate flower decomposing in front of me. I loved him once, and I didn't understand why now. I lived to please a man who couldn't be pleased no matter what I did.

"Where are you my God?" I lamented in tears. "Where are You?"

I struggled in my prayer time asking God to deliver my daughters and me from my husband and this country. I tried to offer up my suffering, as I had been taught in my Catholic faith, for his salvation but I grew angry even at God.

"When are you going to rescue us?" I cried. "I have given up

215

everything for this man and have tried to be the patient, loving wife that I should be. I can't take this anymore, Heavenly Father, I just can't. He is loathing me now. He can't stand me, and I know it won't be long before he does get rid of me and sends me back home without my daughters."

I pulled out my rosary and got on my knees on the hard marble floor, offering up my pain, my suffering for my husband's salvation. "Please Dear Lord, please come into my husband's heart. Make him a new man in Christ Jesus just like St. Paul, who was on his way to persecute and kill Christians, until you blinded him with Your light and told him that You are Jesus and to stop." I prayed the rosary on my knees, fervently begging God for the same miracle I prayed for everyday.

"I am so sorry, my Lord," I cried now, hugging my knees. "Look at the mess I have made of my life so far – and now my daughters are suffering because of my life choices. This is my entire fault! My husband is right – I am not a good Christian, because if I were he would have converted long ago and loved me more every year. He hates me now. He hates me!"

Now I understood what the women at the American Wives Club went through their first year here, and I understood how they felt when they said they had no choice but to convert to Islam to appease their husbands and make peace with their husbands' families. I would deny myself anything to create peace, and I had sacrificed everything for him except the one thing he now demanded – conversion to his religion.

I couldn't do it. Because to convert would mean that I would deny my Lord and my God. How could I deny my Lord and God who laid down His life for me?

To accept Islam would mean to deny Jesus, and I could not do it. I opened my Bible to Isaiah, in the Old Testament, foretelling of Jesus' great sacrifice:

"He was wounded for our transgressions,
He was bruised for our iniquities;
The chastisement for our peace was upon Him,
And by His stripes we are healed." (Isaiah 53:5)

I'll Fly Away

I thought about the torture my Lord endured patiently— The Roman way – 39 lashings with a whip made of several heavy leather thongs with balls of lead attached to the ends that ripped His flesh until He was bloodied beyond recognition. Mocked by Roman soldiers who crammed a crown of thorns on His head and struck Him in his face, laughing. The heavy crossbar of the cross was tied across His shoulders, and He was forced to walk the slow journey along the Via Dolorosa where onlookers jeered at Him and spit in His face. What was His crime? Healing the sick, feeding the hungry, preaching about a God who loves them. He was nailed to a cross and erected on a hill for everyone to see. And as He tried to push Himself upward to avoid the excruciating pain from sagging down on the nails, and gasp for a breath, He looked down at the Roman soldiers that did this to Him and did not curse them but said, "Father, forgive them for they know not what they do." (Luke 23:34)

"Did Jesus suffer all of this for nothing?" I thought. "Was He a liar when He said, "I come to give my life as a ransom for many (Matthew 20:27)" or when He said, "I am the way, the truth and the life. No one can come to the Father except through me. "(John 14:6)

"No," I decided. "He is not a liar. He is the Son of God. He is the Messiah and I will not reject Him."

"But what do I do now, Lord?" I asked. "I do not believe that this is the life You wish for me. I do not believe anymore that I am supposed to suffer in this marriage and be abused this way. This can't be the life you destined for me. I am tired of being a martyr!"

I opened my bible and was drawn to the same scripture He had shown me before:

"For I know the plans I have for you, declares the Lord,
Plans to prosper you and not to harm you.
Plans to give you a hope and a future." (Jeremiah 29:11)

"What plans, dear Lord?" I asked in desperation. "What future?"

I turned on the CD player, and fast-forwarded to my now favorite song, "I'll Fly Away."

**"Some glad morning when this life is o'er,
I'll fly away; to a home on God's celestial shore,
I'll fly away."**

**"I'll fly away oh glory, I'll fly away, in the morning,
When I die, Hallelujah by and by, I'll fly away..."**

**"When the shadows of this life have gone, I'll fly away;
like a bird from prison bars has flown, I'll fly away."**

I sang with all my heart, knowing now for the first time what it felt like to have my freedoms taken away, to be a captive in a foreign land and to prefer death to this life.

In the middle of my singing, Layla walked in on me and looked startled. When she saw me crying and heard the words she rushed over to me and said, "Mommy, I don't want you to die!"

Suddenly, I got a good hard look at myself in her eyes, and I didn't like it. I saw what she must have seen: a weak, depressed, powerless woman – a shadow of the woman I used to be. I was a groveling servant who cowered under the demands of my husband, with nothing to look forward to and everything to fear. And more importantly, I saw my daughters' future.

At that moment, an infusion of strength inundated me. I had daughters to protect, their lives to save. This sense of debilitating powerlessness left me. A flash of righteous anger unleashed a mother's fury. What I couldn't do for myself I could do for my daughters.

"No baby, you are right," I answered her. "Life's not over yet, and we will not surrender. Let's change those words right now."

And we did, singing the song in unison:

**"I'll fly away oh glory, I'll fly away, in the morning.
When I go, Hallelujah by and by, I'll fly away."**

"When we go where Mommy?" she asked.

"When we go home baby, back to America," I answered, hugging her tightly.

NINE YEARS OLD

Layla had reached the age of nine, the same age that one of prophet Mohammed's wives, Aisha, was when he, a 54-year-old man, consummated his marriage with her. He had married her at the tender age of seven. I knew that Islam condoned child marriages, and that Layla could now be married without her permission to anyone her father chose. Sharia law allowed it and it was and is a growing practice in nonMuslim countries as well such as Germany, Canada, the United Kingdom, and the United States. [18] My daughter, in the eyes of Islam, was now seen as a woman, and thus, able to marry. In my eyes, she was a nine-year old girl, still a child, innocent and naïve to the ways of the world. To even think of her being married at this age made me sick to my stomach.

Ibrahim began drawing a black curtain of restrictions around her. A girl at nine in Islam should be praying five times a day and begin covering her hair and body. Boys were allowed six more years and were not required to do this until they were fifteen years of age but she was now considered a woman in Islam and her relationship with her father changed drastically.

He demanded that she pray with him now. One day after afternoon prayers he took Layla into the bedroom and shut the door. He talked to her for an hour, and when he exited he walked by me not saying a word. After he left I asked her what they talked about.

"Baba told me I am nine years old now and that I am supposed to cover!" she blurted out.

"What did you say?" I asked.

"I told him I thought it was my choice, and that I didn't have to if I didn't want to, and he told me that if he tells me to I have to! Mama, I don't want to wear those ugly scarfs! What is so wrong about showing my hair? Why is my hair haram (shameful)?"

"There is nothing wrong with your hair honey," I answered. "If a man looks at a little girl like you with lust because of your hair – he has the problem – not you! Don't worry, I will talk to him."

Layla's eyes filled with panic. "No! No!" she said. "He will get mad at me if he knows that I told you! He always tells me, 'You tell your Mom everything!' He tells me that I can never keep a secret! Please don't tell him, you promise?'"

"I promise," I said. "I won't say a word but you don't have to wear that scarf if you don't want to. There is nothing sinful about a woman's hair. Mary Magdalene washed Jesus' feet with her long beautiful hair, and He saw this as a blessing, not as something sinful."

My mind went back to 1991 when I first visited Kuwait before I had children. It was the day I first visited a mosque. My mother-in-law had invited me, and I was curious. My husband was ecstatic that I was going. Before we left the house she gave me a long drab darrah (a black flowing robe that covered every part of my body). I wore a simple dark scarf pinned neatly under my chin, not showing any neckline. We drove to the center of the city and walked up to a colossal mosque together. When we walked in, the men and women were immediately separated. We, as women, were not allowed to walk in the front door like my husband, so I followed my mother-in-law upstairs to a small, suffocating room with drab green carpet. We removed our shoes and walked in. We were the only ones there, so I sat quietly in the back while my mother-in-law pulled out her prayer rug and began her prayers. I could see beyond the front wall made of wood lattice, the men downstairs praying in the cool, spacious part of the mosque.

I decided to pray myself, so I knelt down and quietly recited a few prayers. Suddenly, a mob of women descended upon us. Kuwaiti women dressed in black abiyas arrived, some only showing their eyes. As they set up their prayer rugs in front of me I sat on my knees watching them. An old, haggard woman spied me in the corner. She walked over to me and grabbed my scarf with her gnarled hands muttering, "Ibe ashoom alaki, (Shame on you!)"

She pulled me to my feet and pushed all of my offending bangs under my scarf, retying it tightly, pinning it to her satisfaction. I sat there passively, allowing this strange woman, her face only inches from mine, to touch me in this way while my mother-in-law watched. I couldn't understand how my few bangs would offend their god while I prayed. It made no sense to me. When my God, my Creator, looked at me saw my heart, my soul, His daughter. How could He could He be offended by the body He created?

I cradled my daughter's face in my hands and told her, "When God looks at you do you know what He sees?" I asked her.

She shook her head.

"He sees His beautiful daughter, His child that He created and loves, and you can come to Him anytime and talk with Him just as you are baby, hair and all."

"Really Mama?" she asked.

"Really," I answered.

PLEASURE MARRIAGES

My mind was made up now. I was determined to leave with my daughters. I saw his game plan now. His family would send me home, like poor Angela, never again to see my daughters. Inside, alone with my thoughts, I worked furiously on a plan, but on the outside I remained compliant and appeasing to Ibrahim and his family. I came when I was summoned, followed when he led and did what I was told. I became like his sisters, docile servants of their husbands.

The next time I was allowed to visit Aisha I dared to ask her some questions about her faith, wondering how she justified her husband's treatment of her.

"Aisha, can you please explain muta (temporary marriage) to me?" I asked.

"Well, it is when a man makes a contract with a woman for marriage," she began. "They agree on a gift, usually money, and how long it will last."

"How long do they normally last?" I asked.

"From one hour up to 99 years," she answered. "It depends on the couple."

"One hour?" I asked putting my teacup down in astonishment.

"Yes, this is possible," she said. "But usually they agree on one day. They are married in the evening and in the morning he simply divorces her."

"Well, in my country, we call that adultery," I said.

"That's because men are only allowed to marry one woman over there," she said.

"So are you okay with this?" I asked.

"What do you mean?" she said looking at me, shocked that I would even think she would question this.

"I mean, if you husband went out and contracted a temporary marriage for one night with another woman, wouldn't you mind?" I asked.

"No, I wouldn't mind. In fact, I encouraged him to do this," she admitted.

"You what?" I asked, my mouth falling open.

"Look," she explained. "My husband is not like Ibrahim. He never tried a woman before we were married. He was pure. I know he was very curious about other women, so when he asked me one day if he could I said, 'Go! Go try and you will see that I am better than any of them!'" She pointed at herself confidently.

"And he did?" I asked.

"Yes," she said nodding her head. "He found a woman and left for a few days, but when he came back he was even closer to me. He said, 'I only love you!' and he told me that I was prettier and better in many ways," she said proudly.

"Oh my God, Aisha," I said. "I could never handle that. I mean it's one thing to have your suspicions that your husband is cheating but for him to come home and tell you about it!"

"It is not cheating in our religion," she explained. "Besides, I have no choice. Look Kelly, I must please my husband or he will go and find someone else, and then where will I be? It will be my fault if he find another woman."

"Your fault?" I said. "Aisha, what about your needs, your wants? Does he please you?"

"I am here to make him happy," she answered. "I don't care about my own pleasure," she confided.

She looked down at the floor and then at me with a worried look on her face. "Kelly you must please your husband," she pleaded. "You must! He is your master! Allah made it that way!"

I bristled, "Aisha, I was not created to be anyone's servant. God designed marriage as a loyal partnership, a covenant between one woman and one man, not a contract that can be broken because your husband doesn't like something you did or if you become too old or not attractive to him anymore."

"What?" she asked, confused. "You don't understand Kelly, and I am worried for you. You must understand and please your husband."

"How are things between you and Khalil?" I asked, changing the subject. "I heard you tried to leave your husband a few years ago…"

"Yes, this is true," she said. "I told my brother Mohammed about everything my husband was doing to me – the hitting – the yelling – the silence – everything… that I couldn't take it anymore."

"So what happened?" I asked gently, hating to see her face turn sad.

"Well, my brother Mohammed confronted my husband and told him that I wanted a divorce," she said. "I was even willing to give up my children then, it was so bad..." Her voice trailed off and she looked into her teacup. "But once this happened, Khalil began crying, and he told me he couldn't live without me – that he loved me so much and would never do those things again. It was amazing! He was like a little boy!"

I sighed, "Are things better now?"

"Well, yes and no," she answered, avoiding my eyes. "He is very jealous of me, but I know this means he loves me too too much. He can't stand for any man to pay attention to me. But I never have any time to myself. Last week I went shopping for clothes, something I haven't done in six months, and he let me go for one hour. I came home after two hours, and he was so angry with me." Her eyes filled with tears. "This was my only chance, you know, to go shopping for myself in six months."

"Of course," I affirmed her, touching her hand.

I never heard what penance she suffered for shopping an hour later than permitted because Ibrahim had arrived to pick me up. Before I left her, Aisha hugged me goodbye and whispered in my ear, "Remember, do it for Allah."

ALLIGATORS

One of Ibrahim's close cousins, Jafar, was visiting from America, and he was on the hunt for a new wife. Ibrahim told me the story the next morning.

"Jafar is visiting from Toledo – do you remember him?" he asked.

"Yes, I do – how are his wife and two boys doing?" I asked.

"Well, he is divorced now and is looking for a new wife," he explained.

"Divorced?" I asked, surprised. "I thought he was so happy with his new, young, Lebanese wife after he divorced his American wife. They seemed really happy together."

"Yeah, well, she became too Americanized," he said. "But anyway, he is here now and he wants me to help him look for a new wife. He trusts my judgment."

"Mm hmm," I murmured. "So you are going to help him how?"

"He is visiting a lot of families with daughters who are eligible for marriage so I need to leave this afternoon. We won't be back until very late this evening," he warned me.

"Fine," I answered, knowing he wasn't asking for permission.

His absence would give me time to think about our escape. As promised, he didn't show up until four in the morning and it became the topic of conversation the next evening sitting on his parents' balcony.

"Did you know Ibrahim came home at four in the morning?" his father asked me, teasingly. My husband translated and I nodded my head placidly.

"Were you too angry at him?" he asked, chuckling.

When I looked confused at my husband, he explained. "He thinks that you were waiting up for me last night, and that maybe you were really angry with me for coming home so late."

"No, no," I answered my father-in-law. "*Huwe min Jafar.*" (He was with Jafar)

Abu Ali looked stunned that I was not upset. I wanted to explain that this was old news to me. I was used to my husband staying out until sometimes four or five in the morning in America. I never questioned him because I was afraid of his angry retributions, but I thought better of this and sat there quietly.

An awkward silence threw a damper on his father's teasing. My husband noticed and said, "Why don't you go downstairs with the girls?"

I rose dutifully and went downstairs to my cell. When he followed me an hour later he had news to share.

"Tomorrow we are going to Jafar's village to visit," he announced.

"I don't want to go," I said quietly, not looking forward to sitting among strangers while they talked Arabic around me.

"You never want to do anything!" he suddenly exploded.

"Oh, I didn't mean it," I answered meekly. "Of course, let's go. It will be a nice outing for us."

We drove the next morning with my in-laws to a small southern village surrounded by banners of martyrs and Hezbollah flags brazenly waving the sword of Islam. We found Jafar's family's home and were welcomed with kisses. We sat on the patio and were offered a bowl of pistachios and soda. The discussion turned to Jafar's search for a wife. Suddenly, a cleric started broadcasting his sermon over loudspeakers. It was so deafening, my husband put his hands over his ears. The others ignored it and continued shouting over the endless sermon.

It was too much for me. I left the patio and walked inside to check on the girls. I found them playing with a few toys while two little boys, around five and nine years old watched sadly. Their shirts were wrinkled and their hair was a tousled mess. They sat slumped over in their chairs with sad expressions on their faces. The five-year-old was trying unsuccessfully to open the pistachios to eat.

"Can I help you?" I asked him.

He handed me the bowl while staring forlornly at me as I began opening them up for him one by one. He greedily ate up the nuts as fast as I cracked them open. Slowly he warmed up to me.

"I don't have a Mommy," he told me.

"I am so sorry, habebe," I said. "I know your parents aren't together anymore."

"Yeah, my Mommy is dead," he said turning a pistachio over in his hands.

"Dead? What do you mean?" I asked.

"The alligators got her," he answered. "One day she was walking toward a swamp, and my father warned her not to go near there, but she didn't listen and she fell in and the alligators ate her up!" He clapped his hands together, mimicking an alligator's jaws.

I was stunned. "Who told you this?"

"My father," he answered. "He told me that he even tried to rescue her. He jumped in to save her but it was too late and she died. But it doesn't matter, he told me that she never loved me anyway."

I put my arms around him, wanting to hold him forever. Anger swelled in my chest as I thought of his seemingly charming father who was telling him these lies. I glanced over toward the balcony and stared angrily at the back of his head as he talked about finding another wife. I didn't dare call his father a liar because I knew the same fate could happen to me. I took the little boy's hand in mine and looked into his melancholy eyes.

"I know your mother loved you very much and that the day you were born, she was so happy she cried, and I know she still loves you," I said.

"Did you know my mother?" he asked, his face now full of hope.

"Yes, I did." I answered. "I stayed with her for a few days when your older brother was just a toddler and I know that she loves you as much as she loved your brother."

His face brightened and he moved closer to sit beside me. I continued cracking nuts for him and when Ibrahim came over to tell me we were leaving I resisted an impulse to take this precious child in my arms and bring him with us. I lingered near him and kept hugging him. Driving away I looked back and saw him waving at me from the balcony.

"What exactly happened with Jafar and his wife?" I asked Ibrahim cautiously.

"She just started having friends that he didn't like," he answered.

"You mean Americans?"

"No, they were Lebanese. She just started complaining to them about her husband and he became upset," he answered. "When he brought her to America, she had nothing. She comes from a very poor family. After she came to America she started getting ideas."

"Yeah, she probably realized she didn't have to be his slave," I thought bitterly.

He continued, "So he told her to take their boys to visit her parents this summer in Lebanon. She went and he followed a week later without her knowing. He showed up unannounced at her parents' home and accused his wife of being too critical and divorced her, taking their boys with him."

"That's terrible!" I said. "What did her parents do?"

"They defended their daughter but they couldn't stop Jafar from taking his sons." He reached for his left pocket, pulled out a cigarette, tilting his head as he lit it up.

"I was sitting with his youngest son while you were talking," I began hesitantly. "He told me that his mother was eaten by an alligator." I waited for his shocked response.

"Oh, you know kids," he murmured.

"No, he sincerely believes this!" I added. "A child wouldn't make something like that up. I can't believe Jafar told him a lie like this."

"Now, now, don't take sides," he answered. "They are both to blame. Remember, it takes two."

"Yeah, it takes two! It is always a given that there are two people in a marriage!" I wanted to shout. *"What does that have to do with anything? A bully always needs another person to pick on!"*

Instead I said, "If your daughter went to school and a bully beat her up would you tell her, 'now, now, it takes two?' No! You would blame the bully and probably want to confront him and have him held accountable for his actions!"

"Now, you're mixing apples and pears," he replied.

"It's oranges!" I replied angrily. "Apples and oranges!"

I had a thought. "Jafar is an American citizen because of his first American wife so I am sure after nine years of marriage he gave this woman citizenship?" I asked.

"I don't know," he replied.

"Does she know that she can return to America and file for divorce and receive at least joint custody? She knows that Sharia law is not acknowledged in America, right?" I asked.

"I don't know," Ibrahim sighed. "I don't want to get in the middle of it."

"So now he is looking for a new wife to replace her?"

"Yeah, poor guy," Ibrahim said. "He has to return to work in the States in one week so he has to hurry up and find one. He started out with the younger ones, of course, but he's already been turned down by several."

"I bet word got out that the last wife was eaten by alligators," I replied sarcastically.

"He can't raise those boys by himself!" my husband snapped. "Those boys need a mother!"

"They have a mother!" I cried.

"I don't want to talk about this anymore. Just drop it," he said, lowering his voice.

I realized that I could be next and instinctively, so did Layla who had been listening to the whole conversation. "Tell us that Fairy Tale you made up last night Mommy," she intervened.

I turned around to face my daughter who had a wide-eyed look on her face. "Once upon a time, there were two little princesses who lived in a far away kingdom…" I began.

BLACK LIST

The next morning while I was fixing breakfast, I implemented my first plan. It was a simple one.

"My parents say hello to you," I began.

"Oh?" he said. "How are they?"

"Good," I replied. "They're going to celebrate their 40th wedding anniversary next month."

"They have been married almost as long as my parents," he said.

"Yes," I replied. "My brother and his wife are going to throw a big surprise party with all their family and friends and they want us to come."

"I don't have the time or the money for that right now," he replied sharply.

"Well, they offered to pay for the plane tickets and any other expenses while we are there," I said as nonchalantly as I could.

He raised his eyebrows in surprise. "They will?"

"Yes," I said. "They just want to see the girls. I don't know – what do you think?"

A deafening silence lingered while I washed the plate I was holding in the sink over and over. "Sure you can go," he answered. "But how long will you stay?"

I stared back innocently. "As long as you want us to – maybe three weeks?"

He nodded and then went back to his book. I tried to hide my enthusiasm and slowly finished cleaning the kitchen talking about other things.

Later that day I told the girls that we were going to go visit Grammy and Grandpa soon.

"In English land Mommy?" Nadine asked, excitedly.

"Yes, baby, in English land!" I responded enthusiastically.

I heard the bedroom door creak open and saw Ibrahim's face. He had been standing outside listening the whole time.

"Baba!" Layla said, running to his arms. "Is that true? Are we going to visit Grammy and Grandpa?"

"Who told you that?" he asked her. An unsettling feeling grabbed my gut.

"Mama," she said softly pointing at me.

"That's exactly what you want. Isn't it?" he said leering at me scornfully.

"Yes… I was telling the girls that you agreed…" I began timidly.

"I haven't agreed to anything," he said staring evenly at me. "I know what you are planning. I know everything." His voice was low and menacing.

Panic raced through me. "*How could he know?*" I thought. "*I haven't told anyone!*"

"I know what your agenda is," he continued pointing his finger at me. "You want us all to go back to America and live."

A sense of relief washed over me. "*He doesn't know,*" I thought.

"Yes, Baba," Layla said. "Let's go back to America!"

He suddenly turned to face his daughter. "Your mother has been talking to you, hasn't she? I know what is going on here. She is poisoning your mind, Layla, against my country, my religion. She wants both of you all for herself. She wants to swallow you!"

"What are you talking about?" I said softly. "All I told them was that we were going to visit my parents."

"Go!" he said loudly. "But you will go by yourself!"

The girls instinctively ran to hug me and Nadine raised her voice, "Don't yell at Mama! You need to be nice!" Layla hugged me tightly.

"Stay with your mother, Layla, and you will see where she will lead you," he threatened. He left the room acting hurt and she ran after him trying to soothe him.

I acted quickly and ran after him. "I didn't know that this upset you," I said. "I won't go if you don't want me to. This can wait. We can go next year. I know that you need us now."

He grunted.

"Yes, I would like to go back to America to try again, but if this is what you want – to fulfill your dream here, then I am behind you," I said. I could see my words were soothing him. I knew that any hope of escaping here depended on him trusting me.

231

I needed to take the next step. The next afternoon I waited until he went upstairs and I quickly logged on the Internet and found the phone number for the U.S. Embassy in Lebanon. I dialed the number.

"May I help you?" a young male answered.

"Yes, um... I would like to speak to someone about passports please," I said hesitatingly.

"Just a minute please," he answered. Click. Click.

"Hello. How may I help you?" a deep male voice with a thick Arabic accent greeted me.

"Yes, um, I would like to speak to an American Consulate please?" I asked.

"And what is this regarding?" he asked.

"Traveling," I responded.

"And what is your name Madame?" he asked.

"I am not giving you my name," I responded, fearfully.

"Well, then how can I tell the Consulate who you are and what you are calling about?" he asked.

"I just need to speak to someone, please," I begged.

"No one is in right now," he answered. "You need to call before one o'clock Madame."

"Okay, thank you," I said. After I hung up my hands started shaking uncontrollably.

The next morning I called earlier, right after Ibrahim left, and was finally transferred to a U.S. Consulate.

"Hello. May I help you?" a female's voice with an American accent asked. I breathed a sigh of relief.

"Yes, hello," I began as calmly as I could. "I am an American citizen who moved here with my Lebanese husband and I just found out he can put a stop on my travel – is this true?"

"Yes, he can," she answered.

"Well I know my husband wouldn't do this," I said, "but for my own peace of mind can you see if he did?"

"Certainly," she answered. "We can check that for you. Just give me your name, your husband and children's names and I will find out. We need your passport numbers also."

"I will get that for you but I don't have it right now," I said, watching the door, straining my ears for Ibrahim's return.

"Fine," she said. "You can email it to us," she said, and gave me her email address. "And we will call you when we find out."

"No!" I said. "Please don't call me. Can you just email me?"

"Okay," she said softly. "I will make a note to not call you. Give me your email address." I hesitated, remembering that Ibrahim knew my email and password. "Well, I will give it to you when I email you – okay?"

"Fine," she responded. "We will start working on it as soon as we receive your email – okay?"

"Thank you," I said shakily and hung up the phone quietly.

I took the piece of paper on which I had written her email address and hid it in the back of my closet. I found my husband's briefcase where he kept all of our passports and important documents. I knew the combination: 0-0-0. He had never changed it, but just as I had opened it I heard the front door open. I quickly snapped it shut and place it back exactly as I had found it. I jumped over to my dresser and opened the top drawer just as he came in the bedroom. I held up a pair of earrings to the mirror hoping he didn't notice my trembling hands. I faked a smile.

"What's up?" I asked casually.

"Nothing," he replied plopping on the bed. "This heat is exhausting. I'm going to take a nap.

After I heard him snoring I went to the computer in the living room and created a new username and password as well as a new email address.

"Mama!" Layla came running in unexpectedly. "Aisha is here with Jasmine and Farah– can I go play with them?"

"Sure honey," I said, logging off.

"Oh, and she needs Baba," she said. "I think Aisha is sick."

I woke my husband up as gently as I could and told him his sister needed him upstairs. Jasmine and Farah came rushing through the front door at that moment.

"You stay here and take care of the girls," he told me. "I will go check on my sister."

While he was gone I opened his briefcase and wrote down our passport information, and as the girls played in the other room I logged on and sent an email to the U.S. Embassy giving them all the information they requested to see if I was on a blacklist for travel.

A few hours later my husband came downstairs and began rummaging through the medicine cabinet. I followed him.

"What's wrong with Aisha?" I asked.

"She is stressed out," he mumbled. "She suddenly collapsed on us and fainted so she is sleeping in one of the bedrooms. I am looking for some muscle relaxants to help calm her."

Much later in the evening, Aisha came down to say goodbye and pick up her girls. She looked exhausted.

"Stay here with us just for a night," I told her. "I will take care of the girls and let you rest."

Aisha hugged me tight. "You are a good person Kelly. Habebti Kelly, please take care of yourself." Her words were sincere and she seemed more concerned for me. She forced herself to smile weakly. We kissed each other goodbye and I walked her to her car.

I walked into the kitchen and saw Ibrahim smoking. "What is going on?" I asked him. "Is it her husband?"

"I asked her this already," Ibrahim answered. "And she screamed, 'No! My husband is a good husband! He's a good man! No it is not my husband!' I think she said it out of fear," he added. "Then I asked her what we could do for her – to name one thing that she wanted more than anything in the world." He paused, taking another puff on his cigarette.

"She didn't answer me," he continued. "So I asked her, 'Is it freedom?' and my sister's eyes widened and she asked, 'How did you know?' and I told her, 'I know, I know.'"

I was stunned. Even Ibrahim saw his sister's plight. Even he recognized the caged bird she had become. I marveled at how he could see so clearly his sister's plight but be so oblivious to mine. I also knew that nothing would come of this. Aisha would be left to fend for herself and no one would come to her rescue.

HOPE

It had been a week, and I hadn't heard anything from the U.S. Embassy. Every free moment all I thought about was escaping. Ibrahim was busy studying for his exam. He was frustrated that he couldn't move ahead with his plans until these tests were passed, and in this heat his temper flared easily.

I kept my plans to myself and didn't tell the girls anything, but I was in a much brighter mood knowing that we would soon be out of this miserable place one way or another. I spent most of the time with my daughters in their bedroom, playing games or reading to make the days go by faster.

One day our fun had reached a point of silliness where we were laughing loudly at each other. All of a sudden the bedroom door swung open.

"You guys are having a good time huh?" Ibrahim asked us, and sat next to Nadine on the bed. He tried to hug her. She slapped him in the face.

He grimaced as if hurt, holding his cheek. "Ouch! Nadine! Why do you always hit Baba?"

Nadine ran away from him into my arms. "Mommy! Mommy! I want Mommy!" she said clinging onto my neck showering me with kisses.

"Are you teaching her to do this?" he asked me.

"No, of course not," I answered.

He stood up pointing to his feet. "Come to your father now!" he demanded.

"No! No! I want Mommy!" she yelled at him.

"Give Baba a hug," I said trying to convince her but she refused.

He grabbed Layla, hugging and kissing her profusely in front of Nadine. "I don't want Nadine. Layla is my best daughter," he said, trying to make her jealous.

"Who do you love more, Baba or Mama?" he asked Layla.

"How come everyone asks me that here?" she responded. "I love both of you the same."

"Well Baba is the one who takes you places and buys you things," he retorted, angrily.

He turned his attention back to Nadine telling her, "Okay, from now on I will only buy things for Layla!" His plan didn't work on her and she just hugged me tighter saying, "Mama! I love Mommy!"

Infuriated, he stood up and yanked her from me, swinging her over his shoulder. "Yalla! I am going to the store, and you and Layla are coming with me!"

Nadine screamed, holding out her arms towards me kicking. I heard the front door slam. A few minutes later, Layla ran back in the room.

"Quick!" she said. "I need a picture of you. Nadine won't leave until she has a picture of you!"

I ran to my bedroom and handed Layla a small photo of me. When they returned a half an hour later, with a few groceries and bags full of candy and cookies, Nadine had a tear-stained face and was clutching my picture tightly in her little hand. When she saw me she ran into my arms crying, "Mommy! I love Mommy!" Ibrahim frowned at her.

I began unpacking the groceries and Ibrahim yelled at Layla to pick up her playroom. He had barked orders at Layla all day and she was tired of it. My compliant child suddenly crossed her arms and said, "I don't want to."

I looked at her in shock. It was the first time I had ever seen her come up against him, and I knew what was going to happen next. I ran across the room as if in slow motion toward her just as he reached down and grabbed his shoe. Nadine ran after me screaming, and Ibrahim took out all his anger on her, whacking her hard on her back. She fell to the ground bursting into tears. I picked up Nadine, grabbed Layla's hand and ran into their bedroom. I shut the door and put them under the covers telling them to stay. I ran back to the kitchen where he was still sitting at the table. I said nothing and started putting the groceries away.

"I have decided that I want to renounce my American citizenship," he said glaring at me. "I want to renounce the girls' citizenship too."

I suppressed my swirling emotions, my mind on the girls crying in the bedroom, and remained calm. "But even your brothers have their American citizenship, save one. A few of them have even flown their wives to America during their last trimester to have their babies in America. It seems important to your family," I replied.

"Well, we should stop doing that as Muslims," he said. "I think that any Muslim who lives in America is a selfish traitor!"

"What do you want for dinner?" I asked him, trying to appease him. "I know – how about chicken and rice with pine nuts?"

"Sure, that sounds good," he said. "I'm going to go lay down. Wake me in an hour, no more. I need to study."

I waited until he left and I heard our bedroom door shut. I immediately went to the girls and found them under the covers, hugging each other. Nadine's body was jerking with hiccups from crying so much, and Layla's eyes were puffy from crying. I climbed between them and held them until we all fell asleep.

I was woken up by Nadine screams. "I want my Mommy! I want my real Mommy!" She was fighting furiously with something in her dreams, kicking off the covers.

"Mommy's here, honey," I whispered to her. "Mommy's right here." She pushed me away until she opened her eyes, putting her little arms around my neck, placing my head on her chest.

Her nightmare scared me to my very core and I hugged them both praying, "God, please get us out of here."

That night I checked my email after everyone was asleep. Finally, an answer from the embassy:

Dear Kelly,

In answer to your question, we have found that your husband has not put any restrictions on your travel. You are not on the blacklist.

The U.S. Consulate

I looked at the words and a surge of hope lifted me. I thanked them for their answer and signed off.

"Thank You God!" I whispered.

KUWAIT

"But Baba, you promised!" Layla whined, reminding her father of his promise to take us to the beach as a family.

"Okay, okay, I will," he agreed. "Go get ready!"

We drove to a small beach club not far from our home. It was occupied with a few families enjoying the reprieve from this August heat. I wore a long summer dress over a modest one-piece swimsuit and spread our towels under the shade of a tree while the girls ran into the water. I watched Ibrahim take the girls farther out into the sea, both girls shrieking in delight as the waves crashed on them.

Suddenly I saw Layla running toward me holding her thigh. "Mommy, look!" she said pointing to her leg.

"What is it?" I asked.

"Jellyfish. There are tons of them out there and I just got stung!" she said.

"Let me see," I said examining the red spots where the spikes had penetrated.

Ibrahim came back with red marks on his legs also. "Everyone is getting stung out there," he said. I looked over and saw swimmers pulling out dead carcasses of huge jellyfish onto the sand. Children were stabbing them with sticks.

He left to get something to eat for us and brought it back. The girls ran off to build a sandcastle while he sat next to me smoking a cigar, wearing my Ray Bans.

"Well, my father is going to go back to Kuwait now and everyone is suggesting that I go with him to look for a job," he told me.

"What about the medical exam in December?" I asked using my hand as a shield from the sun to look at him.

"I am still going to take that exam," he explained. "It's just that my family thinks I can find a job in an America hospital in Kuwait or United Arab Emirates as a physician."

"So now you want to move to Kuwait?" I asked. "But it is

238

dangerous." I panicked. Kuwait had almost a 100% Muslim population with just a few Christians and Hindus and I would have a zero percent chance of escaping there.

"Dangerous?" he asked. "What do you mean?"

"Salam told me that it is dangerous for women. There have been many incidences of women found dead in the desert after being raped. Even boys have to be careful," I explained.

"She exaggerates," he replied.

"I am going to check it out for myself," he said.

A new plan was forming in my mind. "You aren't taking us with you?"

"No, I can't," he explained. "I can't afford it, and I need to concentrate on finding a job. The girls start school soon anyway."

"What school?" I asked.

"The same school Aisha's children go to," he answered.

"Uh-huh," I said. "So how long would you be gone?"

"Just three to four weeks, enough time to put out resumes and make contacts and hopefully have interviews," he answered.

"Well, it looks like you're going no matter what," I answered pretending to be sad. "But I am sure that we will be fine here with your mother and your brother Mohammed." The wheels in my head were turning.

"Yes, and if you need anything, they will be there for you," he said. He leaned back in his chair, with his shades on, puffing on his cigar. "You know, all of these things that have happened to me are unfair, but Allah sees. He sees it all. He knows what happened. He knows I am the victim."

I felt sick to my stomach listening to him cast himself as a victim but I put on my poker face and hid my thoughts as he continued to lament the unfairness of America.

Nadine ran back and forth now with her pink sand pail, throwing water on my arms. She shrieked with laughter as I pretended to be surprised every time.

"You know that my parents aren't accepting you," he said.

"I know," I said cautiously. "You told me already."

"I guess people can only accept so much, and their generation has a hard time with me being married to you," he said. "Well, be ready. Be ready for anything to happen."

I felt my arms bristle. I couldn't tell whether he was mocking me or warning me.

I thought angrily, "*A loving husband would hold me right now and tell me he didn't care what anyone thought, that he would always love me no matter what anyone said.*"

"Yes, my dear husband," I whispered to myself. "I will be ready, more than you realize."

FIRST ESCAPE PLAN

That night I sent an email to my father mentioning my plans to leave. Ibrahim would be leaving soon, taking his briefcase with him and our passports would be going with him. I needed to know if and how we could travel without them.

> Dear Dad,
>
> Can you do me a favor and check to see if the girls and I can travel without our US Passports? Be careful though, and don't call me and only write back to this email address.
>
> Love, Kelly

The next morning I received an email from my father.

> Kelly,
>
> Passports? What is going on? Why just for you and the girls? Where are your U.S. passports? I'll call and find out immediately. Talk to me.
>
> Love, Dad.

My father wrote back the next time I checked my emails.

> Kelly,
>
> Get replacement passports from the embassy. All you have to do is say you lost them. We are praying for you, as are a lot of people.
>
> Dad

The next few days, I worked diligently, preparing Ibrahim's resume to impress prospective employers. This task gave me an excuse to spend a lot of time on the computer, so he wouldn't become suspicious. Once when I was reading a letter from my father, the computer screen froze on me, just as I heard Ibrahim walking in the door. I jumped up from my seat and pulled the plug directly from the wall, and scrambled to my chair just as he walked in.

"Darn surges," I muttered, as he came and stood behind me.

"I know," he agreed. "This will never happen in Kuwait. How are my resumes coming?"

"Great. Just great," I said, pushing the reset button on the computer. "If only this computer would just behave."

Later I wrote to my parents:

Dear Dad & Mom,

I need to tell you what is going on. It's very simple actually - I won't live here and he wants to. He has changed and won't let us return to America. I am being very careful. He is going to Kuwait to look for jobs and will be taking his briefcase with our passports. It will be easier to leave while he is gone, but I contacted the embassy like you said and they told me it would take 1 to 3 months to get new passports.

I am thinking of leaving while he is still here, telling him I am going to the American Wives Club and won't be back until late afternoon. Then we could drive to the airport and take off. Please don't panic. I am panicking enough for all of us, believe me, but keeping my cool somewhat. Already checked to see if he put a stop on our travel - which he hasn't. I am devising a plan so please pray.

Love, Kelly

I knew that this letter would be any parents' worst nightmare: their daughter and only grandchildren being held against their will in a foreign country, but time was running out. I had to let them know the situation we were in now, because I might have to activate my plan on a day's notice. Ibrahim was leaving in a week.

Then an unexpected turn of events gave me another idea. That weekend, the chauffeur's nephew was getting married in southern Lebanon, and he had invited the whole family. The entire village would turn out, and it was going to be an all-night celebration. Ibrahim's family was going to spend the night there and come back Saturday morning.

Ibrahim told me that Layla and Nadine were invited also, so I immediately spoke to the girls.

"Baba is going to tell you to go to a wedding this weekend, and I want you to tell him no," I told the girls.

"But I love weddings," Layla said. "Why don't you want me to go?"

I couldn't risk telling them my plans yet, not even Layla.

"Because you will have to spend the night over there in a strange bed, and you think this house has cockroaches, that house is full of them," I answered quickly.

"Oh, okay," she said, half believing me.

I paused, wondering if I should tell her the truth: that we might have to leave at a moment's notice, but this kind of information would only put her in harm's way, and I couldn't risk jeopardizing our safety. I had to make sure that he was going to the wedding with his parents.

"Do you need me to pack you an overnight bag for this weekend?" I asked him as casually as I could.

"For what?" he asked, frowning.

"The wedding this weekend?" I answered.

"Oh, that," he sniffed. "I've decided I'm not going. I don't even know why my parents are going."

"Oh, of course, you are right in not going," I answered politely. My face did not betray the deep sense of disappointment I felt at this news. I had no time to waste but had to focus on finding another opportunity to leave.

Part X   An Open Door

"So do not fear, for I am with you; do not be dismayed,
for I am your God.
I will strengthen you and help you;
I will uphold you with my righteous right hand."
Isaiah 41:10

SEEDS OF DOUBT

It was the first week of September 2002. I only had one week before he was leaving for Kuwait, and with him, our passports. I heard Tweety chirping louder than normal that morning, so I walked toward her cage. She was responding to the sounds of the other birds outside, and she hopped from one side of the cage to the other, trying to escape and join them.

I leaned over and tried to soothe her. I hated to see any bird in a cage but this was worse. She was not used to these bars that confined her - she knew what it was like to fly, to soar, and she obviously missed it. She was not like the other domesticated birds born in captivity who knew nothing else. She knew what she was created to be and what her wings were for, and she longed to escape back to the freedom she once had.

"You never give up do you?" I said to her, kneeling down to her level.

Tweety tilted her head and fixated one tiny black eye at me, chirping sadly, her little chest heaving. Layla and Nadine saw me and ran over to see what I was doing.

"Can we let her out Mommy?" Nadine asked.

I was about to say no, but I paused. "You know what? Good idea Nadine. Let's set her free." I replied.

Layla raised her eyebrows in surprise and said, "Really Mommy, are you sure?"

"Free! Free! Let's set her free!" Nadine squealed in delight, dancing around the cage.

I opened the sliding glass door to the outside and put the cage in front of it. I opened her door and we waited for her to fly away.

"Fly! Tweety! Fly!" Nadine and Layla squealed, encouraging her by flapping their arms up and down.

Suddenly the front door slammed shut. It was Ibrahim. We turned around in fright.

"What are you guys doing?" he asked.

"We're letting Tweety free, Baba," Layla said excitedly running up to him.

"What?" he roared. "What's the matter with you?" He walked over quickly and grabbed the cage, slamming the door shut.

"Basaam gave this to us as a gift!" he said.

"But he gave it to me," Layla pleaded. "And I want her to go free."

"It's our bird!" Nadine yelled at him, reaching furiously for the cage, trying to take it away from him as he held it just above her reach. Tweety was shrieking, thrashing about in the cage as she was being fought over.

"If you don't want her, I am going to give her back to Basaam!" he said walking to the front door, still clutching the cage in his hands. He slammed the door.

"Go stop him Mama!" Nadine said now crying.

"I can't, baby, I can't," I said, softly crying.

Layla walked over to me and hugged me, "It's okay, Mommy. It's okay," she said.

"I couldn't even free their bird," I thought bitterly. *"How am I going to get my little birds out of here?"*

Ibrahim came back quickly. "Yallah!" Let's go! Everyone in the car!" he ordered.

"Go where?" I asked.

"Shopping," he answered. "I need to buy you enough food to last two or three weeks."

The day before he was leaving all I could think was any chance to escape would soon be gone with him in that briefcase. For the first time I faced the dark reality that we might never be free. I was trapped, and there was nothing I could do about it. He noticed my sadness and mistook my tears of hopelessness for sorrow at his leaving.

"Don't worry, my mother will be here, and Mohammed is always downstairs," he said. "You are in good hands."

I nodded somberly as I watched him model suits for his interviews, asking for my advice as I helped him pack. I eyed him closely as he took his silver briefcase from the back of his closet. He pulled out our U.S. passports and a few papers in Arabic and handed them to me. I looked up at him, surprised.

"These are for the girls. They need these to enroll them at the new school," he explained. "Oh! And don't forget this!" he said, grabbing the Lebanese passports for the girls, placing them in my hands. "They will probably need both just in case. Keep them in a safe place, and don't lose them."

I tried to hide the surge of hope now rising within me.

"Layla is scheduled to take an entrance exam next week," he continued. "She won't be accepted unless she passes."

I hid my trembling hands. "What day next week?" I asked.

"On Wednesday, at 9 o'clock," he answered. "You must not be late. And don't forget to go to the front office and have them copy all of these passports I gave you."

"Am I driving?" I asked hopefully.

"No, Mohammed will drive you," he answered. He brought in his duffle bag to fill with his toiletries.

My mind went into overdrive. "Mohammed can't drive us," I said. "He leaves for work early in the morning and doesn't return until nine, and Fatima doesn't drive. I just don't want to bother him."

"Well then, the chauffeur will drive you," he said hesitantly.

I knew that Ibrahim did not like the chauffeur, and I had to think quickly to make him feel insecure about another man driving me.

"Oh Basaam?" I said smiling and giggling shyly. "That's better. You know he and I are really getting along now. We talk now whenever we can. He is so intelligent. Maybe I can ask for his advice while you are gone about some things."

My arrow hit its mark. Ibrahim stuck his head out of the bathroom to peer at me, frowning. "Well, I don't know. Let me discuss this with my father."

"If your father disagrees, I understand," I said. "You know I can save everyone the hassle and just drive the girls myself. It's not far, and I know the way," I suggested casually, holding my breath.

"You don't have a driver's license here," he snapped, obviously not liking the idea.

"Neither did you for three months, and you drove," I answered smiling. "I have my American license, and I have yet to see a policeman stop anyone here for traffic violations, but if they did I could show them my American license and just pretend I don't know any better."

"No, no," he said shaking his head. "I don't like it."

"Yeah, you are probably, right," I backed down immediately. "I don't want to cause any trouble. Basaam will be just fine. In fact, I feel very protected with him around. I know he will take good care of me." I walked casually into the kitchen letting my words linger with him, hoping seeds of doubt were planted in his mind.

LAST GOODBYE

It was a sleepless night. I vacillated between hope and fear. I had the passports but I was still locked in my own home forbidden to drive. I prayed all night that God would deliver us, begging Him to convince my husband to let me drive.

The next morning I jumped out of bed early, showered and put make up on, fixed my hair and looked as attractive as I could. After breakfast we carried Ibrahim's things downstairs to the courtyard where Basaam was waiting, smoking a cigarette.

"Go ahead and put my suitcases in our car," Ibrahim ordered me. I obeyed, picking one of them up, and just as I opened our trunk, Basaam approached me.

"Shoo amtamli?" (What are you doing? he asked me. "Huta hayda, (Put them over there)." He pointed to Abu Ali's car. I smiled and said, "Okay."

Ibrahim was watching this exchange and glared darkly at Basaam. He didn't like the way the chauffeur was ordering his wife around. "Leave them there," he said to me. "Wait for my father." I put down the suitcase and went to sit with my husband.

When Abu Ali came down to the courtyard Ibrahim immediately walked over to his father, pulling him aside. I watched as he discussed something in Arabic with him. I saw his father lurch back and shake his head no, but Ibrahim kept talking, leaning forward as if he wasn't giving up on convincing him of something. After about ten minutes, Ibrahim came back to me and said, "Put the suitcases in our car. My father says that you will be allowed to drive the girls to school."

I immediately did as I was told, every cell in my body wanting to sing out with gladness, but I remained calm. Ibrahim drove our car behind Abu Ali and the chauffeur all the way to the airport. I stayed alert, paying close attention to landmarks as we drove.

While Ibrahim checked his bags, my father-in-law stood beside me, his hands clasped behind his back watching people. He was troubled about something and turned to address me.

"I am friend too much with the top man here," he said in broken English, touching his chest importantly, his one bad eye ogling me.

"Abu Ali has many friends in top places," I said, nodding my head.

"Yes, he is very high, the top, top man here! He is my friend too much this man!" he repeated.

It struck me that with my newfound freedom he was worried and was giving me warning that he had connections here at the airport. I pretended not to understand, feigning ignorance. "Abu Ali is a very important man," I said smiling. "Lucky man who knows Abu Ali."

I turned my attention back to Nadine who was playing a game of cat and mouse with one of the security guards. She kept teasing him by running over the security line only to have him order her back. With a sly little grin, she put her toe over the line and then would run back, laughing.

Ibrahim walked over to us and bid farewell to his father and made plans to meet him in Kuwait the next day. Abu Ali was leaving tomorrow and would join him then. We still had an hour to wait, so we walked downstairs to the café. He gave Layla some money to get her and Nadine a doughnut. As we sat down he handed me a hundred dollars.

"Remember, Layla has to take a test next Wednesday at nine o'clock and she needs to be there on time. Otherwise she won't be accepted," he warned me. "Nadine will be in pre-school there so it isn't a problem."

"I understand," I said, nodding my head.

"School will start a week before I return, so you will have to drive them for that week," he continued. "But there is a very important rule you must follow. Before you leave the house to take them to school, you must check in with my mother so she knows when you left and when to expect you back. You must do this so she doesn't worry."

"Of course," I said. "Don't worry. I can handle this," I assured him. "I will check in with your mother as you ask."

He handed me the car keys and said, "I will call you to check in on you and see how you are doing," he said, pushing his chair away from the table. It was time to board. "Well, I better get going. Come, I will walk all of you to the door."

I rounded up the girls to bid their farewells. We stood in front of the blue-tinted windows of the exit doors. He bent down to give the girls a kiss goodbye. Layla hugged him and Nadine wiped his kiss off and reached up for me to hold her. With Nadine on my hip, I waited for him to kiss me goodbye and leaned my face toward his. He looked nervously around, as though embarrassed, and pulled away from me not allowing me to kiss him.

"*Perfect,*" I thought, bitterly.

We walked away, our back to the airport as he watched us walk to the car. Layla turned around to wave goodbye to him, but I kept walking forward and never looked back.

When I put the keys in the ignition and started the car's engine I felt empowered. It had been almost a year since I had driven.

Nadine looked surprised. "Mommy, you can drive?" she asked.

"You better believe it baby," I answered. "Most of my life honey – since I was fourteen."

I drove home carefully, and as I pulled into the driveway of our building I saw Basaam waiting in the courtyard, sitting at a table, drinking tea with his wife. I smiled politely as we walked past them and waved hello, but Basaam just stared darkly at me, frowning, and took another drag on his cigarette.

LAYLA'S CHOICE

Once inside our apartment I jumped for joy. Yesterday I was a prisoner without any hope of leaving. Today I had the passports and the keys to the car. My prayers were being answered.

"What do you girls want for dinner tonight?" I asked.

"Tuna fish casserole Mommy, please!" Layla asked.

"Yes, tuna fish casserole it is!" I said. "Tonight we eat what we want!"

"Can we listen to The Little Mermaid tape?" Layla asked excitedly. Ibrahim frowned on any American music, even Disney.

"Of course we can! No one is here to tell us we can't!" I exclaimed happily.

I brought the CD player into the kitchen and plugged it in. We danced around the kitchen in a conga line to Sebastian the crab singing.

We were giddy with freedom from strict rules and regulations.

The next day I emailed the U.S. Consulate and told her the truth; that I had been held prisoner by my husband, and that he would never allow us to return to America, and I wanted to know how I could leave.

I received an email back:

Dear Kelly,

If you are thinking about leaving, you need to do it immediately. Please do not hesitate. Do you have any family in the U.S. who can buy the tickets for you?

Sincerely,

The U.S. Consulate

This was harder than I thought it was going to be. Somehow I had the idea that as an American citizen I was protected, and that an employee could just drive to our building and drive us to the airport, tickets in hand. This was real now. I needed to make a plan and let Layla know what was going on. I took her aside into the bedroom alone. I wasn't sure if she would be on the same page as me, so I tested her first.

"Layla, we have to take you to school next week so you can take an entrance exam," I began.

"What? What school?" she asked giving me a hurtful look.

"Jasmine and Farah's school," I replied.

Unexpectedly, she burst into tears. "But I don't want to go to school there! I don't want to! I will have to wear a scarf and it is a Muslim school!" she said. "You promised that we were going back to America!"

"You don't want to go to school or stay here any longer?" I asked her, happy at her response.

"If I stay here one more year, I will die!" she yelled at me. She looked at me accusingly, "You lied to me!"

I was happy to hear this. "It's okay, honey," I said looking into her tear-stained face, flushed red from her emotional outburst. "We are going home. You do not have to go to school here. We are going back to America!"

"Really?" she asked. "What do you mean?" She stopped crying and rubbed her eyes with her sleeve.

"We are going to leave here with some help," I said. "But no one can know about it, not even your sister. She is too little and might tell everyone. We are going to escape, my love, we are going back home!"

"We are?" she asked, her voice rising with hope. "When Baba gets back?"

It was too late. I couldn't retract my words. "Baba is not coming with us, Layla," I said holding her shoulders. "He said he would never go back to America."

Slowly, the realization of what I was saying seemed to sink in. Her countenance changed from one of joyous expectation to one of terrified apprehension.

"But what about Baba?" she asked. "Won't he be mad if we leave without him?"

"Honey, I don't care if he is furious," I answered her strongly. "I will not be held prisoner in my own home, watched constantly. I won't have my daughters forced to become Muslims against their will. I don't want this life for you and Nadine, dominated and controlled by men who see it as their right to treat you like possessions, like servants!"

"So you two will divorce?" she said quietly.

"Yes, we will," I said anxiously.

"I knew this was going to happen," she said sadly wiping away a tear. "I knew it wouldn't last. I knew he didn't love you." I was startled by her words, surprised that a child saw what took me so long to realize.

"I need to know if this is what you want too?" I asked. "I need your help."

I realized that having all of this information thrown at her was overwhelming for child of nine years old, but I believed she deserved to know the truth. Divorce was an ugly word to hear for any child, no matter what kind of home they had. I waited patiently for her to respond and she motioned for me to sit next to her on the bed.

"Baba is mean to you, isn't he?" she asked. Her question caught me off guard. I had been so good at covering up his abuse to protect them, explaining noises in the bedroom as accidents or using makeup to cover bruises that I thought she had no idea.

"Yes, he is," I answered.

"I know he is always yelling at you and calls you an idiot, but what else has he done?" she asked.

"Many things that I have kept secret," I whispered.

"Tell me," she asked. "Tell me everything."

She wanted me to tell her things about her father no one knew but me. I told her a few stories that she didn't know about and she asked for more. I told her enough for her age, and it hurt me to divulge these stories to my daughter.

"But why did you stay when he hurt you so much Mommy?" she asked.

Her question caught me by surprise. "Because I believed that he would change and that I had no choice," I told her truthfully. "I thought that it was my place to offer up all of this suffering for him. I thought that by now things would be different, but they only got worse. And I couldn't bear the thought of losing both of you."

"But it's not right that he hurts you, Mommy," she said, speaking the truth to me.

I looked into her big sad eyes and said, "You're right baby, It's not."

Here all these years I thought that I was doing the right thing, staying with an abusive man for the sake of my daughters, but I saw now that even she at nine years old knew that it was wrong for me to stay. She could see that I deserved more - that I wasn't created to live a life of sorrow at the hands of a man who despised me. I put my head in my hands and just wept.

"I am with you Mommy," she said putting her little arms around me. "I am with you."

REVENGE

The morning of Layla's exam I rose early. I was aware that this was my first trip in the car to show everyone that I could be trusted. Before we left, we walked upstairs together to check in with my mother-in-law. After receiving her blessing we drove to the school. I gave the school office the passports and papers that Ibrahim had given me and waited until they took copies of each. After registering both daughters, Layla took her test. After she finished, we drove home, dutifully checking in with Amu Ali. So far so good. The next part of my plan was to make my mother-in-law comfortable with me driving the car for small errands.

In the morning I told Layla to run upstairs and tell her grandmother that we needed to run to the store to buy milk for Nadine and that we would be right back.

We lingered at the neighborhood grocery store and returned home thirty minutes later immediately knocking on my mother-in-law's door to let her know we returned. She seemed satisfied. I made it a point to drive to the grocery store almost every day asking my mother-in-law if she needed anything.

One day Hala invited us to join her and her children for a picnic. I knew that she was still not on any speaking terms with my mother-in-law and I didn't want to make my mother-in-law mad at me, so I declined. Ibrahim called me from Kuwait that evening telling me that Hala was complaining to her husband that I refused her invitation. He told me to go with her to please his brother. I went upstairs with Layla to explain to Amu Ali what my husband's wishes were. She wasn't happy about me going with her enemy, but because her son wanted it, she grudgingly agreed.

The next morning, Hala drove up to our building, honking her horn but before we went with her we ran upstairs to say goodbye to Amu Ali. Hala was not allowed even in the courtyard so she waited patiently while I backed out my car and pulled in behind her.

"Kelly!" she exclaimed. "I am so happy to see you! I am sorry we all can't fit in one car, but my mother is with me and I had to bring Sandra. Just stay close to me and follow me."

"No problem," I answered. "I am happy to drive actually."

We drove about a half an hour, up winding hills and stopped at a picnic area near a grove of pine trees on the crest of a hill. When I saw Sandra we exchanged knowing glances as I stared at the long pink scar on her forearm. Sandra made a fire and prepared dinner for us. I felt uncomfortable having her wait on us.

After dinner our children ran off to explore. Hala and I sat together, drinking coffee and talking until the shadows of the trees lengthened and the warm afternoon breeze turned cold. We finally packed up the cars and meandered slowly back down the mountain. By the time we arrived home, it was already dark.

As I pulled in the driveway, a whole entourage of my husband's family was sitting in the courtyard: Mohammed and his family, Basaam and his family, and Salam with her sons and Amu Ali. Mohammed was pacing nervously, talking on his cell phone. Oblivious that I was the reason for their gathering, I walked over to them to say hello.

Salam saw me first and ran to me. "Habebti, Kelly!" she said, relieved. "Where were you?"

"I was with Hala and her family," I said quickly. "I told Amu Ali – she saw us leave."

"Habebti, we were so worried about you," she said. "You are late."

"I am so sorry," I said. "We didn't realize how late it was."

I walked over to Amu Ali to apologize but she was glaring furiously at me. I averted my eyes and kissed her on both cheeks while she pouted like a hurt child and sniffed. I sat with them for a while, and told them about our picnic, apologizing over and over. Amu Ali asked Salam to translate for her while she asked questions about Hala. I gave her pat, bland answers, not wanting to start any arguments between these two strong women.

Finally, frustrated with my answers, she rose to go back upstairs. I followed behind her, motioning for Layla and Nadine to come with us. The four of us rode the elevator up together, in an awkward silence. The elevator stopped on the fourth floor and as we walked her to her door and kissed her goodnight, her dark eyes lingered on me, wavering angrily as if to say, "I am watching you."

I was to pay for the crime of being out late. Amu Ali complained to my husband and he called me.

"My mother was worried about you and the girls," he admonished me. "This is not good for her health!"

"I am so sorry," I said. "It will not happen again, but I was just doing as you asked me to do, going with Hala for your brother's sake."

"From now on, I do not want you to take the girls out this late anymore," he said firmly."

I bit my tongue as I listened to his chiding, furious that this picnic almost cost me my right to drive. Amu Ali was not on my side and she was jealous of the fact I had more freedoms than her husband allowed her. She was furious that I had gone out with Hala and was now wreaking her revenge on me.

MATH EXAM

I knew I had better act quickly before any more freedoms were taken away from me so the next day I put my plan to action. It seemed easy at first: I had the car, the passports, I was not on the blacklist and my parents could buy the plane tickets but I was worried about someone recognizing me at the airport. I also recalled from my conversations with the women in the American Wives Club that I couldn't leave the country with my children alone unless I had a document signed by my husband giving me permission. So I emailed the U.S. embassy:

> Dear U.S. Consulate,
>
> I am about to have my parents buy the tickets. I just have one concern: I know that I am not on the blacklist, but I am afraid that I will be stopped at the airport without a document allowing me to travel alone with the girls.
>
> Sincerely,
>
> Kelly

The U.S. Consulate emailed me within the hour:

> Dear Kelly,
>
> Do not worry about this. We will be there to escort you through security checkpoints. With us there, you won't need this paper.
>
> Sincerely,
>
> U.S. Consulate

When I got off the computer I felt better but I now needed to choose a day that would draw the least attention. The longest I had been gone to the grocery store was almost an hour and now I was forbidden to leave in the late afternoon so I had to pick a day with a flight leaving in the morning, but which one?

That night I couldn't sleep. I lay awake wondering how I was going to pull this off without drawing suspicion. Then, like an unexpected gift, I received a phone call the next morning from the girls' future school.

"Mademoiselle Kelly?" It was the secretary.

"Yes?"

"I am calling to inform you that Layla did not pass her Math exam and we would like to discuss this with you," she said.

"Certainly," I replied.

"Could you come meet with us tomorrow?" she asked.

"Of course, I will be there," I replied.

I called Ibrahim to tell him to relay this information to his mother so I could go.

The President received us into her office to discuss Layla's exam. After I looked it over I realized what the problem was immediately. On the addition problems, instead of using commas to show the place value for a thousand, the school used a blank. 10,000 was written as 10 000. She shared my analysis but still insisted on her taking another exam. We scheduled this for the following Monday at eight a.m. September 16th, 2002. I had my departure date.

I immediately emailed my parents when I arrived home:

Dear Dad,

I need you to look into airline tickets leaving Beirut, September 16th. Please let me know what you find.

Love, Kelly

He responded immediately:

Dear Kelly,

Do you need four tickets round trip? Talk to me.

Love Dad

I responded:

Dear Dad,

Just 3 tickets one way for the girls and me. Ibrahim will not be coming with us. I am leaving him while he is gone in Kuwait. I can't explain everything right now but I am in contact with the U.S. Embassy. You can secure the money with the embassy for the tickets and they will make sure we get on the plane.

They have your information and will be contacting you.

Love, Kelly

Later that day I checked my emails and my father had written back:

Dear Kelly,

British Air leaves Beirut at 9:45 every morning and arrives in London at 1 p.m. Then you can take a flight from there to Chicago then Boise. How does this sound? When is Ibrahim supposed to be back?

Love Dad

I immediately wrote back:

Dear Dad,

Sounds good. Please buy three tickets for this coming Monday, September 16th.

Layla is supposed to take a test at 8:00 a.m. so his family will think that we are at the school. He isn't expected back until October 5th, but he could come home sooner.

Please pray for us.

Love, Kelly

COWARDS

It was September 11, 2002, and Salam had invited us over for lunch with her sons. The TV played in the background while we ate lunch in her living room. It was the one-year anniversary of the 9/11 attacks and BBC News was showing excerpts from the terrorist attack on the Twin Towers of the World Trade Center. I watched as they showed the planes flying into the buildings and the devastation that followed.

"What do you think of this?" I asked one of Salam's sons as I pointed to the TV.

"I think they are courageous," he said proudly.

My mouth fell open but I thought he misunderstood. "Courageous?" I asked. "I think the word you are looking for is cowardly?"

"Maybe I am saying the wrong word in English," he began. "I am trying to say that these men had no fear. To take a plane like this and crash it into a building knowing that you are going to die, that took a lot of guts!" he exclaimed smiling.

"These men were not courageous," I said my voice rising higher. "These men were cowards. Anyone can take a life – the men who risked their lives like the firemen who died trying to save those people – they were courageous. They were the heroes!"

The room became uncomfortably silent. Salam smiled politely and told her son to change the channel. She went to the kitchen and the boys changed the subject, talking about the scuba diving they had done the day before. As I looked at my nephews I felt shocked by their last words about their 'heroes' of 9/11. They were highly educated Lebanese young men, studying hard subjects in Engineering and Science. They were well traveled throughout Europe and dressed modernly and spoke fluent English. My hope that this newer generation was not tainted with the prejudices and hatred for America plummeted. They followed the same ideology as their religious leaders who only saw Sharia law as the law to follow in any country.

I had always prided myself on my ability to get along with people from all walks of life. I had believed that people everywhere all had the same basic ideology as I did. This naïve altruistic outlook now came crashing down around me just as the towers on the television had. It was hard for me to comprehend that anyone could believe that in any way shape or form that the Al-Qaeda terrorists who killed more than 3,000 innocent civilians (at least 18 were American Muslims)[19] was a courageous act.

I could no longer naively believe that our ideologies were just different versions of the same thing. Maybe it was because I was a woman raising two daughters that I saw the world differently than these men, or maybe it was because after fourteen years of trying to understand and love a man who only saw me as a kifir, an unbeliever, a piece of property, I realized that I would never change his mind. I was angry because I knew I was much more than this, and so were my daughters. I knew intrinsically, deep down that I was created for so much more than to please a man. I believed in a loving Father who cherished me and loved me just as much as He loved his sons.

As I watched Salam humbly serving her sons I thought back to every home we had visited here replaying the same scene: women running around submissively serving the men of the family. Not once did I see a Muslim man prepare and serve the meals, pour tea or wait on the women. Not once did I see any man get up to help with the dishes, or insist that their wife sit while they waited on the company. The more important the man in the family, the more he was waited on. I thought about how the most important Man who ever lived waited on his disciples, humbly washing their feet at the Last Supper, showing them how real men serve others.

The doorbell rang. It was Amu Ali arriving with Salam's other son Mehde. I quickly jumped up to welcome her; thankful that her arrival had interrupted what could have been a volatile discussion.

A CLOSE CALL

It was time to pack. Layla knew the plan. We were going to pretend to go to her school Monday morning to take an exam, but instead drive to the airport. We decided to keep this from Nadine who was too young to understand.

After making sure the front door was locked, and all of the blinds were down in the house, I grabbed two small suitcases and began packing what I thought was important – photos and videos of the girls. All of a sudden the phone rang. It was Ibrahim.

"How are you?" I asked him, while Layla sat next to me on the bed.

"Great!" he answered. "I found a job for you in Kuwait."

"You found me a job?" I asked. "I thought you were looking for a job?"

"I am, I am," he answered. "I have an interview on Monday, but I found you a job teaching English at a grade school here."

"So it looks like we are moving to Kuwait?" I asked. "Where would we live?"

"With my parents until we get our own apartment close by," he answered.

I cringed, imagining living with my in-laws in the same apartment, the same in-laws who weren't accepting me. I would be under the thumb of my mother-in-law who hated me.

"Let me talk to the girls," he said.

Layla talked to her father, hiding the fact that we were leaving on Monday, but then Nadine bounced in the room and grabbed the phone from her.

"Hi Baba!" she exclaimed. "Guess what we're doing? We're packing!" I froze in terror as Layla shot me a look of horror. She quickly pulled the phone away from Nadine.

"Hi Baba," she said, laughing and giggling. "What? Oh Nadine? She is just being silly, always playing games." She continued to giggle and quickly changed the subject.

She handed me the phone and said, "He wants to talk to you."

"Okay," he began. "I will call you when I can and…."

I interrupted him, bursting into tears. I knew this would be the last time we spoke.

"I know you miss me," he said. "Just take my photo off the dresser and hug it tonight as you sleep."

"Ibrahim?" I asked.

"Yes?" he said.

"I just hope that your dreams finally do come true, and that you do find a fantastic job," I said sobbing.

"Okay, well go spend time with my mother," he answered. "She is complaining that you never go upstairs to visit her. She wants to take you out for ice cream Sunday night."

"Okay, that would be great," I whispered softly.

"Okay, then, goodbye," he said.

"Goodbye, Ibrahim, goodbye," I whispered.

After I hung up the phone, my body shook uncontrollably. All the previous fourteen years of loving this man came rushing back. I had loved him to the point of my extinction. I had given him everything: my obedience, my fidelity, my love, and my life. I had given up my culture, my country, my family, my freedom, everything. But I refused to give him anymore. I walked over to the dresser, picked up his photograph, and talked to it between heavy sobs.

"I loved you Ibrahim… I loved you so much. I loved you more than I loved myself. But loving you is killing me, and it is killing my daughters."

I placed his picture face down on the dresser and finished packing.

Part XI   Taking Flight

"We have escaped like a bird from the fowler's snare;
the snare has been broken, and we have escaped.
Our help is in the name of the Lord,
The Maker of heaven and earth."
Psalm 124:7-8

A MAD RACE

It was Friday, Islam's holy day, and I woke up to the call of men
wailing from competing mosques. Their voices seemed louder than
normal, and an unsettling sense of foreboding hung over me. I went to
the computer immediately to check my emails. I wasn't prepared for
what I read from the U.S. Embassy.

> Dear Kelly,
>
> We need to have the passports in hand today in order to expedite this for
> your flight on Monday. Can you get them to us today?"
>
> U.S. Consulate

"Can I get them to you today?" I screamed at the computer. "I
don't even know where you are!" I looked at the city in the
correspondence – it was from Junea which was a good hour and half
away.

265

Dear Consulate,

No one can get the passports to you but me. I have no one here that I can trust. I will try and see what I can do.

Kelly

    I panicked. Today Salam was coming by at 2 pm to say goodbye before she returned to Kuwait. I needed to get these passports to the embassy before then.
    I immediately emailed my Dad and told him my dilemma, explaining to him that there was no way I could drive to the U.S. Embassy. I did not know how to get there and it would be a three-hour round trip.
    My father wrote back telling me that he called his Christian Lebanese friend to see what he suggested. His friend offered to call some of his extended family members who lived in Beirut, and see if one of them could meet me at the local grocery store. The plan was to hand one of them the passports so they could take them to the U.S. embassy for me. I was relieved and thankful; this was perfect. I waited by my computer watching my inbox, hitting the reset button over and over, anxious to hear which grocery store I should go to and what time to meet them.
    I watched the clock nervously, waiting for a response. Finally, I emailed my dad and asked what was taking so long. His response hit me in the gut, hard.

I'm sorry Kel,

But it looks like they can't meet you. They are too afraid that after you leave they will find out who helped you escape and they don't want to endanger their family.

Not sure what to do now.   Love, Dad

    "What?" I screamed at his message. "They can't help me? What am I going to do?"
    My daughters turned their heads in my direction, sensing something was wrong.
    "What's wrong, Mommy?" Layla asked.

"Cowards, that's what!" I said angrily to her, but then reminded myself that in this country, they were right. They had every reason to be afraid.

I had to make a decision. I realized at that point that no one was going to come and rescue me. No one. There was no white knight in shining armor on a white horse. I turned to the Lord, my God and cried out, "Lord, I need your help! I cannot do this on my own! Please help me!" Suddenly, a new sense of strength rose within me, as if a protective shield now encompassed me. I knew I was not alone.

"Come on, hurry up!" I directed the girls. "Get your shoes on. We're going to the store! Layla go up and tell Teta (your grandmother) we are going to the grocery store! Hurry!"

I knew this would buy us some time, but not much. I threw all the passports in my purse as well as my temporary residency card and we raced down the stairs and climbed in the car. I raced to the freeway. It was 10:45 am. I had three hours before anyone would become suspicious.

I drove like a madman down the freeway, out-speeding men who tailed my bumper to punish me for passing them. I didn't care. I drove even faster; thankful for the first time this country had hardly any traffic lights or policemen to stop us.

I remembered our one trip to Junea when my husband mentioned that the U.S. Embassy was behind a French grocery store off the main highway. The highway went straight into Beirut before exiting for Junea though, so when I neared Beirut, I guessed and took the wrong exit. We somehow ended up in the middle of downtown Beirut.

"Oh my God! I took the wrong exit!" I said. "Never mind, I'll find the way," I assured the girls.

The traffic slowed, and I took another wrong turn that brought us to a narrow alley where only a single car could squeeze by the parked cars on either side. I felt trapped, lost, constricted on every side. I took another turn veering right toward a busy road, but again it led me toward the Hamra area away from Junea. I was totally lost.

"God please help us," I cried out.

Suddenly I saw a wizened old man with a white beard stooping over on the side of the curb, watching me intently. I slowed down, and rolled down my window.

"Btismahli, y haj, Anna baddi ruhh a Junea (Excuse me, one who has been to haj, but I want to go to Junea)," I said in my broken Arabic.

He came closer and peered in the car, looking at my daughters. "Junea?" he repeated.

"Naam, Junea (Yes, Junea)," I repeated, smiling.

"Junea ktiir baad! (Junea is very far from here!)," he exclaimed, pointing the way with his weathered hands.

"Baraf, bass laazam (I know, but it is necessary)," I said hoping I made sense.

He pointed up ahead, talking slowly to me, telling me I needed to go down and take the second right and it would take me directly to the main highway toward Junea.

"Shukran! Shukran! (Thank you! Thank you!) I said driving away. I saw him waving in my rearview mirror, watching me.

Soon we were on the main highway, the sea on our left. I pressed on the gas and we flew. We drove for what seemed an eternity. It was now 11:30 am.

"What are we looking for?" Layla asked, knowing what was at stake.

"The French grocery store," I told her. "Look for a giant red grocery cart filled with huge cartons of milk and eggs."

Layla spotted the huge landmark and pointed it out to me. I drove into the parking lot and found a small narrow road behind it that lead up an incline, forking into two different directions. I chose the right one and soon we spotted a concrete building with metal gates, two men standing guard. There was no American flag, so I drove right by it. The road dead-ended and I passed by the building again, eyeing the soldiers who were watching me carefully. They were tall, Arab men wearing tan military uniforms.

"Maybe they can help me," I told the girls. We parked and approached them.

"Hello, um, do you speak English?" I asked nervously.

"Yes, we do," one soldier responded.

"Can you tell me what building this is?" I asked.

"This is the American Embassy, Madame," he answered.

My heart skipped a beat. "Well, I am here to see someone," I told them.

I gave them the person's name and they had us pass through a metal detector before walking down a narrow sidewalk into a small building. We entered a tiny waiting room with a few folding chairs. A man sat behind a bulletproof window staring at me. I walked up to the counter.

"What is your purpose here, Madame?" he asked.

"I am here to give our passports to an American Consulate," I said repeating her name.

"She is not here right now, but you can leave them with us and we will make sure that she receives them," he said.

I didn't trust him. The other men were now behind him staring at me seriously. What proof did I have that this really was the American embassy? What if this was just a Lebanese government office and they would soon be calling my husband's family to tell them of my intention to flee?

"No, I don't want to leave these with you," I said. "I want to speak to the American Consulate."

They looked at each other and one spoke, "We will call her. Answer the phone if it rings."

Ten minutes later the phone rang. I picked up the receiver.

"Hello?"

"Hello, Kelly?" She answered. I recognized her voice.

"Hi, I am here with our passports as you asked and I want to hand them to you," I said.

"Don't worry, I will be right there," she said.

Fifteen minutes, twenty minutes passed and then I saw her rush into the room. She hugged me. "Good for you! You made it!" she said. "And these must be your beautiful daughters!" She took turns kissing my girls on their cheeks.

I handed her our U.S. passports and my temporary residency card. I felt so relieved that she was real and that she was helping me. "Thank you," I said, tears in my eyes. "Thank you."

"Your flight will leave at 9:45 am Monday morning," she told me. "Can you be there at 8:00 am to check in?"

"Yes," I answered. "We will be there at 8:00 am."

"Okay, but in the meantime please be careful," she warned me.

"I will," I said. "Thank you for everything."

We walked back through the gates and into our car. It was 1:30 pm already. Salam would be arriving at 2 pm. I had to hurry. I sped off in the car back down the highway and raced against the wave of traffic, swerving in and out of lanes, passing people who were going 90 miles an hour.

Finally, I took the exit to our neighborhood, but then realized I had no groceries to bring into the house. Three hours gone and no groceries would look suspicious. I drove to the neighborhood grocery store and we ran in, grabbed a cart and threw in the biggest items I could find: huge rolls of paper towels and toilet paper, and giant bags of chips, etc. We checked out quickly. I was dripping with sweat and my heart was racing when we pulled in the driveway. I didn't see Salam's car. "*Yes! Thank God she is late!*" I thought. We flew up the stairs and I had Layla check in with Amu Ali.

When she came back down I asked her how Teta seemed. "Fine, she had just finished praying and told me that Aunti Salam would be over soon," she said.

I was too nervous to eat but I fed the girls. I sent an email to my parents, letting them know I had just delivered the passports to the embassy by myself.

When Salam arrived we went down into the courtyard to say goodbye to her. My mother-in-law's maid, Baseera, poured us tea while we conversed quietly. Salam's flight to Kuwait would take off in a few hours and she was waiting for her two sons to drive her to the airport. When she embraced me, she noticed the strained look on my face and mistakenly thought it was because I missed my husband.

"You miss Ibrahim don't you?" she asked.

I choked up, tears escaping my eyes. I felt guilty for what was about to happen but I had to somehow let her know why.

"Talk to me habibti," she said.

"Salam, I need to tell you something," I began. "I need to tell you that things have not been so good between your brother and me. There are things that he has done to me that no one knows about -not even my parents or daughters. I never told anyone because I always protected him…"

Salam's face fell as she heard my words. She put her arms around me, placing her face close to mine, pulling me away from her mother. "Habebti Kelly, we must talk," she whispered. "Not here. Not now. I will call you from Kuwait. Give me a few days and we will talk."

Her sons drove up the driveway and honked the horn. She shot me a worried glance and grabbed her purse, rushed over to her mother to say farewell and gave me one last kiss. As I watched her drive away, still with a worried look on her face, tears streaked my face. I waved goodbye to my best friend in this country, knowing we would never see each other again.

MY REAL MOMMY

I jolted out of bed, running from the dark shadows that were pursuing me. I looked over at my daughters who were sleeping with me and watched Nadine fighting furiously with her own nightmares again.

"No! No!" she screamed, thrashing her arms and legs. "I want my real Mommy!"

It was the same nightmare and it scared me. She had no idea how real this could be. I could be caught trying to escape and then she would have another mother.

It was Saturday. Only two more days until we left. I was too nervous to eat and sipped my third cup of instant coffee that morning. My suitcases were packed and I put each in a big blue garbage bag, tying them at the top. From a distance, they looked like all the other bags of garbage I had put in my trunk to take to the dumpster a few meters away. I just needed an opportunity to put them in the trunk of the car when no one was around. I wanted to take these pictures and videos and I knew that having suitcases would look normal to any airport security, better than traveling without luggage.

I decided to take the girls into the courtyard, pretending to read a book while they played, so I would have a better vantage point to watch the comings and goings of the family. Sometime after noon, Mohammed came downstairs with his wife and children following.

"Ask them where they are going," I whispered to Layla.

"They are going to visit Fatima's mother in her village," she reported back.

This left the chauffeur and Amu Ali. As I sat there mulling over whether I should sneak the suitcases out while they were in the building, I heard the elevator door slam open. Amu Ali walked toward us, her maid behind her.

"Where are they going?" I asked Layla.

"She told me that she is going to the store and will be back in an hour," Layla said.

"Where are the chauffeur's wife and his children?" I asked her.

"They are gone to her home village and won't be back until next week," Layla answered.

After waving goodbye to Amu Ali, I sat in the courtyard alone with my daughters. The impossible had happened. Everyone was gone except us. We quickly raced upstairs and carried the suitcases wrapped in blue garbage bags to the elevator. When we got to the courtyard I had Layla check for an all clear before I opened the door.

I walked casually to the car, holding each bag by the unseen handle and placed them in the trunk of my car. As I shut the trunk I looked up and noticed a man leaning over his balcony in the building next to us watching me. He smiled at us as he smoking his cigarette and waved. I froze and waved back weakly. On the way back up the elevator, my hands started shaking.

"What have I done?" I wailed. "I just jeopardized our safety by wanting to take these things with us! He was watching me the whole time!" I prayed that he would just think they were garbage bags.

MERCY

Sunday, and all was quiet. I busied myself cleaning the house, listening for any noise at the door, half expecting authorities to come arrest me at any minute. The girls noticed my apprehension and tiptoed around me, playing quietly. Every time I heard a strange sound I would admonish them to be quiet. I cleaned the house thoroughly, irrationally wanting to leave an immaculate house before we left.

Early that afternoon I went to check my emails and I couldn't believe what I read:

> Dear Kelly,
>
> The visas on the U.S. passports for you and your children have expired. Your temporary residency card will get you through security, but not the children.
>
> Also, can you tell us the name of the official at the airport your father-in-law said he knows?
>
> Sincerely,
>
> U.S. Consulate

"What?" I gasped, rereading the email over and over again.

"I knew it! I knew it! I can't believe this!" I slammed my fist on the desk. "What am I going to do?" I wrote them back frantically:

> Dear U.S. Consulate,
>
> I have Lebanese passports for the girls and they are current. Will this help?
>
> I do not know the name of the official my father-in-law knows. I have no idea who it could be.
>
> Are we going to call the whole thing off? What should I do? I am bursting into tears at this news!
>
> Kelly

I hit send and sat there waiting, watching my inbox.

"So what was that whole life-threatening drive to the embassy all about?" I thought. *"I had the Lebanese passports with me the whole time. Why didn't they just ask me for them? Do they even know what they are doing?"*

I sat staring at my computer screen for a long time, checking and rechecking my inbox. After an hour I walked in a daze to the couch and lay down, staring up at a bare light bulb dangling above me. I began to laugh hysterically as I recognized the absurdity of the situation. "After all this!" I said out loud. "After all of this careful planning, the visas have expired!" My laughter quickly turned to sobbing.

"Sweet Jesus, please have mercy on us!" I cried. "Please get us out of here!"

I rose to check my inbox again. It read:

Dear Kelly,

Dry your beautiful eyes and don't worry. Just bring the Lebanese passports with you Monday morning and all will be fine.

Your father-in-law was probably playing head games with you. Please don't worry. And please....be very careful.

The U.S. Consulate

I dried my tears, relieved. I heard knocking at the front door and signed off. The girls ran for the door but stopped when they saw me approach and look through the peephole. It was Amu Ali's maid, Baseera. I hesitated.

"Mama!" Layla said. "Remember? Teta is taking us out for booza (ice cream)!"

"Booza?" I answered. "Oh yes, that's right – Ibrahim said she was taking us out tonight."

I opened the door and the girls pulled me into the hallway, excited. I fixed my hair in the elevator mirror. A gaunt, pale face with frightened eyes stared back at me. I didn't look like myself. I had lost so much weight that my clothes hung on me.

Downstairs I greeted Amu Ali politely, kissing her on each cheek. She shifted her shoulders back and sniffed as though taking us out was a great effort on her part. Mehde drove us to an outdoor ice cream parlor where we sat outside listening to Lebanese music. She spoke only to her grandson, ignoring me completely. I found it so ironic that my husband's refusal to enroll me in Arabic classes was the reason we sat here in silence. I would have loved to visit with her all this time, asking her stories about her childhood, her family, my husband but we sat separated by this frustrating language barrier. I told Mehde to remind her that in the morning we had to go take a test at 8 am in the morning.

As soon as the girls ate their last bite of ice cream, my mother-in-law rose from the table. "Yalla, ann tahbani (Let's go! I'm tired)."

We followed her back to the car and after Mehde dropped us off, we rode up the elevator in silence, stopping on her floor first. I knew this would be the last time we would see each other, and I took another look at this woman who found me so unworthy of her son. I gazed upon her tired face and rough chapped hands that belied the hard life she had led. Her breathing was labored and heavy as she avoided my eyes, watching her granddaughters. I knew she would never understand what I was going to do in the morning and I knew it would hurt her deeply. I wished at that moment I could communicate heart-to-heart with her and explain that I didn't want my daughters to follow in her path. I didn't want the life that her daughters Salam and Aisha were forced to live. I knew that my leaving would only reinforce her belief that all Americans were evil and nothing I could ever say would change her mind. A part of me wanted to save her too, save her from this prison but I knew that she was like a domesticated bird that grew up in this cage and to her this prison was her home. She knew nothing else.

I reached out to kiss her warmly on her cheeks and our eyes locked, her dark beautiful Arabian eyes, trembling and sad, met mine, and I forced myself to hold back tears as she kissed her granddaughters goodnight.

FREEDOM

It was Monday morning and the first buzz of the alarm jolted me out of my sleep. It was 5:00 a.m. I lay there frozen in suspense, listening for any stirrings from my mother-in-law up above. Nothing. I rose noiselessly and dressed quickly before I went to wake up Layla. She put on the clothes I had picked out the night before.

"I'm sorry we have to leave everything else behind, honey," I smiled sadly.

"That's okay Mommy," she said. "It doesn't matter." She hugged her favorite stuffed animal, a little white lamb, before putting it in her backpack. I walked over to Nadine's bed to wake her up, but thought better of it when I saw her murmuring angrily in her sleep. I dressed her while she slept and pulled the blankets back over her.

I covered my tracks, and logged onto the computer, making sure every email had been deleted, dumping my recycle bin and changing all of the passwords. I went to the kitchen to fix some coffee just as I heard Nadine's high-pitched wailing. Layla and I ran to her, racing down the hallway. Nadine was in a terrible mood so I held her over my shoulder and rocked her until she stopped crying.

"Where are we going?" she demanded loudly when she saw Layla dressed with her backpack on.

"We're going to the school so Layla can take her test and you can play with the other kids," I lied, hoping that would please her.

She looked down and noticed that she had on tennis shoes. "I don't like these shoes!" she said angrily kicking them off.

"You need to leave those on because we're going to do a lot of walking today," I tried to reason with her.

"Noooo!" she screamed at the top of her lungs. I cringed knowing she might wake everyone up in the building.

"Shh. Shh. Okay," I whispered. "Go pick out whatever shoes you want." Layla rolled her eyes at her stubborn sister. She chose some impractical white sandals and demanded a backpack like her.

I'll Fly Away

It was 7 am. It was time to leave. I turned off the lights and slowly inched the front door open. We avoided the elevator and tiptoed down the stairs. At the bottom of the stairs, I motioned for them to wait as I turned the key to the courtyard lock. The heavy metal door creaked slightly.

"Okay," I whispered. "Quickly now, to the car!"

We raced across the courtyard down into the driveway. I unlocked the car and motioned for the girls to get in. I slid in and shut the door softly.

Suddenly, Basaam was standing at my car door window. I jerked back, startled. I rolled down the car window, my hands shaking. He gazed at me boldly.

"Sabah el hare (good morning)," I said, smiling weakly.

He pulled the cigarette from his mouth still staring at me. "Sabah el noor (Good morning)," he replied. He motioned for me to wait, moving his hand up and down touching his thumb and two fingers. He walked toward the back of the car.

"Oh my God!" I thought. "He's going to open the trunk!" I panicked.

I watched in the rearview mirror, and saw him move a garden hose and then walk over to the driveway gate. He took out some keys and unlocked it.

"I didn't have those keys," I whispered to myself. "I couldn't have driven out of here if I wanted to!"

I waited until he swung the gates open, and then backed out carefully until I was halfway in the street. I put the car in drive and turned to wave at him. He gazed at me darkly, returning my wave with a cold stare, just taking a drag from his cigarette.

We drove past the Syrian soldiers, who waved us through. We reached the bottom of the hill and hit a traffic jam. It was half past seven and cars were bottlenecked at this major intersection, coming in every conceivable direction. The two-lane highway was jammed with cars making their own five lanes, disregarding the white lines. Men, late for work, pulled in front of me, missing my car by mere inches. I found a large white bus filled with passengers and pulled directly behind it until our bumpers almost touched. I ignored the men screaming and honking at me on either side.

"I'm not moving!" I yelled at them. "Just try to cut in front of me!"

"That's right Mommy!" Nadine yelled. "Honk back at them!"

277

Soon traffic came to a complete standstill. It was 7:45 and we were not moving. 8:00 came and went. We were late. I started to panic. Horns were blaring, people yelling, and no one was going anywhere.

Suddenly the bus lurched forward. I tailgated behind it until we reached the highway exit where I floored it. I found the familiar airport exit and turned into the airport's parking lot. A security guard motioned for me to stop. I rolled down my window while he peered inside and motioned with a nod of his head for me to proceed. I saw another guard patrolling the area so we parked as far away from him as possible. I popped open the trunk quickly and pulled the suitcases out of the blue garbage bags.

We walked to the airport and went upstairs where we saw the U.S. Consulate waiting for us. When she saw us she immediately walked over to us and kissed me on both cheeks, whispering in my ear, "Pretend we are family. Just relax, smile, and act natural."

"You managed to bring suitcases!" she said, lifting her eyebrows into high arches. "Okay, we need to check these bags in. Give me the girls' Lebanese passports so we can start."

I handed her the burgundy Lebanese passports, with trembling hands. Nadine bounced around the airport while Layla watched her nervously.

Two tall Lebanese men in dark suits approached us. She introduced us as they firmly shook my hand. "They are here to help us."

She gave them our suitcases and tickets, and motioned for us to sit down on the chairs lining the wall. She sat beside me, pretending to be engrossed in a pleasant conversation. I kept glancing over at the check-in counter nervously until these men walked toward us and handed us our tickets. This was the first checkpoint.

"Follow us," my advocate directed, rising to her feet. I picked up Nadine and held Layla's hand, walking right behind them. We came to the first security checkpoint and placed our purses and the girls' backpacks on the conveyer belt before stepping through a metal detector.

"Okay, we need to pass through two more checkpoints," she whispered tensely. "These men will do all the talking while we stand here chatting. Try to look calm," she said, placing her hand on my shoulder.

We followed our two tall bodyguards, who approached another security booth, where a man in uniform sat. I watched how they leaned over the counter talking amiably to the guard who smiled and laughed with them. Finally, the security guard placed a stamp on our passports. The U.S. Consulate smiled with relief as we continued down the hallway to the next checkpoint.

It was the last checkpoint, but the official sitting behind the glass window had a sour expression on his face when our guardian angels walked up. I avoided his stare and smiled at my friend, hoping I looked casual. This time the conversation between the men didn't sound so friendly. The tone of this guard was surly and serious. He shot forth questions rapidly, and the men responded quickly.

The U.S. Consulate began to visibly sweat. "This is taking too long," she said. When I looked into her eyes I saw fear. She was frightened for us. Her reaction made my knees start to buckle.

"Don't they know what is going on?" I asked her. "I mean isn't it obvious?" I whispered to her through a clenched smile.

"No, they don't," she answered. "We are passing you off as a U.S. diplomat with certain immutable rights."

"A U.S. diplomat? But I look like a mother with her two daughters," I whispered.

"You look just fine actually," she assured me. "You should have seen the woman we helped out last week. She had five children with her, and only a diaper bag."

We were interrupted by the shrill voice of the official who was addressing her in English. We walked over to the counter and he asked her in English, "If this is legitimate, they may go. But if not, they stay, here," he said narrowing his eyes at me.

"Of course this is legitimate," she exclaimed, extending him a warm smile. "What else would it be?"

The official grumbled to himself, not liking the situation at all. I flashed a weak smile and opened my eyes in what I hoped was an innocent expression. He hesitated for what seemed an eternity, then shrugged his shoulders, and allowed us to pass with a nod. We took our cue and shuffled past him quickly, before he changed his mind.

I was in a state of shock. We walked as a group to the cafeteria and my friend sat with us, while the men ordered coffee and pastries for all of us.

"I want a chocolate donut with sprinkles!" Nadine told one of the men.

Our advocates sat at another table next to us, watching the hallway warily. It all seemed so surreal to me, sitting in Beirut's airport drinking coffee, chatting quietly. She asked me why I was leaving and I relayed my years of abuse and recent prison I had found myself in. I listened somberly as she shared stories of other American women who had tried to escape. Most were successful, but some had been caught at the airport, found out by an anonymous phone call to the husband's family.

My ears heard it before I saw it. Our plane had arrived. I watched the British Airway airplane descend on the runway, as I had never watched a plane before. I held it with my gaze, my heart racing wildly within my chest. I got up to get in line but my friend motioned for me to sit down.

"Wait until everyone has boarded," she advised me. "Pretend like you are in no hurry."

I waited impatiently until all the other passengers had boarded. My friend finally rose and grabbed both of my shoulders, kissing me warmly on each cheek.

"Take care of yourself, Kelly," she said. Tears of gratitude gushed down my cheeks as I thanked all of them for their help.

We walked down the narrow corridor into the British airplane, my heart pounding against the walls of my chest. All of the Lebanese passengers stared curiously at us as we took our seats. Nadine took the window seat and Layla sat beside her.

"Where are we going Mommy?" Nadine asked, realizing we were leaving.

"We're going to America baby!" I exclaimed excitedly.

Nadine frowned and stood up in her seat. "No! I don't want to go to America!" she said loudly. "America is evil! America Shaytani (America is Satan)!"

I was shocked. She had already been brainwashed by the anti-American rhetoric she had heard living here. The other passengers around us chuckled at her words.

"No, Nadine," Layla said thinking quickly. "We're not going to America. We're going to English land to see Grammy and Grandpa!"

"English land?" Nadine asked. "Where everyone speaks English?"

"Yes baby," I said hugging Layla. "Where everyone speaks English."

Satisfied, she sat back down and put her seatbelt on, looking out the window. The plane shuddered and began to roll down the black pavement. The rumble of the wheels grew in intensity and then a forceful thrust shoved us back in our seats as we lifted off the ground.

We were ascending quickly now, and I could see the city of Beirut beneath us, fading away, until it was nothing but a shadow of a past nightmare. I drew in a deep breath. We had done it. The door to our cage had been opened. We were free.

"But this is what the LORD says:
"Yes, captives will be taken from warriors,
and plunder retrieved from the fierce;
I will contend with those who contend with you,
and your children I will save."
(Isaiah 49:25)

SAFE HAVEN

"Are you travelling without your husband's permission?" the U.S. customs official at the O'Hare International Airport in Chicago asked me accusingly, in a familiar foreign accent. His words and demeanor took me aback. Startled, I faced my accuser warily.

He narrowed his eyes at me, demanding a reply. He knew. He knew what the other passengers waiting in line, didn't. He knew that I had broken Sharia law. He knew that I, a woman, had dared to defy those laws and escape our prison and master. Layla shot me a look of terror. My throat tightened. I held my breath.

"Would this man betray me to Lebanese authorities?" I thought. "Had we made it this far only to be sent back to my husband?"

I averted my eyes to a few inches below his collar, avoiding his stare. I had learned my place as a woman.

"Quick! Think! What should I say?" I thought.

As I struggled to come up with an answer, a small American flag stitched above his left shirt pocket commanded my attention.

"Wait a minute! What is the matter with you, Kelly?" I thought. "His employer is the U.S. Government for God's sake and I'm an American citizen. I have rights here!"

Like a weary warrior, hardened from many battles, I slowly, steadily raised my head, defiantly meeting his dark, condemning eyes. I hadn't surmounted impossible odds, planned an escape down to the minutest details, weathered setbacks and risked everything for my girls and their freedom to be stopped by this – this man. His arrogant leer struck fresh wounds, which were still raw and weeping from another man, who also believed that his male birthright gave him dominion over me.

"I don't need his permission," I thundered above the crowd. "I don't need his permission to do anything anymore. We are in American now and we are American citizens!"

He flinched as if struck, frowned, and lowered his eyes. Defeated, he pressed the entry stamp against our passports grudgingly. "Well, welcome back," he mumbled, sullenly plopping our passports on the counter.

"Thank you," I replied, still staring at him, daring him to deny me my rights. Turning my back to him and some confused onlookers I steered my daughters through the swarming crowd, dodging travelers rushing to make their flights. I checked a computer monitor and realized we had a three-hour layover before boarding the plane bound for Boise. After securing our seats, I found a remote waiting area all but abandoned, except for a young couple snuggled up near the far wall.

"I'm tired, Mommy," moaned Layla, as we collapsed on the floor. Tucked away, hidden behind the backdrop of a deserted airline check-in counter, we were relieved to find a safe haven far from the clamor of the crowd.

I instinctively encircled my daughters as they huddled next to me, nestling in my arms. Hot tears of exhaustion rippled down my face, mingling with theirs.

"Everything is going to be all right now," I choked out the words hugging them tighter. "We made it little ones. We made it. Thank God, we're free... and soon we will be home."

I was exhausted, physically, mentally and emotionally. I had hit the brick wall days ago and all of my adrenaline reserves were spent. My muscles began to convulse, protesting the large amounts of caffeine I had been forced to dump into my system. We had made it, clawed our way to victory, but my overwrought nerves were still laced up, ready for a fight, and pacing the cage.

Suddenly, a rush of relief washed over me, saturating every pore of my being with an emotion that had long lain dormant. Now it burst forth fearlessly, brazenly reclaiming lost territory. I surrendered to this overwhelming feeling of liberty. Like a prisoner seeing the light of day for the first time in years, I was blinded by the intensity of its force. The cage that had bound us dissipated, for it had no power here, no authority.

We boarded the last leg of our flight and headed home to Boise. When we landed it was dark, almost midnight and as the plane's wheels touched the ground I could breathe again. We were home.

283

Epilogue

Even though we were back home the battle wasn't over. When Ibrahim realized what we had done, he immediately called my parents' home. My father was ready for him.

"Where are they?" Ibrahim demanded. "I just want to speak to them."

My father who prided himself on always telling the truth answered, "They are somewhere between Los Angeles and New York."

Seeing that he wasn't going to be able to talk to me and convince me to come back, Ibrahim took the first plane over. We were way ahead of him. Friends of my parents opened their homes for us to stay in so we could hide until I could file for divorce. I was afraid that he would try to kidnap the girls and fly them out on their Lebanese passports.

After almost a year of legal battles and the help of my parents and Stan, a wonderful friend and lawyer, I was granted full legal and physical custody of my girls. The testimony heard in court was such that Ibrahim was only allowed to visit the girls twice a month for two hours at a time under strict supervision by a third party. I found out that he had hired a private detective to find out where the girls were going to school. During his visits, he repeatedly asked Layla where they were attending school and she avoided the question. On his first visit he even asked Nadine if she wanted to go on an airplane ride with him and she stubbornly said, "No, I don't like Arabic land. I like English land." Seeing that his daughters weren't cooperating with him, on his second visit his last words to them were, "I am going to go back to my country to marry a real wife and have children who really love me."

That was the last the girls saw of him and that was over thirteen years ago. My daughters are almost grown now and I know they realize how blessed they are to be in America where they are not considered the property of their father or future husbands. I am very proud of these little birds that are now trying out their wings, going after their dreams. There is nothing more lovely than watching them grow in God's grace and I am truly blessed to have such compassionate, strong, beautiful daughters.

Layla has grown into a beautiful, confident young woman and is now 23 years of age. She has found great success in sales and is now managing her own store. She is driven, hard working and loves working with her customers. She loves doing anything outdoors, camping, hunting, hiking or fishing. She has been gifted with a beautiful voice and loves country music.

Nadine is still as feisty and outspoken as ever and has blossomed into a beautiful young lady of 18. She loves competitive sports and her favorite is golf. She is on her way to college and is confident in her abilities, and in her own words says, "You know mom, I know that I can be anything I want. I just have to decide what that is." She also has been gifted with a beautiful voice and dreams of singing professionally with her sister.

Both girls have sung the national anthem many times for the local university games. I can't even begin to tell you how I feel when I see my daughters sing to the stars and stripes of America, with their hands over their hearts because when I watch them I realize that on the other side of the world they would have been taught to hate America and everything it stands for. It is true; no one appreciates their freedom as much as someone who has had it taken from them.

My daughters have also chosen to be Christians and they follow the one called Jesus who radically altered the world with his love and respect for women, the one who on this earth not only taught and respected women but ministered to them, healed them and defended them.

***

Leaving someone that you have sacrificed for, struggled to make a life with, raised children and loved for over fourteen years was not easy, especially when all I had to my name were two small suitcases and the clothes on my back. My parents opened their home to us and helped us until I could get back on my feet again. After I won the legal battle with their help, I began to reconstruct my life. I worked hard to reenter the workforce and was finally able to provide for my daughters on my own.

Although now financially stable, I struggled with the aftermath of this marriage: posttraumatic stress disorder, feelings of inferiority, guilt and just plain loneliness. I knew that my life choices had put my daughters in a home being raised by a single mom with no father and I felt guilty for all of the past mistakes that had led me here. Even though we were free, I was still bound by my sin-consciousness thinking and suffered from depression. I was forever carrying a heavy burden of my failings, and my sins were ever before me. My inferiority complex and insecurities were deadly when I finally allowed myself to date. I learned that when one has come out of abuse, what feels familiar should not be trusted. I struggled and fell along the way many times in my search for a good man who would love me and be a father to my girls. I truly believe that God reached down once again and rescued me before I fell into the same trap again.

In 2006 I met Dave, who had also just come out of a bad marriage, and we comforted each other in ways that only people who have been betrayed understand. We married in 2007 and at first, the way he treated me didn't feel familiar or normal to me, and this was sad because all he tried to do was love me. During the first few years of our marriage he described me as being "like an abused little girl backed up in the corner with my fists out ready to strike anyone trying to hurt me." The pendulum had swung too far the other way. Thankfully, I was at the point in my life where I wouldn't stand for any abuse. The trouble was, everything and everyone seemed threatening to me.

Dave introduced me to his church: a nondenominational bible-based church. I was reluctant to go because I had heard about "those Protestants", but it was unlike any mass I had been to. The first time I heard the worship music I began crying. The band was playing, "Oh How He Loves us," by John Mark McMillan, and I felt the Holy Spirit like never before. When the Pastor spoke, he applied the bible to my life and it became alive for me for the first time. I never realized how thirsty I was until that moment and I wanted more.

I finally broke free from the shackles of living in the bondage of scrupulously confessing my every sin, thought and desire and stepped into God's forgiveness for the first time understanding that Jesus Christ died for all of our sins once and for all, that no more sacrifices were needed, just the one great sacrifice that He paid for on the cross. I was free to step forward into living with joy, not condemnation and how easy it was then to align myself with the Holy Spirit living in me. I realized that the view of my God was flawed: He was not demanding an accounting of my every failure every time we met, asking for daily sacrifices from me.

How confidently I approach my Father now, knowing how much He loves me. When my own daughters approach me, I do not keep a list of all of their wrongdoings and demand confessions and sacrifices for every transgression. I let natural consequences be felt, but always with love. If I as a mother can love like this, how much more so does our God?

"Their sins and lawless acts I will remember no more. And where these have been forgiven, sacrifice for sin is no longer necessary."
(Hebrews 10:18)

  I have given up religion for a relationship and now walk confidently in my Father's footsteps and take great delight in knowing that despite all of my sins and failings, He loves me just as I am - I don't have to earn His love but just accept it. Like a young child running to her Father's arms, I know that each time I seek Him, He picks me up in his arms, smiling, lavishly showering me with kisses sweeter than honey. And when we truly come to Him and confess our sins and decide to follow Him, He places our sins as far away from us as the east is from the west. Oh how He loves us.

  Unbeknownst to me, telling my story has created some controversy, none of which I intended. Apparently today, in polite society, it is politically incorrect to have a religious belief and disagree with another's. Religious tolerance is the mantra of the day but we are fortunate to live in America where church and state are separate and our government respects our inherent right to believe in what we want to. It is also called free will.

  We are left to decide who this Jesus is. Is He just a nice guy, a false messiah, a prophet, or is He who He says He is: the Son of the living God who spoke the universe into creation and laid down His life for our sins and is coming back as King and Judge. They can't all be true.

Jesus turned to His disciples and said, "But what about you? Who do you say I am?" Simon Peter answered, "You are the Messiah, the Son of the living God!" (Matthew 16:15,16 NIV)

Acknowledgements

First and foremost, I would like to thank my husband, Dave, who encouraged me greatly through this whole writing process. Writing this made me relive a lot of painful memories and you were there for me in the midst of all of these emotions. You were my rock during this difficult time and I could not do this without you. Thank you for being a wonderful father and loving husband. I love you.

I would like to thank my parents for taking us in when we came back, opening up their home to us and helping us financially until I could get on my own two feet again. Thank you for your patience and generosity, for being there for us, and thank you for starting me on my journey towards my faith.

I would also like to thank the following friends:

Bob, Kathy, Judy & Harold. Thank you for opening your homes and finding safe places for us to stay when we needed it.

Stan, my lawyer, who understood my situation and offered to help us. Thank you for helping me to gain legal custody of my girls. I will never forget what you have done.

To the U.S. Consulate and the two Lebanese guardian angels who helped us escape. I am forever indebted to you.

Mary McColl who was the first friend to encourage me to rewrite my story. Every time we met she asked me how my book was coming along. Because of her persistence I began rewriting. She was my first editor and insisted on doing it free of charge. In the middle of my writing she was diagnosed with leukemia and I watched her fight for her very life. She battled with this terrible disease, and courageously endured rounds of chemo and transfusions with the help of her loving family. The last time I saw her she was smiling and happy and that is how I want to remember her. She passed away May 9, 2015 and she will be missed greatly. Thank you Mary for your encouragement and for your friendship.

Kat Heatherly, my editor, whose eye for detail is unparalleled, who is not only my editor, but a good friend who inspires me everyday with her attitude of gratitude despite life's many challenges that she faces.

Lori, Keri, Kindal, Morgan & Jana who were my initial readers of my first rough draft. When I wanted to quit, they didn't let me. When I became discouraged, they uplifted me. I am blessed to have such friends.

My two daughters: Layla & Nadine. It was by finally looking through their eyes that I woke up to see my reality. Because of you I had the courage to leave an abusive marriage. I love you fiercely and I am so proud of the young women you are becoming.

To Salam and Aisha: Thank you for being a friend to me while I was in Beirut and making my days brighter. I truly wish the best for you and your children. May you find freedom - true freedom by knowing Whose you are and that you one day understand how much God loves you.

To my pastor, Doug Peake, who continues to courageously stand firm in the faith and is not afraid to preach the truth with conviction. Thank you for making the bible come alive for me today in this life. To his wife Kim, who works tirelessly to end modern day slavery and sex trafficking. Thank you both for letting His light shine in your lives so brightly that we are inspired to follow.

And last but not least to my Heavenly Father who rescued us from the fowler's snare. I thank Him for His constant provision and protection in my life. He is my refuge and my fortress, my God in whom I trust.

Footnotes

[1] And in their footsteps, We sent 'Iesa (Jesus), son of Maryam (Mary) confirming the Taurat (Torah) that had come before him, and We gave him the Injeel (Gospel), in which was guidance and light and confirmation of the Taurat (Torah) that had come before it, a guidance and an admonition for Al-Muttaqun (the pious - see V.2:2). S. 5:46 Al-Hilali & Khan; cf. S. 57:27
He [Jesus] said, "Lo, I am God's servant; God has given me the Book, and made me a Prophet." S. 19:30 Arberry
It is He Who has sent down the Book (the Qur'an) to you (Muhammad) with truth, confirming what came before it. And he sent down the Taurat (Torah) and the Injeel (Gospel). S. 3:3 Al-Hilali & Khan

[2] The Dead Sea Scrolls are a collection of 981 texts discovered between 1946 and 1956 at *Khirbet Qumran* in the West Bank. They were found inside caves about a mile inland from the northwest shore of the Dead Sea, from which they derive their name. (Down, David. "Unveiling the Kings of Israel." P.160. 2011.) Nine of the scrolls were rediscovered at the Israel Antiquities Authority (IAA) in 2014, after they had been stored unopened for six decades following their excavation in 1952.[] http://www.foxnews.com/science/2014/03/13/nine-unopened-dead-sea-scrolls-found/ ["Nine manuscripts with biblical text unearthed in Qumran". *ANSAmed.* 27 February 2014. Retrieved 13 March 2014.] The texts are of great historical, religious, and linguistic significance because they include the earliest known surviving manuscripts of works later included in the Hebrew Bible canon, along with deuterocanonical and extra-biblical manuscripts which preserve evidence of the diversity of religious thought in late Second Temple Judaism.
The texts are written in Hebrew, Aramaic, Greek, and Nabataean, mostly on parchment but with some written on papyrus and bronze.[From papyrus to cyberspace *The Guardian 27 August 2008.*] The manuscripts have been dated to various ranges between, Greg, " the Scrolls on the Basis of Radiocarbon Analysis", in The Dead Sea Scrolls

after Fifty Years, edited by Flint Peter W., and VanderKam, James C., Vol.1 (Leiden: Brill, 1998) 430–471.

3 The Dead Sea Scrolls and the Masoretic Text by Dr.Patrick Zukeran

http://www.probe.org/site/c.fdKEIMNsEoG/b.4223603/k.B3EE/The_Dead_Sea_Scrolls_Shed_Light_on_the_Accuracy_of_our_Bible.htm

The Dead Sea Scrolls play a crucial role in assessing the accurate preservation of the Old Testament. With its hundreds of manuscripts from every book except Esther, detailed comparisons can be made with more recent texts.

The Old Testament that we use today is translated from what is called the Masoretic Text. The Masoretes were Jewish scholars who between A.D. 500 and 950 gave the Old Testament the form that we use today. Until the Dead Sea Scrolls were found in 1947, the oldest Hebrew text of the Old Testament was the Masoretic Aleppo Codex, which dates to A.D. 935. (Randall Price, *The Stones Cry Out* (Eugene, OR.: Harvest House Publishers, 1997), 280.

After years of careful study, it has been concluded that the Dead Sea Scrolls give substantial confirmation that our Old Testament has been accurately preserved. The scrolls were found to be almost identical with the Masoretic text. Hebrew Scholar Millar Burrows writes, "It is a matter of wonder that through something like one thousand years the text underwent so little alteration. As I said in my first article on the scroll, 'Herein lies its chief importance, supporting the fidelity of the Masoretic tradition.'" Millar Burrows, *The Dead Sea Scrolls* (New York: Viking Press, 1955), 304, quoted in Norman Geisler and William Nix, *General Introduction to the Bible* (Chicago: Moody Press, 1986), 367.

A significant comparison study was conducted with the Isaiah Scroll written around 100 B.C. that was found among the Dead Sea documents and the book of Isaiah found in the Masoretic text. After much research, scholars found that the two texts were practically identical. Most variants were minor spelling differences, and none affected the meaning of the text.

One of the most respected Old Testament scholars, the late Gleason Archer, examined the two Isaiah scrolls found in Cave 1 and wrote, "Even though the two copies of Isaiah discovered in Qumran Cave 1 near the Dead Sea in 1947 were a thousand years earlier than the oldest dated manuscript previously known (A.D. 980), they proved to be word for word identical with our standard Hebrew Bible in more than 95 percent of the text. The 5 percent of variation consisted chiefly of obvious slips of the pen and variations in spelling." Gleason Archer, *A Survey of Old Testament Introduction* (Chicago, IL.: Moody Press, 1985), 513-517.

Despite the thousand-year gap, scholars found the Masoretic Text and Dead Sea Scrolls to be nearly identical. The Dead Sea Scrolls provide valuable evidence that the Old Testament had been accurately and carefully preserved.

[4] The Dead Sea Scrolls and the Masoretic Text by Dr. Patrick Zukeran http://www.probe.org/site/c.fdKEIMNsEoG/b.4223603/k.B3EE/T he_Dead_Sea_Scrolls_Shed_Light_on_the_Accuracy_of_our_Bible.ht The Messianic Prophecies and the Scrolls

One of the evidences used in defending the deity of the Christ is the testimony of prophecy. There are over one hundred prophecies regarding Christ in the Old Testament.{ J. Barton Payne, *Encyclopedia of Biblical Prophecy* (Grand Rapids, MI.: Baker Books, 1984), 665-670. } These prophecies were made centuries before the birth of Christ and were quite specific in their detail. Skeptics questioned the date of the prophecies and some even charged that they were not recorded until after or at the time of Jesus, and therefore discounted their prophetic nature.

There is strong evidence that the Old Testament canon was completed by 450 B.C. The Greek translation of the Old Testament, the Septuagint, is dated about two hundred fifty years before Christ. The translation process occurred during the reign of Ptolemy Philadelphus who ruled from 285 to 246 B.C. {Millar Burrows, *The Dead Sea Scrolls* (New York: Viking Press, 1955), 304, quoted in Norman Geisler and William Nix, *General Introduction to the Bible* (Chicago: Moody Press, 1986), 503-504} It can be argued that a complete Hebrew text from which this Greek translation would be derived must have existed prior to the third century B.C.

The Dead Sea Scrolls provided further proof that the Old Testament canon existed prior to the third century B.C. Thousands of manuscript fragments from all the Old Testament books except Esther were found predating Christ's birth, and some date as early as the third century

B.C. For example, portions from the book of Samuel date that early, and fragments from Daniel date to the second century B.C.{ Geisler and Nix, 137 } Portions from the twelve Minor Prophets date from 150 B.C to 25 B.C.{ Ibid., 138-139. } Since the documents were found to be identical with our Masoretic Text, we can be reasonably sure that our Old Testament is the same one that the Essenes were studying and working from.

One of the most important Dead Sea documents is the Isaiah Scroll. This twenty-four foot long scroll is well preserved and contains the complete book of Isaiah. The scroll is dated 100 B.C. and contains one of the clearest and most detailed prophecies of the Messiah in chapter fifty-three, called the "Suffering Servant." Although some Jewish scholars teach that this refers to Israel, a careful reading shows that this prophecy can only refer to Christ.

Here are just a few reasons. The suffering servant is called sinless (53:9), he dies and rises from the dead (53:8-10), and he suffers and dies for the sins of the people (53:4-6). These characteristics are not true of the nation of Israel. The Isaiah Scroll gives us a manuscript that predates the birth of Christ by a century and contains many of the most important messianic prophecies about Jesus. Skeptics could no longer contend that portions of the book were written after Christ or that first century insertions were added to the text.

Thus, the Dead Sea Scrolls provide further proof that the Old Testament canon was completed by the third century B.C., and that the prophecies foretold of Christ in the Old Testament predated the birth of Christ.

The Messiah and the Scrolls What kind of Messiah was expected by first century Jews? Critical scholars allege that the idea of a personal Messiah was a later interpretation made by Christians. Instead, they believe that the Messiah was to be the nation of Israel and represented Jewish nationalism.

The Dead Sea Scrolls, written by Old Testament Jews, reveal the messianic expectations of Jews during the time of Christ. Studies have uncovered several parallels to the messianic hope revealed in the New Testament as well as some significant differences. First, they were expecting a personal Messiah rather than a nation or a sense of nationalism. Second, the Messiah would be a descendant of King David. Third, the Messiah would confirm His claims by performing miracles including the resurrection of the dead. Finally, He would be human and yet possess divine attributes.

A manuscript found in Cave 4 entitled the *Messianic Apocalypse*, copied in the first century B.C., describes the anticipated ministry of the Messiah:

> "For He will honor the pious upon the throne of His eternal kingdom, release the captives, open the eyes of the blind, lifting up those who are oppressed… For He shall heal the critically wounded, He shall raise the dead, He shall bring good news to the poor."

This passage sounds very similar to the ministry of Jesus as recorded in the Gospels. In Luke chapter 7:21-22, John the Baptist's disciples come to Jesus and ask him if He is the Messiah. Jesus responds,

> "Go tell John what you have seen and heard: the blind receive their sight, the lame walk, the lepers are cleansed, the deaf hear, the dead are raised, the poor have the good news brought to them."

But, with the similarities there are also differences. Christians have always taught that there is one Messiah while the Essene community believed in two, one an Aaronic or priestly Messiah and the other a Davidic or royal Messiah who leads a war to end the evil age. James Vanderkam and Peter Flint, *The Meaning of the Dead Sea Scrolls* (San Francisco, CA.: Harper Collins Publishers, 2002), 265-266}

The Essenes were also strict on matters of ceremonial purity while Jesus criticized these laws. He socialized with tax collectors and lepers, which was considered defiling by the Jews. Jesus taught us to love one's enemies while the Essenes taught hatred towards theirs. They were strict Sabbatarians, and Jesus often violated this important aspect of the law. The Qumran community rejected the inclusion of women, Gentiles, and sinners, while Christ reached out to these very groups.

The many differences show that the Essenes were not the source of early Christianity as some scholars proposes. Rather, Christianity derived its teachings from the Old Testament and the ministry of Jesus.

The Dead Sea Scrolls have proven to be a significant discovery, confirming the accurate preservation of our Old Testament text, the messianic prophecies of Christ, and valuable insight into first century Judaism.

5 The merits gained by Christ were enough to expiate all sins, and these merits, combined with the merits of Mary and the saints that were in excess of what they needed, form the Spiritual Treasury of the Church. (CCC 1476). It is from this treasury that the Church grants indulgences for the remission of temporal punishment, when a certain prayer or work is performed. A plenary indulgence (ie. The Stations of the Cross) remits all of one's punishment, while a partial indulgence (ie. reading Scripture for 15 minutes) remits a portion of one's punishment. (The Council of Trent (Sess. XIV, Can. Xi) reminded us that God does not always remit the whole punishment due to sin together with guilt. God requires satisfaction, and will punish sin, and this doctrine involves as necessary consequence a belief that the sinner failing to do penance is this life may be punished in another world (purgatory).

6) http://en.wikipedia.org/wiki/Lebanese_nationality_law
https://www.passportsusa.com/family/abduction/prevention/prevention_560.htm

7) http://www.divorcesource.com/ds/newjersey/how-to-fight-an-international-removal-case-3823.shtmlrequires compliance
http://travel.state.gov/content/childabduction/english/preventing/faq.html

8 The Children's Passport Issuance Alert Program is a service for the parents and legal guardians of minor children. It enables the Department of State's Office of Children's Issues to notify a parent or court ordered legal guardian, when requested, before issuing a U.S. passport for his or her child. The parent, legal guardian, legal representatives, or the court of competent jurisdiction must submit a written request for entry of a child's name into the program to the

Office of Children's Issues.

Passport Issuance to Children Under Age 18 On July 2, 2001, the Department of State began implementation of a new law regarding the passport applications of minor U.S. citizens under the age of 14. A person now applying for a passport for a child under 14 must show that both parents consent to the issuance or that the applying parent has sole authority to obtain the passport. Passport applications made in the U.S. and at consular offices abroad will the new law cover both. Exceptions to this requirement may be made in special family circumstances or exigent circumstances necessitating the immediate travel of the child.

Once a passport is issued, its use is not tracked or controlled by the Department of State. There are no exit controls for American citizens leaving the United States. If you believe that your child may be abducted internationally, immediately contact the Office of Children's Issues and inform appropriate law enforcement officials. Information regarding the issuance of a passport to a minor is available to either parent, regardless of custody rights, as long as the requesting parents' rights have not been terminated. The Department of State's Children's Passport Issuance Alert Program is a program to alert us when an application for a United States passport is made. This is not a program for tracking the use of a passport. This program can be used to inform a parent or a court when an application for a United States passport is executed on behalf of a child. The alert program generally remains in effect until each child turns 18. It is very important that parents keep us informed in writing of any changes to contact information and legal representation. Failure to notify CA/OCS/CI of a current address may result in a passport issuance for your child without your consent.

Dual Nationality for Children Many children, whether born in the United States or born abroad to a United States citizen parent, are citizens of both the United States and another country. This may occur through the child's birth abroad, through a parent who was born outside the United States, or a parent who has acquired a second nationality through naturalization in another country. There is no requirement that a United States citizen parent consent to the acquisition of another nationality.The inability to obtain a United States passport through the Children's Passport Issuance Alert Program does not automatically prevent a dual national child from obtaining and traveling on a foreign passport. There is no requirement that foreign embassies adhere to United States regulations regarding issuance and denial of their passports to United States citizen minors who have dual nationality. If there is a possibility that the child has another nationality, you may contact the country's embassy or consulate directly to inquire about denial of that country's passport. .

https://www.passportsusa.com/family/abduction/resources/r esources_554.html

Many U. S. citizen children who fall victim to international abduction possess dual nationality. The Department cannot prevent other countries from issuing their passports to children who are also their nationals. You can, however, ask a foreign embassy or consulate in the United States not to issue a passport to your child. Send the embassy or consulate a written request; along with certified complete copies of any court orders you have which address custody or the overseas travel of your child. In your letter, inform them that you are sending a copy of this request to the United States Department of State. If your child is only a United States citizen, you can request that no visa for that country be issued in his or her U.S. passport. Keep in mind that no international law requires compliance with such requests, although some countries may comply voluntarily. For more information:

http://travel.state.gov/content/childabduction/english/preven ting/faq.html

[9] Muhammad has been often criticized outside of the Islamic world for his treatment of the Jewish tribes of Medina.[John Esposito, *Islam the Straight Path*, Oxford University Press, p.17-18] An example is the mass killing of the men of the Banu Qurayza, a Jewish tribe of Medina. The tribe was accused of having engaged in treasonous agreements with the enemies besieging Medina in the Battle of the Trench in 627.[Sahih al-Bukhari, 5:59:362][Daniel W. Brown, *A New Introduction to Islam*, p. 81, 2003, Blackwell Publishers, ISBN 0-631-21604-9] Ibn Ishaq writes that Muhammad approved the beheading of some 600-900 individuals who surrendered unconditionally after a siege that lasted several weeks.[Ibn Ishaq, A. Guillaume (translator), *The Life of Muhammad*, p. 464, 2002,

Oxford University Press, ISBN 0-19-636033-1] (Also see Bukhari 5:59:362) (Yusuf Ali notes that the Qur'an discusses this battle in verses [Quran 33:10]).[Yusuf Ali, "The Meaning of the Holy Quran", (11th Edition), p. 1059, Amana Publications, 1989, ISBN 0-915957-76-0 They were buried in a mass grave in the Medina market place, and the women and children were sold into slavery. Yusuf Ali, "The Meaning of the Holy Quran", (11th Edition), p. 1059, Amana Publications, 1989, ISBN 0-915957-76-0

10 https://www.ewtn.com/faith/teachings/marya4.htm
St. Pius X said she was the "dispensatrix of all the gifts, and is the "neck" connecting the Head of the Mystical Body to the Members. But all power flows through the neck. Pius XII said "Her kingdom is as vast as that of her Son and God, since nothing is excluded from her dominion." These and many other texts speak in varied ways of Mary as Mediatrix of all graces, so often that the teaching has become infallible..."

11 World Political Almanac, 3rd Ed, Chris Cook.
UN Human Rights Council. "IMPLEMENTATION OF GENERAL ASSEMBLY RESOLUTION 60/251 OF 15 MARCH 2006 ENTITLED HUMAN RIGHTS COUNCIL"
Commission of Enquiry on Lebanon, 23 November 2006, p.18.
CIA World Factbook. "CIA World Factbook: Lebanon: Refugees and internally displaced persons". CIA World Factbook, 10 September 2012.
"Things Fall Apart: Containing the Spillover from an Iraqi Civil War" By Daniel Byman, Kenneth Michael Pollack, Page. 139
Islam and Assisted Reproductive Technologies, Marcia C. Inhorn, Soraya Tremayne - 2012, p 238
"Beware of Small States: Lebanon, Battleground of the Middle East", p.62

12 Reference Abu Huraira Vol 4, Book 54, Hadith No 491

13 (Quran 43:36).

14 William Muir (2003), *The life of Mahomet*, Kessinger Publishing, p. 317, ISBN 978-0-7661-7741-3

Ibn Kathir, Saed Khalil -Rahman (2009), *Tafsir Ibn Kathir Juz'21*, MSA
Publication Limited, p. 213, ISBN 978-1-86179-611-0(online)
Kister, (1990), Society and religion from Jāhiliyya to Islam p. 54.
Rahman al-Mubarakpuri, Saifur (2005), *The Sealed Nectar*, DarusSerah
Publications, pp. 201–205 (online)

15 Harel and Isacharoff (2004), p. 247
"Timeline: Bethlehem siege". *BBC.* 10 May 2002.
Rees, Matt; Bethlehem; Bobby Ghosh, Gaza, Jamil Hamad, Aharon
Klein (2002-05-20). "The Saga of the Siege". *Time.* ISSN 0040-781X.
Retrieved 2008-09-26.
'Monks urge end to Bethlehem siege,' BBC News 12 April, 2002
Cohen, Ariel (April 24, 2002). "The Nativity Sin". National Review
Online. Retrieved 2012-07-01.

16 *Article 19 of 36{FOUNDITEMS:-0}, Article ID:*
200205151103290017
Published on May 15, 2002, The Washington Times
{PUBLICATION2}
'Greedy monsters' ruled church Militants feasted, drank while civilians,
clergy suffered

The Palestinian gunmen holed up in the Church of the Nativity and
later deported by Israel seized church stockpiles of food and "ate like
greedy monsters" until the food ran out, while more than 150 civilians
went hungry. They also guzzled beer, wine and Johnnie Walker scotch
that they found in priests' quarters, undeterred by the Islamic ban on
drinking alcohol. The indulgence lasted for about two weeks into the
39-day siege, when the food and drink ran out.

17 US Department of State 2006, *International Religious Freedom Report
2006 – Lebanon*, September, Section II – Attachment 1).

18 Pedophilia according to Wikipedia is a psychiatric disorder in which
an adult or older adolescent experiences a primary or exclusive sexual
attraction to prepubescent children.

Parvin Darabi - Ayatollah Khomeini's Religious Teachings on Marriage,
Divorce and Relationships - Dr. Homa Darabi Foundation (The late

Ayatollah Khomeini of Iran was the Supreme Leader of the Islamic Revolution) "A man can marry a girl younger than nine years of age, even if the girl is still a baby being breastfed. A man, however is prohibited from having intercourse with a girl younger than nine, other sexual acts such as foreplay, rubbing, kissing and sodomy is allowed. A man having intercourse with a girl younger than nine years of age has not committed a crime, but only an infraction, if the girl is not permanently damaged. If the girl, however, is permanently damaged, the man must provide for her all her life. But this girl will not count as one of the man's four permanent wives. He also is not permitted to marry the girl's sister."

In many Islamic countries, child marriages are common practice. (WikiIslam) Girls far below the age of puberty are often forcibly married to older persons (sometimes in their 50s and later) for various personal gains by the girls' guardian or with the intention to preserve family honor by helping her avoid pre-marital sex. Pedophilic Islamic marriages are most prevalent in Pakistan and Afghanistan, followed by other countries in the Middle East and Bangladesh. [1][2] This practice may also be prevalent to a lesser extent amongst other Muslim communities, and is on the rise among the growing Muslim populations in many non-Muslim countries, such as the United Kingdom[3] and the United States.[4]

1)America Magazine: Child Marriage in Afghanistan and Pakistan, by Andrew Bushell; March 11, 2002

2) Americans For UNFPA: Virtual Slavery: The Practice of "Compensation Marriages" by Net Community of AfUNFPA; last retrieved Monday, 08 December 2008

3) Ten-fold rise in forced marriages in just four years - The Daily Mail, July 2, 2009

4) Christine Vendel - Man charged with statutory rape in 'marriage' to 14-year-old girl - The Kansas City Star, November 8, 2009

More than 3,000 women and girls in Germany, most from Muslim families and many of them minors, faced forced marriage in the course of a year, official research released this week indicates.

The first federal study of its kind found 3,443 recorded cases in 2008 - the most recent year with sufficient data - in which people living in Germany were forced to wed or threatened with a forced marriage. Most were between the ages of 18 and 21, although nearly a third of them were under the age of 17.

More than half were beaten or otherwise physically abused to convince them to marry, while more than one in four were threatened with weapons or told they would be killed if they did not go through with the marriage.[Young women face forced marriage in Germany - Agence France-Presse, November 12, 2011Germany)

United Kingdom

According to 2009 government figures in the UK, forced marriages have seen a ten-fold rise in just four years. One-third of these cases involve victims aged under 18, and one-sixth under the age of 16.

The number of forced marriages has increased more than ten-fold in just four years, government figures have revealed.

More than 770 suspected cases were reported to the Forced Marriage Unit this year, up from 152 in 2005.

If the trend continues, by the end of this year more than 1,540 Britons will have been coerced into a marriage they do not want to enter - an increase of more than 913 per cent.

The practice affects mainly young Asian women, with more than a third of cases involving those fewer than 18. One in six victims are under 16. Advisors said they are dealing with hundreds of schoolchildren who have confided to teachers that they fear they will be taken abroad in the summer holidays and forced to marry. [Ten-fold rise in forced marriages in just four years - The Daily Mail, July 2, 2009)

One has to agree that whatever reasons and justification people may give for the prevalence of child marriages in Muslim-majority nations, without Islam this practice would have long been discarded as immoral and unacceptable in the modern world.

[19] http://islam.about.com/od/terrorism/a/Muslim-Victims-Of-9-11-Attack.htm